Resilience of Sustainable Power Plant Systems in Catastrophic Events

by Naim Hamdia Afgan

RoseDog🐾Books
PITTSBURGH, PENNSYLVANIA 15238

RoseDog Books
585 Alpha Drive
Suite 103
Pittsburgh, PA 15238
Visit our website at *www.rosedogbookstore.com*

ISBN: 978-1-4809-6416-7
eISBN: 978-1-4809-6438-9

CONTENTS

AUTHOR BIOGRAPHY

Prof. Naim Hamdia Afgan, visiting professorof Instituto Superior Tecnico, Lisbon, Portugal, Member oof Academy of Science and Art of Bosnia and Hezegovina, Srajevo, Bosnia and Herzegovina, Fellow of Islamica Academy of Science, Amman, Jordan, Ellow of World Academy of Art and Science Napa, USA.

In his academic career Prof. Naim Afgan has been a scholar, a scientist and an engineer. He hold the chair for Energy Engineering at the Mechanical Engineering Faculty, University of Zagreb. Prof. N. Afgan has joined VINCA Institute of Nuclear Science, Belgrade in 1957, where he has spent most of his academic career. Prof. Naim Afganhas published more than 200 scienctific papers.

In the field ofSustainable Energy Development Prof. Afgan has published a following books:

1. Sustainable Assessment for Energy Systems; Indicators,Criteria and Decision Making Procedure, NaimHamdiaAfgan, Maria Graca Carvalho, Kluwer Academic Publisher,2000
2. Quality, Sustainability and Indicators of Energy Systems, NaimHamdiaAfgan, Maria Graca Carvalho, Begell House Publisher,inc, New York, 2007
3. Sustainable Resilience of Energy Systems, NaimHamdiaAfgan, NOVA Science Publishers, New Youk, 2010
4. Sustainable Nuclear Energy Dilemmas, NaimHamdiaAfgan,LAP LAMBERT Academic Publishing, Sarbrruken Germany, (accepted for publication), 2014

FOREWORD

This book is aimed to the reader interested to learn about progress the development of new toll for the evaluation and assessment of the power plant accident and catastrophe. It is aimed to give an overview of the present state of art this field. As the readers will notice the book is devoted to the professionals in the power engineering. Also, book is written to postgraduate student willing to learn more about present knowledge in the field of the accident of power plants.

The book is written as an overview of the state of art the power plants accident engineering. The special attention was devoted to the evaluation and assessment of the recent accidents of the different power plants including: nuclear power plants, coal fired power plant, wind power plant, solar power plant, and power transport systems.

The book comprises 10 chapters devoted to the following subjects: First chapter takes note about review of the accidents history presents photography the different accident.Second chapter is devoted to the catastrophe phenomena which are defined as the state of the system resulting from the mal function of control system. Tried chapter presents engineering systems that are subject to the catastrophe resulting from potential mal function of its elements. It is of paramount importance to predict potential event which may be cause for the catastrophic event.Fourth chapter is devoted to the energy resilience as the ability of energy system to provide and maintain an acceptable level of service in the face of various to normal operation. Fifth chapter describes the catastrophic event resilience is a monitoring parameter for the assessment of state of the system. It implies the capacity of the system reflecting the ability of the system to withstand changes of indicators leading to the catastrophe development.

Sixth chapter comprise hazards related to extreme weather conditions occurred most frequently and often affected the largest areas. Most of these events lead to disasters but did not led necessarily to environmental catastrophes. Seventh chapter represent current studies of the resilience in social view as the capacity of the system to re-organize and incorporate the idea of adaptation, self-organization and learning. These studies perceive the response of the social system to ecosystem change from diverse perspectives, including understanding of social processes such as social learning, mental models and knowledge-system integration, visioning and scenario building, agents and actor groups and adaptive capacity. Eight chapter is devoted to the global system resilience refers to the capacity of a global system to withstand perturbations from e.g. climatic, economic, technological and social causes and to rebuild and renew itself afterwards. Ninth chapter is presented to the urban systems which are centered in urban areas; in terms of ecosystem services, urban areas are primarily sites of consumption. This contrasts with the other systems assessed in this report (such as cultivated systems, drylands, and coastal systems), which primarily generate and supply ecosystem services. Tenth chapter comprise risk management as a process for identifying, assessing, and prioritizing risks of different kinds. A variety of strategies is available, depending on the type of risk and the type of business.

ACKNOWLEDGMENT

I would like to express my high appreciation to the Institute Superior Tecnico in Lisbon, Portugal and Prof. Maria GracaCarvalho for her active role in promotion activities which has contributed to preparation and writing the book.

It is my great pleasure of my students and colleges with whom I have exchange many ideas in the process of writting this book.

On the personal side, the large multiyear effort of writing this book I was continuously supported and intellectually enhanced by my wife Bahrija Afgan (Djulbegovic) as well as to my daughter Aida Afgan. I would particularly I would like express my thanks to my grandson Aleksander Stefanovicfor his software organization.

CHAPTER I

INTRODUCTION

This book is devoted to the subjects relevant to the main expression in title of the book, namely: SUSTAINABLE RESILIENCE CATASTROPHE OF POWER PLAN SYSTEM:

a) To the World Commission on Environment and Development (Brundtland Commission) [1] it is"development that meets the needs of the present without compromising the ability of future generation to meet their own needs."

b) To the United Nations Conference on Environment and Development, Agenda21, Chapter 35 [2], "development requires taking long-term perspectives, integrating local and regional effects of global change into the development process, and using the best scientific and traditional knowledge available."

c) To the Council of Academies ofEngineering and Technological Sciences, Declaration of the Council Engineering and Technological Sciences, 1995 [3], "It meansthe balancing of economic, social, environmental and technological consideration, as well as the incorporation of a set of ethic values."

d) To the Franciscan Center of Environment Studies (The Earth Chapter, 1995) [4],it is, "The protection of the environment is essential for human well-being and the enjoyment of fundamental rights, and as such requires the exercise of corresponding fundamental duties."

e) Thomas Jefferson, March 4, 1801(Jenkinson C.S., 1987) [5] said, "Then I say the earth belongs to each generation during its course, fully and in its right no generation can contract debts greater than may be paid during the course of its existence."

The concept of resilience has been introduced by

Holling (1973) [6,7] in the field of ecology. *"resilience determines the persistence of relationships within a system and is a measure of the ability of these systems to absorb change of state variable, driving variables, and parameters, and still persist".*

According to a relatively recent work of Lebel Louis [7] the term resilience is defined as *"the potential of a particular configuration of a system to maintain its structure/function in the face of disturbance, and the ability of the system to re-organize following disturbance-driven change and measured by size of stability domain".*

Folke Cark et al [8] a defined resilience as,

"resilience for social-ecological systems is often referred to as related to three differentcharacteristics: (a) the magnitude of shock that the system can absorb and remain in within given state;(b) the degree to which the system is capable of self-organization, and(c) the degree to which the system can build capacity for learning and adaptation. "

Catastrophe is a sudden and widespread disaster: the catastrophe of war, any misfortune, mishap, or failure, fiasco.

This is a strong word for terrible, harmful, devastating things. Tornadoes, hurricanes, earthquakes, and tsunamis are catastrophic weather events. A depression is catastrophic for the economy. In sports, if the star player is injured, that's catastrophic for the team. If a parent dies, that's catastrophic for a family [9]. Scientists worry that climate change will have a catastrophic effect on the planet.

Contemporary science does not deny altogether this relationship and its cosmology based on a . primitive universal catastrophe:

The Big Bang. The model is motivated and observationally. Theoretically justified explosion It is based on specific actions that support the idea of an explosion is supported by a strong and proven corpus, essentially based on the theory Einstein's gravity: general relativity [10] is not trivial as physics, following the course of history it intends to describe, leads in inexorably.

CATASTROPHIC EVENTS

Catastrophe phenomena are events which are defined as the state of the system resulting from the mal function of control system. In the normal life of a system it is not uncommon to experience random catastrophe failures of a system [12]. However, events such as a power outage can have a major impact on a system. It is very common to experience lighting strikes during summer months that can randomly affect a process control or network system.

Catastrophic events are very often natural phenomena [13]. In the normal life of a system it is not uncommon to experience random catastrophic failures of a system. Statistically, random catastrophic events appear rarely. However, events such as a power outage can have a major impact on a system. It is very common to experience lighting strikes during summer months that can randomly affect a process control or network system.

In the normal life of a system it is not uncommon to experience random catastrophic failures of a system. Statistically, random catastrophic events appear rarely. However, events such as a power outage can have a major impact on a system. It is very common to experience lighting strikes during summer months that can randomly affect a process control or network system.

In other to demonstrate different groups of catastrophic event a following accidents are presented [14]:

Nuclear Accidents

Chernobyl [Date: April 26, 1986]

An explosion and fire at the nuclear power plant in the former Soviet Republic Ukraine resulted in the deaths and injuries of 56 people.However, due to the massive amounts of released radiation, the long term effects will not be known for some time.Chernobyl is a district in North-Western Ukraine in Eastern Europe. On 26th April 1986 a test was being carried out at Reactor Number Four in the Chernobyl Nuclear Power Station. The aim of the test was to see if, in the event of an unexpected loss of electric power, the turbines would provide sufficient electric power to keep the cooling system operating for the few seconds it would take the diesel generators to kick in and to provide backup electric power for the cooling water pumps. This test was being carried out because it is imperative that the fuel rods in a nuclear power plant are kept cool at all times.

Three Mile Island [Date: March 28, 1979]

Unit 2 of the Three Mile Island nuclear power plant melted down. The accident began at 4 a.m. on Wednesday, March 28, 1979, with failures in the non-nuclear secondary system, followed by a stuck-open pilot-operated relief valve (PORV) in the primary system, which allowed large amounts of nuclear reactor coolant to escape. The mechanical failures were compounded by the initial failure of plant operators to recognize the situation as a loss-of-coolant accident due to inadequate training and human factors, such as human-computer interaction design oversights relating to ambiguous control room indicators in the power plant's user interface. In particular, a hidden indicator light led to an operator manually overriding the automatic emergency cooling system of the reactor because the operator mistakenly believed that there was too much coolant water present in the reactor and causing the steam pressure release. The scope and complexity of the accident became clear over the course of five days, as employees of Met Ed, Pennsylvania state officials, and members of the U.S. *Nuclear Regulatory Commission* (NRC) tried to understand the problem, communicate the situation to the press and local community, decide whether the accident required an emergency evacuation, and ultimately end the crisis.

Fukushima Nuclear Accident [Date: 11 March 2010]

On 11 March at 14:46 JST, Unit 1 scrammed successfully in response to the earthquake] though evacuated workers reported violent shaking and burst pipes within the reactor building At 15:37 all generated electrical power was lost following the tsunami leaving only emergency batteries, able to run some of the monitoring and control systems. It was later learned that Unit 1's batteries were damaged and unavailable following the tsunami. At 15:42, TEPCO declared a "Nuclear Emergency Situation" for Units 1 and 2 because "reactor water coolant injection could not be confirmed for the emergency core cooling systems."The alert was temporarily cleared when water level monitoring was restored for Unit 1 but it was reinstated at 17:07 JST." Potentially radioactive steam was released from the primary circuit into the secondary containment area to reduce mounting pressure.

Floods

Yangtze River, China 11 [Date: Summer 1998]

More than 4,100 people were killed. The floods submerged 21 million acres of land, affected 53 million acres and destroyed 11 million acres of crops. More than 5.8 million houses were destroyed.

Midwestern USA [Date: May to September 1993]

The 1993 Midwest flood was one of the most significant and damaging natural disasters ever to hit the United States. Damages totaled $15 billion, 50 people died, hundreds of levees failed along the Mississippi and Missouri Rivers and thousands of people were evacuated, some for months.

South and Southeast Texas [Date: October 17 – 18, 1998]

In October 1998, Texas Flooding occurred across parts of South and Southeast Texas. It was one of the costliest storms ever recorded. Rainfall totaled over 20 inches and caused over $750 million in damages. 31 people were killed as a result of the storm, mostly from drowning.

Russian Dam Disaster [Date: September 4, 2009]

On August 17th one of the world's largest hydroelectric plants, Sayano–Shushenskaya in Russia, suffered a major catastrophe. The disaster has resulted in 73 confirmed dead and two missing. It has also resulted in the destruction or damage of 9 of the 10 turbines, a transformer fire and extensive flooding in the turbine hall as well as collapsing a major part of its roof. Additionally a large amount of insulating oil is traveling downriver. The cause of the accident

is still unknown but evidence is pointing toward a failure of the #2 turbine or its control system. 70% of the hydroplants electric generation was used to power 4 aluminum smelters. The accident will result in a cut of 500,000 tons of production. Early estimates are that it will take 4 years and 1.3 billion dollars to repair the facility.

Three Gorges Dam Disaster, Chine [Date: June 12, 2007]

It is the virtual definition of a monumental project — a dam one and a half miles wide and more than 600 feet high that will create a reservoir hundreds of feet deep and nearly 400 miles long. The reservoir, its engineers say, will enable 10,000-ton ocean-going freighters to sail directly into the nation's interior for six months of each year, opening a region burgeoning with agricultural and manufactured products. And the dam's hydropower turbines are expected to create as much electricity as 18 nuclear power plants. China's huge Three Gorges Dam hydro-power project could spark 'catastrophe' unless accumulating environmental threats are quickly defused, senior officials and experts have warned, according to state media.

The Three Gorges project is seen as an important future source of energy for China's growing electrical consumption. It is also expected to tame the fabled Yangzi River. The Yangzi's notorious floods have been recorded for millennia and have claimed more than 1 million lives in the past 100 years.

Meteor

Chicxulub [Date: 65 Million Years Ago]

A meteor approximately 10 miles across slammed into the Yucatan Peninsula (Mexico) creating a crater 110 miles wide and 12 miles deep. This impact wiped out 90% of all ocean species and 70% of land species.

Tunguska [Date: June 30, 1908]

A large explosion caused by what many believed to be a meteor occurred over Siberia, Russia. The explosion had the same force as setting off 10-15 megatons of dynamite. 800,000 acres of forest burned from the explosion.

Volcano

Tambora [Date: 1815]

92,000 people were killed just from the eruption of the volcano. The ash from the explosion caused Europe to not have a summer.

Anak Krakatau [Date: 1883]

This volcano pushed ash about 50 miles into the air and its collapse caused a massive Tsunami that hit 295 villages in the vicinity and killed over 36,000 people. In April 2009, 4060 explosions were recorded at Krakatau.

Considered to be the deadliest and economically costly volcano in American history. The eruption destroyed the northern face of the mountain and killed 57 people as well as thousands of animals. Hundreds of square miles were reduced to wasteland.

Earthquake

Chile [Date: May 22, 1960]

Considered to have been the largest modern earthquake in the world. The initial quake killed 1,655 and left over 2 million people homeless. The resulting tsunami caused 61 deaths in Hawaii and 138 deaths in Japan.

Prince William Sound, Alaska [Date: March 28, 1964]

This large earthquake caused the deaths of 128 people from the quake and resulting tsunami. It also caused about $311 million in damages.

San Francisco, California [Date: October 17, 1989]

57 people died as a direct result of the earthquake; there were 3,757 injuries as a result of the earthquake. 42 people died when a double-deck portion of the freeway collapsed, crushing the cars on the lower deck. The quake caused an estimated $6 billion in property damage. Four people died in San Francisco's Marina District, four buildings were destroyed by fire, and seven buildings collapsed.

Tornado

Missouri, Indiana and Illinois [Date: March 18, 1925]

Traveled 219 miles across three states and lasted for about 3 ½ hours. The storm was responsible for the deaths of 689 people.

Daultipur and Salturia [Date: April 26, 1989]

In Bangladesh, a massive tornado wiped out everything in its path and caused 1,300 deaths.

Hurricane

Galveston, Texas [Date: September 8, 1900]

This hurricane was the deadliest weather disaster in United States history. Storm tides of 8 to 15 ft inundated the whole of Galveston Island, as well as other portions of the nearby Texas coast. These tides were largely responsible for the 8,000 deaths attributed to the storm. The damage to property was estimated at $30 million.

Hurricane Katrina New Orleans, LA [Date: August 29, 2005]

It produced catastrophic damage - estimated at $75 billion in the New Orleans area and along the Mississippi coast - and is the costliest U. S. hurricane on record. Katrina is responsible for approximately 1200 reported deaths, including about 1000 in Louisiana and 200 in Mississippi. Storm surge along the Mississippi coast caused total destruction of many structures, with the surge damage extending several miles inland. The surge overtopped and breached levees in the New Orleans metropolitan area, resulting in the inundation of much of the city and its eastern suburbs. Wind and water damage from Katrina extended well inland into northern Mississippi, Alabama and Florida.

REFERENCES

[1]   *Report of The United Nations Conference on Environment and Development*, Rio de Janeiro, Brazil, Vol. 1, Chapter7, (June 1992.

[2]   Agenda 21, Chapter 35, *Science for Sustainable Development*, United Nations Conference on Environment and Development, 1992.

[3]   *The Role of Technology in Environmentally Sustainable Development, Declaration* of the Council of Academies of Engineering and Technological Sciences, Kiruna, Sweden, June 21,1995.

[4]   *The Earth Chapter: A Contribution Toward Its Realization, Franciscan Center of Environmental Studies*, Rome, Italy (1995),http://www.globalsustainability.org

[5]   Jenkinson C.S., *The Quality of Thomas Jefferson's Soul*, White House Library, 1987.

[6]   Holling, C.S. (1973) Resilience and Stability of Ecological Systems. *Annual Review of Ecology and Systematics* 4, 1-23.

[7]   Walker, B. H., C. S. Holling, S. Carpenter, and A. Kinzig. 2004. Resilience, adaptability, and transformability in social-ecological systems. *Ecology and Society* 9 (2):5. http://www.ecologyandsociety.org/vol9/iss2/art5/

[8]   Louis Lebel, 2001. *Faculty of Social Sciences.* Chiang Mai University. November 2001.

[9]   Folke, C., S. Carpenter, T. Elmqvist, L. Gunderson, C.S Holling and B. Walker (2002). Resilience andSustainable Development: Building Adaptive Capacity in a World of Transformations. *Ambio*, 31(5), pp. 437- 440.

[10] Luciana L. Braga, Jose P. Fiks, Jair J. Mari and Marcelo F. Mello,*The importance of the concepts of disaster, catastrophe, violence, trauma and barbarism in defining posttraumatic stress disorder in clinical practice*http://www.biomedcentral.com/1471-244X/8/68.

[11] Heller M, *Where did the Big Bang come from ?,*., Standpoint, Cosmos, April 2012.

[12] *Catastrophic Events Impact on the Ecosystem* (NXPowerLite).ppt.

[13] Leah R. Gerber* And Ray Hilborn Catastrophic events and recovery from low densities in populations of otariids: implications for risk of extinction.*Mammal Rev.* 2001, Volume 31, No. 2, 131–150.

[14] *Catastrophic events*, www.stms.si.edu/ce/ce/htm.

[15] *Catastrophic events*, www.stms.si.edu/ce/ce/htm.

CHAPTER 2

ENGINEERING SYSTEM ACCIDENTS

Every complex system features indicators that reflect specific states of the system. In a normal state the system *resilience* is a parameter that corresponds to a specific value. When catastrophe strikes, the resilience of a system is an overriding value that corresponds with the destruction of the system.

Engineering systems are subject to catastrophe that may result from a malfunction of its elements. Every element of the system can be envisaged as a potential trigger for the catastrophic event. It is of paramount importance to anticipate any potential causes of a catastrophic event. For this reason, the evaluation of the resilience of any element of the system is of great importance. It is of special interest to validate energy system as the potential catastropheaccidents. For this reason every engineering system is exposed to assessment and verification of the potential accident of the system,

2.1. ENERGY SYSTEM ACCIDENTS

The evaluation of an energy system is designed to provide a comprehensive list of all plausible catastrophic events, as the following evaluations demonstrate.

Nuclear weapons [1] were the first technology to be developed that allowed our species to render itself extinct by choice. Besides the technology for nuclear weapons there is a need to establish full control of their dissemination. There is now world consensus that the development of new nuclear weapons will be limited to vertical dissemination. The Non-Proliferation Treaty (NPT) has become the essential marker to prevent nuclear technology dissemination. In accordance with NPT is a definition of horizontal and vertical development of nuclear technology. However, we survived the Cold War, and the political climate between the major powers has improved. The fact we survived the brinkmanship of the Cold War suggests that the leaders of major nuclear powers can be trusted to behave responsibly with their arsenals. After all, it isn't easy to become a leader of a major power. Someone who does so will have survived years of infighting; such a person is normally ambitious, smart, rational, and power-hungry enough that they won't choose to sacrifice their ideals, their countries, and their lives, in a haze of mushroom clouds. So, while a large scale nuclear war is possible, and it could cause the end of civilization or of our species, it isn't nearly as serious a threat as some of the others we face.

*Bioweapons*are the threat oftomorrow. [2] Like nuclear weapons, the first truly calamitous bioweapons will be (or have been) created and stored in secure government-run facilities. Unfortunately, unlike nuclear weapons, within the next three or four decades incredibly infectious and lethal bioweapons will probably be available to anyone with a few million dollars and a couple of well-trained scientists. There is very active development of potential biological weapons. But there is also an understanding among countries to limit the development of bioweapons. The U.S. Department of Defense (amongothers) is working on ways of protecting against bioweapons, including vaccines that could be effective against almost any virus. That said, advancements in bioweaponry still seem more certain than the advancements in biological defenses. If bioweapons do become readily available to small numbers of individuals, as seems likely, then one or two hate-filledideologuescould end our species.

Many optimists envision a future in which self-replicating tiny machines areubiquitousand perform a wide variety of tasks, from building perfect objects molecule by molecule to swarming in your bloodstream and quickly repairing any damage to your body. The research is promising and there are high expectations for this field of biomedicine. So far, however, it has been very difficult to build useful self-replicating nanoscale machines. Quantum effects complicate the attempt, and the effort could achieve little success. Of course, there is a darker side to the possibility of self-replicating nanoscale machines. Designed as a weapon, these invisible machines could chew through organic flesh and leave behind millions of copies of themselves. Or, designed to do a constructive task, these machines, if their constituent elements were common, could replicate out of control and consume a significant fraction of our planet, destroying our species in the process. Many futurists view nanotechnology as ultimately more dangerous than bioweaponry, however, the danger is almost certainly several decades away.

Global warming is not likely to drive us to extinction. [3] However, we can't accurately predict how all of the world's feedback mechanisms will respond to adrasticallyincreased amount of CO_2 in the air and to a warmer planet. One possible outcome of global warming is runaway temperaturechange (either warming or cooling). Although we don't know for certain how much of a global temperature change would create an ecological disaster, such a change certainly isn't out of the question. We do know that a warming world will probably lead to increasingly violent weather patterns and to substantial desertification. Any of these changes could easily disrupt food supplies for much of the world, and thereby cause the collapse of civilization. Even if climate change doesn't prove to be catastrophic, our increased CO_2 levels are increasing the acidity of the oceans and if the acidity level increases too much, it could have a deadly effect onocean life. This would, in turn, have majorrepercussions on other ecosystems and on our food supply.

Civilization today is dependent on abundant *cheap sources of energy*. It is essential for man to develop new resources. Without supplies of energy, the world's economy would collapse; we wouldn't be able to grow and transport even a fraction of the food the world's 6 billion plus people need to survive. The most important source of energy right now is oil. Yet our supplies of oil are limited and many oil reserves are located in unstable parts of the world. Policymakers have finally begun realizing the urgency of the development of alternative sources of energy. That said, if we face unforeseen technical or political difficulties and we fail to end our dependency on oil before supplies of it run low, our civilization will face collapse.

The economic future of the world looks bright right now. Europe, America, Japan, and several other regions of the world have modern, industrialized economies which enable their people to enjoy easy access to all of the necessities, in addition to good educations and many luxuries. The economies of China and India are growing rapidly and those two regions combined contain over a third of the world's population. Nevertheless, there is some uncertainty about the future of the world's economy. America is deeply indebted to foreign lenders, perhaps dangerously so. Both European and American governments have made large financialcommitmentsto their people; commitmentsthat are easy to grow and difficult to shrink. Thesecommitmentscould necessitate burdensome taxes thatstifletheir economies. Furthermore, advancements in technology may lead to a future where machines replace workers in most professions, rendering a large sector of society almost unemployable. Large scale economic disruptions have had cataclysmic effects in the past, and they may again.

There are a number of situations that could lead to *widespread crop failure*, [4] such as adverse effects of global warming. Other ways in which we could imperil food supply also exist. We couldaccidentally(or purposely) kill off an important pollinating agent (e.g., bees, birds). Or we could become increasingly reliant on one or two strains of a small number of plant species, placing ourselves at the mercy of pests that could decimate that particular strain of plant. If crop failure, for any reason, is sufficiently widespread and affects enough species, it would cause the end of modern civilization.

A potential threat exists of *suicide by scientific experiment with possible catastrophic effects*. Though scientists are, in general, responsible, reasonable, moral people, [5] their job is to conduct experiments, and, very infrequently, an experiment may contain a potential fordisastrousresults. This situation can occur in any branch of science, but the possibility of destruction can be particularly spectacular when it results from a physicsexperiment. For an incredibly short period of time, the protons and neutrons in ions are torn apart into a sort of *quark soup*. Physicists don't know all that much about the behavior of this "soup," which is why they want to experiment. Several unlikelyscenarioshave been raised for how experiments of this nature could cause a catastrophe. The most likely of these possibilities, and the one that is still given the most credence from the greatest number of physicists, is that a negatively charged strangelet could be created. If this strangelet had areasonablylong half-life, it could potentially convert the entire Earth into strange matter, destroying everything in the process. Another particularly horrifying, although even more unlikely, possibility is that an experiment couldinadvertentlytrigger a transition to a lower vacuum state. In layman's terms this would mean the end of everything in the universe (the catastrophe would propagate at the speed of life, so most of the universe would continue to exist long after we were gone).

The *adoption of new technology*normallyprecedescomplete knowledge of therepercussionsof the technology. [6] For example, we adopted a new system of raising and feeding animals only to discover that the system helped spread a prior that decayed brains (including, apparently human brains). Imagine if prions had spread far more rapidly and had less effect on cattle and greater effect on humans: anyone who has eaten beef would be at real risk of having their brain turned to sponge. Likewise, new evidence continues to come to light that cell phones have a greater effect on the brain than was previously thought. Will two or three decades of frequent use from an early age lead to widespread health problems among our youngest generation? There is speculation that cell phones may be the cause of our current bee shortage; a shortage that threatens a number of crops. We are adopting new technologies every day and any one of them could haveunforeseeneffects. In the worst-case scenario, one of thesesurprisescould threaten our civilization.

*Rapid developing of faster computers*and better machines will lead to to the potential of information system. The use of information technology has become an essential step in the development of modern society. If these advancements continue, machines will probably replace humans in the workplace. This has already begun to happen with unskilled workers and it will eventually happen at all levels of the workforce. Advances in computer technology make it likely that we will develop computers that are smarter than ourselves in every way, and which are capable of completely emulating the thought processes of a human brain. Once thisoccurs we will have, in some fundamental way, lost control of our machines. If these machines do not make good decisions for us we will be unable to effectively oppose them. We may be unable torealisticallypredict what end thissituationwill lead to.

Recently, a *new development of space program* was developed a new expectation for an extra intelligent life [7]. One possible explanation for the lack of evidence of extra terrestrial intelligent life is that technologically advanced species exist but those species did not lose the violent edge to theircompetitivedrive as they expanded into space. In such a universe, the galaxy is a dangerous place and technologically advanced species may remain hidden for fear of attracting unwanted attention. An advanced intelligent species might reasonably conclude that it is safer to eliminate potential competitors before they can become a threat. We have happily obliged anyspeciesthat wants to destroy us by providing a century's worth of radio signals, and, indeed, we've gone further than that to proudly send out signals to the stars in an attempt to contact other species. As a result, we may be awaiting the arrival of an alien attack. Unlike as depicted in Hollywood movies, this attack probably won't be something we can fight against. A large mass accelerated up torelativisticspeeds and aimed at Earth would hit us almost before we knew it was coming, and it could easily wipe out all life on our planet. Advanced self-replicating machines could overwhelm our defenses, and, in fact, consume our planet. Thus, if an intelligent species knows about us and wants to kill us, it could be very easy for it to do so (as long as we are dependent on a single planet, at least). Two possible versions of this event exist. One is the mystical version: God exists, he is angered at the people of Earth for their sinful ways, he destroys Earth (or the entire universe) in his rage. The alternative version is that our planet doesn't actually exist as a physical entity; instead we exist in a virtual reality simulacrum (we might be biologicalentitieshooked into a virtual reality system, like in the movie *The Matrix*, or we might simply be complex computer simulations). In this case, the plug couldliterallybe pulled on the computer and, therefore, our world. It's very hard to predict the likelihood of thesescenarios.

Asteroid impacts are believed to havecaused the extinction of the dinosaurs and they may have been responsible for some of the other mass extinctions in Earth's history. [8] Anasteroidlarge enough to wipe out human civilization might have as high as a 1 in 300 chance of hitting us in 2880. We haven't charted many of the comets and asteroids that could potentially hit us. That said, the odds of significant harm to our species from an asteroid impact are extremely low for theforeseeablefuture. A slightly greater threat is that many nuclear nations don't have the technical capacity to tell an asteroid explosion from a nuclear explosion. In a tense situation, it's possible that an asteroid entering our atmosphere could trigger a nuclear war.

Any energy system is subject to potential malfunction events that may lead to a catastrophic event. It is important to be aware that the resilience capacity of an energy system is the assessment tool for any potential events that might reflect deficiency of a complex system. In particular, any complex system is subject to a number of potential sudden changes of individual indicators leading to the resilience capacity change.

There are a number of potential changes of indicators of a complex system. [9] Every system as the complex system is imminent to the potential malfunctions which are result of the sudden change of the respective indicators. An agglomeration of sudden changes of indicators will lead to the destruction of an energy system. It is important to develop an appropriate methodology for the evaluation of any eventual energy system structure change; this will lead to a better understanding of the functionality of the energy system. The *resilience index* is a parameter that is defined as the capacity of a complex system to withstand sudden change of individual indicators.

Energy system resilience is a set of characteristic parameters which define the causes of the destruction of the energy system and its functionality. Generally it is envisaged that the quantitative measurement of the resilience of the energy system includes economic, environmental, and social indicators. Within the economic indicator are certain sub indicators: energy cost sub indicator, capital invested in the energy system sub indicators (i.e., energy cost), efficiency of energy system sub indicator, and so on. The environmental indicator comprises CO_2 emission sub indicator, NO_x emission sub indicator, waste sub indicator, and resilient heat sub indicator. Social indicators include a manpower sub indicator and an income sub indicator.

2.2. NUCLEAR POWER PLANT ACCIDENT

Remarks: Yellow marked text is used from INSAG -7: The Chernobyl Accident: Updating INSAG-1: Safety Series No. 75- INSAG-7, 1992 [10]

"The catastrophic events whichhas happen on the April 1986 disaster at the Chernobyl nuclear power plant in Ukraine a flawed Soviet reactor design coupled with serious mistakes made by the plant operators [11]

The accident of Chernobyl 4 reactors was killing number of operators and firemen within three months and causing several additional killing. Acute radiation syndrome (ARS) was originally diagnosed in 237 people onsite and involved with the cleanup and it was later confirmed in 134 additional cases. Of these, 28 people died as a result of ARS within a few weeks of the accident. Nineteen more subsequently died between 1987 and 2004, though their deaths cannot without uncertainty be attributed to radiation exposure. Nobody offsite suffered from acute radiation effects although a large proportion of childhood thyroid cancers diagnosed since the accident is likely to be due to intake of radioactive iodine fallout. Furthermore, large areas of Belarus, Ukraine, Russia, and beyond were contaminated in varying degrees.

The Chernobyl Power Complex, lying about 130 km north of Kiev, Ukraine and about 20 km south of the border with Belarus, consisted of four nuclear reactors of the RBMK-1000 design Units 1 and 2 were constructed between 1970 and 1977, and units 3 and 4 of the same design were completed in 1983. More RBMK reactors were under construction at the site at the time of the accident. This area of Ukraine is described as Belarusian-type woodland with a low population density. About 3 km away from the reactor in the new city of Pripyat, there were 49,000 inhabitants. The old town of Chernobyl, which had a population of 12,500, is about 15 km to the southeast of the complex. Within a 30 km radius of the power plant, the total population was between 115,000 and 135,000.

The RBMK-1000, a Soviet-designed and built graphite moderated pressure tube type reactor.

Source: OECD NEA.

The RBMK-1000 nuclear reactor used is a Soviet-designed and built graphite moderated pressure tube type reactor that uses slightly enriched (2% U-235) uranium dioxide fuel. It is a boiling light water reactor with two loops feeding steam directly to the turbines, without an intervening heat exchanger. The water acts as a coolant and also provides the steam used to drive the turbines. The vertical pressure tubes contain the zirconium alloy clad uranium dioxide fuel around which the cooling water flows. The extensions of the fuel channels penetrate the lower plate and the cover plate of the core and are welded to each. A specially designed refueling machine allows fuel bundles to be changed without shutting down the reactor.

The core itself is about 7 m high and about 12 m in diameter. In each of the two loops, there are four main coolant circulating pumps, one of which is always on standby. The reactivity or power of the reactor is controlled by raising or lowering 211 control rods, which, when lowered into the moderator, absorb neutrons and reduce the fission rate. The power output of this reactor is 3200 MW thermal, or 1000 MWe. Various safety systems, such as an emergency core cooling system, were incorporated into the reactor design.

There are components that contribute to the overall power coefficient of reactivity, but the void coefficient is the dominant one in RBMK reactors. However, at the time of the accident at Chernobyl 4, the reactor's fuel burnup, control rod configuration. The power with a positive void coefficient large enough to overwhelm all other influences on the power coefficient.

The design characteristics of the reactor were such that substantial damage to even three or four fuel assemblies can result in the destruction of the reactor. There is some dispute among experts about the character of this second explosion, but it is likely to have been caused by the production of hydrogen from zirconium-steam reactions[12].Intense steam generation then spread throughout the whole core (fed by water dumped into the core due to the rupture of the emergency cooling circuit) causing a steam explosion and releasing fission products to the atmosphere.

The accident caused the largest uncontrolled radioactive release into the environment ever recorded for any civilian operation, and large quantities of radioactive substances were released into the air for about 10 days. This caused serious social and economic disruption for large populations in Belarus, Russia, and Ukraine. Two radio nuclides, the short-lived iodine-131 and the long-lived cesium-137, were particularly significant for the radiation dose they delivered to members of the public.

It is estimated that all of the xenon gas, about half of the iodine and cesium, and at least 5% of the remaining radioactive material in the Chernobyl 4 reactor core (which had 192 metric tons of fuel) was released in the accident. Most of the released material was deposited close by as dust and debris, but the lighter material was carried by wind over Ukraine, Belarus, Russia, and to some extent over Scandinavia and other parts of Europe.

The main task was cleaning up the radioactivity at the site so that the remaining three reactors could be restarted and the damaged reactor shielded more permanently. About 200,000 people ("liquidators") from all over the Soviet Union were involved in the recovery and cleanup during 1986 and 1987. They received high doses of radiation, averaging around 100 millisieverts. Some 20,000 of them received about 250 mSv and a few received 500 mSv. Later, the number of liquidators swelled to over 600,000 but most of these received only low radiation doses. The highest doses were received by about 1000 emergency workers and onsite personnel during the first day of the accident.

Initial radiation exposure in contaminated areas was due to short-lived iodine-131; later cesium-137 was the main hazard (both are fission products dispersed from the reactor core, with half lives of 8 days and 30 years, respectively; 1.8 EBq of I-131 and 0.085 EBq of Cs-137 were released). About five million people lived in areas contaminated (above 37 kBq/m^2 Cs-137) and about 400,000 lived in more contaminated areas of strict control by authorities (above 555 kBq/m^2 Cs-137).[13]

The history of the Chernobyl issue since the accident indicates the importance of continuing high-level research; both to meet the needs of the affected populationsand also to address questions of importance for humanity. Major health and environmental issues remain unresolved and, if the evidence is not to be lost forever, it is essential that they be investigated according to internationally recognised protocols and in a timely manner. Concern for the effects on health of ionising radiation delivered in low doses and at low dose rates has grown over the past 15 years. These concerns reflect the fact that there is no direct basisfor determining risks associated with exposures of the kind resulting from the Chernobyl accident.

Over the past decade, progress in radiobiology and radiation epidemiology has been considerable. This research presents important challenges to existing concepts upon which risk estimation is based. In addition, little serious consideration has been given by the research community to ameliorating the psychosocial effects of accidents such as Chernobyl.

2.3. HYDROPOWER PLANT ACCIDENT

The accident at Russia's Sayano–Shushenskaya hydroelectric power station occurred on 17 August 2009 at 08:13 local time). There was a loud bang from turbine 2. [14] The turbine cover shot up and the 920-tonne rotor also shot out of its seat. Water spouted from the cavity of the turbine into the machinery hall. As a result, the machinery hall and rooms below its level were flooded. At the same time, an alarm was received at the power station's main control panel, and the power output fell to zero, resulting in a local blackout. The steel gates to the water intake pipes of turbines, weighing 150 metric-tonnes each, were closed manually by the opening of valves of hydraulic jacks and keeping them up from 08:35 to 09:20 hours (09.30 by the official report). The operation took 25 minutes, which is near the minimum time (highest speed) allowed for this operation. The emergency diesel generator was started at 11:32. At 11:50, the opening of 11 spillway gates of the dam was started and was finished at 13:07. Seventy-five people were later found dead.

The scene of the Sayano–Shushenskaya hydroelectric power station where the accident took place.

Nine out of the 10 turbines were operating at the time, with a total output of 4400 MW. Turbine 6 was undergoing scheduled maintenance, but was ready for a restart. A survivor of the accident, Oleg Myakishev, described it as follows [15]:

...I was standing upstairs when I heard some sort of growing noise, then I saw the corrugated turbine cover rise and stand on end. Then I saw the rotor rising from underneath it. It was spinning. I could not believe my eyes. It rose about three meters. Rocks and pieces of metal went flying; we started to dodge them... At that point the corrugated cover was nearly at roof level, and the roof itself had been destroyed... I made a mental calculation: the water is rising, 380 cubic meters per second, so I took to my heels and ran for the Number 10 turbine. I thought that I wouldn't make it, I climbed higher, stopped, looked down, and saw everything getting destroyed, water coming in, people trying to swim... I thought: someone must urgently shut the gates to stop the water, manually... Manually, because there was no power, none of the protection systems had worked.

On 9 September 2009 at 17:40 local time (09:40 GMT), a fire started in the turbine hall during repair works. [16] Around 200 people were evacuated. There were no fatalities or injuries. According to RusHydro the fire was extinguished "within a few minutes."

The official report states that the accident was primarily caused by the turbine vibrations that led to the fatigue damage of the mountings of turbine 2, including the cover of the turbine. It was also found that at the moment of the accident at least six nuts were missing from the bolts securing the turbine cover. After the accident 49 found bolts were investigated from which 41 had fatigue cracks. On 8 bolts, the fatigue damaged area exceeded 90% of the total cross-sectional area.

According to the report, on 17 August 2009 at 01:20 (local time) there was a fire at the hydroelectric power station of Bratsk which broke both communications and the automatic driving systems of other power plants in the region, including Sayano–Shushenskaya. The situation was recovered on 17 August 2009 at 15:03. At 08:12 localtime, turbine 2's output power at Sayano–Shushenskaya was reduced by the turbine regulator and it entered into the no recommended power band II. Shortly after this, the bolts keeping the turbine cover in place were broken causing an underwater pressure of about 20 bars (2000 kPa); the spinning turbine with its cover, rotor, and upper parts started to move up, destroying machinery hall installations. At the same time, pressurized water flooded the rooms and continued damaging plant constructions.

2.4. COAL-FIRED POWER PLANT ACCIDENT

Coal has been an integral part of world power generation since the late 1800s. While that technology has in some ways benefited our society, we now recognize the ecological hazards and health risks associated with using coal as an energy source. Coal by itself is not harmful, however, the byproducts of burning coal raise serious health and environmental issues. Another cause for concern are the vague laws governing the disposal of the toxic byproducts of coal-fired power plants, laws that allow each state to determine its own rules for its plant sites. [16]

Coal-burning plants are some of the worst industrial polluters in the United States, producing approximately one-third of its carbon dioxide (CO_2, a major contributor to global warming), 40% of its mercury (highly toxic if ingested or inhaled), one-quarter of its nitrogen oxide (an ingredient found in smog), and two-thirds of its sulfur dioxide (a component of acid rain). The Environmental Protection Agency (EPA) contends that sulfur dioxide promotes heart disease and asthma, while nitrogen oxides destroy lung tissue.

Additional hazardous byproducts produced by coal-burning plants include arsenic, chromium, cobalt, lead, manganese, zinc, radionuclide's, and particulate matter. Each type of coal produces different levels of these pollutants, all of which negatively impact both the environment and our health.

Mercury, a known carcinogen, is of particular concern as it poisons fish in bodies of water miles away. Greenpeace reports that even at minimum levels, this neurotoxin has been shown to cause reduced intelligence in hundreds of thousands of children born annually. Mercury emissions occur at rates of approximately 25 pounds per 100 megawatts at the average coal plant, making coal-fired plants the largest single contributor of mercury pollution in the United States.

The American Lung Association (ALA) released a report in March 2011 offering this startling statistic: "Particle pollution from power plants is estimated to kill approximately 13,000 people a year." The ALA report singled out coal-fired power plants as among the worst offenders. [17]

Beyond the day-to-day danger of burning coal to produce energy, there is the devastating impact of plant malfunctions. In December 2008, the Tennessee Valley Authority (TVA) reported the failure of a holding pond used by a coal-fired electric plant. When heavy rains washed away the holding-pond dike, more than 2.2 million pounds of hazardous waste flooded 300 acres in east Tennessee. Even after the best cleanup effort, the area will remain polluted with dangerous byproducts for decades.

It remains impossible to quantify the amount of poisons released by the above incident, but in one year, this plant reportedly produced 45,000 pounds of arsenic, 49,000 pounds of lead, 1.4 million pounds of barium, 91,000 pounds of chromium, and 140,000 pounds of manganese, much of this held in the holding pond and all of which can cause cancer, liver damage, neurological trauma, and more.

To reduce the devastating ecological and health effects of coal-fired power plants, coal-industry advocates are touting new "clean coal" technologies. As a start, many coal-powered plants are recycling some of their dangerous byproducts into useful materials. For example, the byproducts of fly and bottom ash—previously dumped into landfills—are being transformed into concrete, asphalt, and masonry blacks. Another byproduct, synthetic gypsum, is being used in the production of drywall and chalk.

Greenpeace and other environmental groups, however, believe there is no such thing as clean coal. They claim the coal industry's touting of the term "clean coal" in their advertising is "greenwashing" or propagandizing. These environmental advocacy groups favor phasing out coal-burning power plants entirely. As an alternative, they are pushing for the expansion of environmentally friendly power sources such as solar and wind energy.

One way or another, the days of coal-fueled power plants are numbered. Even if the dream of "clean coal" is achieved, it is only a matter of time before the finite supply of coal, like that of oil, runs out. In the meantime, it behooves us to work for increased safety regulation of coal plants to prevent the release of dangerous byproducts into our environment and our bodies, and to develop alternative energy technologies to replace coal.

2.5. SOLAR CYCLE ACCIDENTS

Storms of less severity [18] occurred in September 1989, March 1991, and October 1991, but they were still strong enough to hinder utility operations. These events have caused the industry to become more aware of the reality of geomagnetic storms and the destruction they can wreak on unprepared infrastructure components.

Solar cycles are consecutive groups of geomagnetic storm activity that repeat approximately every 11 years. Solar cycle 22 occurred between September 1986 and May 1996. Currently, we are in solar cycle 23 and April 2000 was thought to be the peak of this cycle's activity. Recently, it was discovered that solar cycle 23 is peaking for the second time. The second peak of this cycle appears to be only a few percent smaller than the first peak. This double-peaking phenomenon was last observed during solar cycle 22. The first peak occurred in 1989 and the second peak occurred in 1991. Past observations have indicated that odd-numbered solar cycles are more severe than numbered ones. Since events of the last solar cycle were above average, it can be expected that the current cycle has the potential to be severe as well. [17,18]

Two major infrastructure groups are discussed in this section: energy and communications. The effects of geomagnetic activity on energy and communications, the extent to which these infrastructures are vulnerable to geomagnetic storms, and the action that can be taken to minimize the negative effects of geomagnetically induced currents (GICs) are examined. We explore various practices that Canada is utilizing to mitigate effects of geomagnetic storms on the country's critical infrastructure.

During a geomagnetic storm, several important elements of the energy sector can suffer adverse effects if they are not protected. Intense electric currents flowing throughout the ionosphere can induce voltage surges on power grids, trigger the melting or malfunctioning of transformers, and cause the overloading of electrical grids. As a consequence of this activity, blackout conditions can result over a large area and pipelines can suffer cumulative damage from corrosion.

Geomagnetic storms can affect power operations when GICs flow through power lines to substation transformers, saturating the transformer core with electricity. The extra voltage fluctuations produced in the transformer cause relay operations that can suddenly prevent power lines from functioning. As well, the stability of the entire system can be compromised when compensators switch out of service due to irregularities in voltage levels.

Power stations may experience increased vulnerability due to advances in technology. [19] Modern power systems are interconnected in such a way that they are quite stable and are safeguarded against localized failures. This interconnectedness, however, can lead to increased vulnerability in some circumstances. When a solar storm damages one system, systems connected to it can experience failure as well. Also, some systems that experienced problems during the last peak in Solar Cycle 22 may be stressed because they are currently increasing the electrical load on their systems and, in turn, can be more affected by geomagnetic events that happen during Solar Cycle 23.

Preventative measures have been implemented to avoid events such as the 1989 Québec blackout. System operators in Canada have developed and implemented procedures to respond to these emergencies, thereby reducing potential damage due to GICs. Since 1989, Hydro-Québec has spent more than $1.2 billion installing transmission line series capacitors. These capacitors block GIC flow to prevent them from causing damage to the system.

Hydro-has also installed monitoring equipment that spots voltage fluctuations and immediately notifies operators so that they may redistribute the load to other parts of the network. Additional protective measures include disconnecting the links between power grids, desensitizing automatic control systems, delaying power station maintenance, and delaying the replacement of equipment. Utilities are also relying on space weather forecasting to help remain operational during geomagnetic storms. Operators can implement conservative operating procedures once they have received an advance warning of a storm thread threat.

Geomagnetic storms have the ability to cause cumulative damage to pipelines in the form of corrosion. Significant efforts have focused on reducing corrosion by maintaining pipelines at a negative voltage relative to surrounding soil. Electric currents induced by geomagnetic field variations can cause large voltage fluctuations damaging the pipeline and initiating corrosion. These electric currents are driven along the pipe resulting in the buildup of current that raises the electric potential at the end of the pipe and creates a potential gradient that drives the charge back along its length. In addition, some of this charge buildup can leak into surrounding soil through the pipeline's electrical insulator coating. This leak can cause changes in the charge buildup and initiate fluctuations in the pipeline electric potential. As a result, the corrosion process is initiated and the pipeline will suffer cumulative damage over time.

Pipelines that have insulating flanges can be more vulnerable to damaging electric currents. The flanges are meant to interrupt current flow, however, it has been discovered that the flanges create an additional site where the electric potential can build up and force the current flow to ground. The flanges lead to an increased risk for corrosion. The length of the pipeline also adds to its vulnerability due to the increased potential for corrosion.

A geological perspective is useful in determining which energy systems will be more vulnerable to GICs. System vulnerability can be increased because GICs from geomagnetic storms have the ability to induce an electrical charge in a rock deposit. An example of such a rock deposit is the North American Central Plains (NACP) anomaly. It is one of the world's longest strips of conductive rock, which winds underground from Wyoming through Saskatchewan and Manitoba to the Hudson Bay area. It is extremely conductive because of the presence of sulfides and graphite, which make it up to 1000 times more conductive than the surrounding Canadian Shield. Critical infrastructure elements that are positioned in or on the anomaly may be at increased risk to

GICs due to the high electrical conductivity of the rock. Currently, a detailed map of the electrical conductivity running through the Manitoba portion of the NACP is being developed. This map will help power and pipeline companies better predict how the North American power and pipeline grids can be affected during a geomagnetic storm event.

Communication technology can be vulnerable to the effects of a geomagnetic storm. Since the introduction of coaxial cables in the twentieth century, the bandwidth of communication systems has increased but cables now require repeater amplifiers along their length. These amplifiers compensate for the loss of signal strength over distance and are connected in series with the center conductor of the cable. Amplifiers are powered by a direct current supplied from terminal stations at either ends of the cable. The varying magnetic field that occurs during a geomagnetic storm induces a voltage into the center of the coaxial cable increasing or decreasing the voltage coming from the cable power supply. The induced voltage experienced during a geomagnetic storm can produce an overload of electricity on the cable system and, in turn, cause a high current shutdown.

Geomagnetic storms can also impact satellites and spacecrafts. Geosynchronous satellites are at risk of being exposed to a hostile environment. Changes in the Earths magnetic field confuse navigational sensors such as the Global Positioning System (GPS) and the sensors on satellites. Satellites can experience orbital decay problems such as increased drag as a result of the increasing atmospheric temperature and subsequent expansion.

Protons and electrons become extremely energized when contacted with solar flares or coronal mass ejections (CMEs). When these solar particle events are fired toward Earth, they are capable of damaging spacecraft microelectronics or solar cells in one collision. These events can intensify radiation inside a spacecraft with severe or even lethal consequences. Mitigation efforts regarding space activities include putting satellites to "sleep," turning sensitive spacecraft subsystems off, increasing satellite monitoring for anomalies, and calculating the best time to adjust a low Earth orbit for drag. Space flight activities can also be delayed to avoid exposing astronauts to dangerous levels of radiation.

Aerial navigation systems can also be damaged by geomagnetic storms. To minimize negative effects from GICs, the flight altitude on polar routes can be adjusted to minimize health hazards and alternatives to GPS-based takeoff and landing procedures can be implemented.

Surveying practices rely heavily on technology for activities such as mapping. This sensitive technology, however, can be vulnerable to the effects of GICs. To safeguard surveying activities and avoid magnetic disturbances that can produce false results, high-resolution land surveying, magnetic surveying, and exploration can be delayed until the threat from GICs is no longer significant.

The prediction and advance warning of geomagnetic storms assist industry and public in avoiding adverse effects of GICs. There have been numerous technologies developed that gather data to support prediction activities. For example, x-ray based observations provide a very detailed and inclusive picture of the magnetic structure of the sun and its CMEs. This tool provides forecasts two to three days in advance with approximately 50% accuracy.

Geomagnetic storms, although infrequent, have the potential to severely impair critical infrastructure. In Canada, it has been demonstrated that power systems, pipelines, and communications are at risk from the damaging effects of CMEs and GICs. Consequences of geomagnetic storm activity can include widespread power failures, pipeline corrosion, the shutdown of cable systems, an increased drag on satellites, inaccurate navigational sensors, and the loss of millions of dollars.

2.6. WIND POWER ACCIDENTS

Wind is the movement of air mass from a high pressure area to a low pressure area and is mainly caused by differences in temperature within the atmosphere. A high difference in pressure results in an increased wind velocity. Climate changes, location, region, and height are all factors that have a significant effect on wind speed and direction.[20] A wind turbine is a rotating mechanical device that converts the wind kinetic energy to practical mechanical energy, resulting in the production of electricity. The main advantage of vertical-axis wind turbines is that the gearbox and transmission systems are placed at ground level. Another advantage is their ability to capture the wind without considering wind direction. However, maintenance of these turbines is not straightforward as removing the rotor is often required. In addition, the captured energy is not efficient and large areas are compulsory for those turbines situated on land as guy-wire is necessary for supporting the structure. shows the likelihood of various wind power plant failures.

Chart showing the breakdown of wind power plant failures. [21]

Alternatively, the most recent wind turbines used are horizontal-axis-based with two or three blades. Having the rotor positioned on the top of the tower creates a more efficient system as more wind energy is produced. These turbines also have a nacelle, which is held up by the tower and contains the gearbox and generator. A yaw system, which is turning the nacelle and rotor to face the wind, enables the turbine to capture the highest amount of energy. Additionally, some wind turbine blades have moveable blade tips, which are used as air brakes. A condition monitoring system (CMS) is used in machine maintenance and is becoming a long-term service package for components. CMS provides information on what the condition of a component is and can also predict an impending failure within the system. This includes service and maintenance, inspection, measuring and evaluating the machine conditions, and estimating the remaining service life. process is extensively utilized within the turbine industry and includes operations such as rotating, milling, drilling, and grinding. For example, it is considered to be state-of-the-art for rotary machinery to be equipped with vibration-based condition monitoring. The monitoring process involves sensor measurements to determine the condition of the process. Analyzing measured signals, detecting a process anomaly, and detecting faults are necessary factors of the monitoring process. Within the control part, regulating of the processes are considered, which requires process variables and a model of the system for various techniques.

A fault refers to a mistake. In terms of the engineering world, more technically, it is an unpermitted anomaly or deviation of any system parameters from an acceptable condition. Detecting the fault kind, determining size and time of occurrence, and determining location in a system are factors involved in fault detection and isolation (FDI). In fault detection and diagnosis systems (FDD) the certain tasks must be followed, as described next.

In mathematical-based methods, mathematical descriptions of the system are implemented in the form of various equations or similar transformed representations. Analytical redundancy is being relied on for most of the model based FDD methods. Measurements from sensors and results from models can be extended to the comparison of two generated quantities, obtained from different sources that comprise the same behavior. The differences in results are called *residuals* and indicate faults within the system. Relying on parameter estimation has been considered a successful method.

Supervisory Control and Data Acquisition (SCADA) [22] is an application that collects data from a system and sends them to a central computer for monitoring and control usage. Remote measurements, reporting data, and monitoring information are known as *telemetry*. In industrial processes and modern manufacturing, public and private services, and security and leisure industries telemetry is usually required to connect equipment and systems that are located far away from the center, from a couple of meters to hundreds of kilometers. In general, SCADA is a mixture of data acquisition and telemetry. SCADA software can be separated into two types: *open source* or *proprietary*. Proprietary software is developed by companies to communicate to the specific hardware. The key problem with this system is the overwhelming reliance on the supplier of the system. Interoperability is the main reason that open source software systems have increased in popularity. Interoperating allows different manufacturers' equipment to be used on one system. SCADA software has some important features, such as user interface, graphics displays, alarms, RTU interface, database, networking and communication, and Server and client distributed processing.

A system is a way of doing things. Each system may have any number of inputs and outputs. In the case of computer system, the input could be the keyboard and the output might be the printer or the monitor. The early detection of faults and having enough time for maintenance, implementation of the fault detection system (FDS) is critical. The FDS has to have an appropriate action depending on the severity and importance of the fault.

Faults can be categorized with different levels of urgency and system responses. [23] For instance, they can be caution, warning, or alarm. *Cautions* indicate that there is a need of service or adjustment of a component in the system; not having the service done within a certain period would not affect the system. *Warnings* indicate that there is a measurement within the system that is not acceptable and it is outside of the normal operating limits. Continuing in this situation will lead to serious damages or failures in the system. *Alarms* indicate a malfunction in the system that could be an immediate failure.

The operational costs of an offshore (away from or at a distance from the coast) wind turbine can be very high. The costs for operation and maintenance (O&M) are around 30 to 35% of the cost of electricity, whereas the repair costs for onshore wind turbines (on dry ground) are much lower.

Knowing the condition of the machinery is the main function of CMS. Early fault detection reduces the costs for corrective maintenance of wind turbines.

When faults are detected and identified early on, the consequences of breakdown and damages are reduced and the repair costs are less. In Offshore wind turbines, early failure detection allows repairs to be better planned, leading to shorter downtimes and fewer revenue losses.

A condition monitoring system for wind turbines that predicts or detects incipient critical failures is the state-of-the-art in system safety, and remains one of the most important attributes of the wind energy industry. Condition monitoring can either be used to enhance safety or to make the current level of safety more affordable. [24]

Fault is defined as the termination of the capability of an object to complete a function. When a failure occurs inside the wind turbine (e.g., high oil temperature in a gearbox) the control unit logs the failure directly or registers the consequences of the fault, and responds referring to the type of the malfunction. Sometimes, to avoid safety hazards or main system breakdowns, the turbine has to be shut down. Often a turbine is restarted because of wrong failure detection, which could be caused by noise within the system, and therefore these faults are not considered as crucial problems. If the failure is serious, a visual inspection has to be made which can be carried out by the operators or by authorized personnel. Finally whenever a major failure has happened, a report is documented. This describes the failure reasons, parts involved, and downtime associated with the fault. Here are two different examples of various failures that can happen within wind turbines [25]:

The base unit of a CMS should provide a number of functions. Analogue or pulse signals from sensors must be converted to digital information, and some of these conversions might need filtering. Digitalized and filtered values will be analyzed for CMS purposes and must be saved in databases for additional evaluation. Moreover, an assured communication between the data acquisition and a remote central server or operator must be considered.

2.7. HIGH VOLTAGE TRANSMISSION SYSTEM ACCIDENTS

Electric power systems are critical infrastructures in the same way as gas and oil networks, water networks, transportation networks, telecommunications, and computer systems. [26,27,28,29] As the digital society matures on a global scale, these complex networked systems are becoming increasingly interdependent. Consequently, their vulnerability and security are raising major concerns worldwide. For instance, the normal operation of water and telecommunications systems is maintained only if there is a steady supply of electrical energy. On the other hand, However, the generation and delivery of electric power cannot be ensured without provision to power plants and power networks of fuel, water, and various telecommunications and computer services for data transfer and control purposes. These interdependencies increase as the usage of the internet, intranet, and other wide area computer networks becomes more prevalent.

The strong reliance of critical infrastructures on each other may turn a local disturbance in one of them into a large-scale failure via cascading events, which may have a catastrophic impact on the whole of society. The risk of such a disastrous domino effect is growing due to the current trend of operating critical infrastructure systems closer to their stability or capacity limits. One compelling reason for this practice is, of course, economics. Providing these infrastructures with some degree of robustness comes at a price, which entails the achievement of the required level of redundancy.

A typical example of a critical infrastructure that undergoes rising vulnerability to catastrophic failure is the electric power transmission network. [30] There are several reasons for this. Firstly, as witnessed in developed countries, there has been a very slow expansion of the high voltage transmission grid during recent decades due to stringent regulations put forward in response to environmental concerns. Government institutions have issued new regulations to transform the vertically integrated utilities into independent generation, transmission, and distribution companies. In these emerging competitive electricity markets, the wholesale market is the first to flourish and expand at a rapid rate, boosted by transmission's open access and the existence of a large variability in electricity prices between the U.S. states. This price discrepancy has resulted in a growing amount of bulk power being transferred over long distances throughout the transmission grid, worsening a shortage of reserve margins in transmission that have prevailed since the mid 1980s. Consequently, blackouts and brownouts in the eastern and western parts of the United States have been increasing in number at an alarming rate in recent years.

In bulk power transmission system planning and operation, the present practice is to carry out an N-1 contingency analysis. Occasionally, security analysis is employed in some stringent cases. However, it is implemented not via an exhaustive search but rather via a partial assessment of the system reserves over a small portion of the transmission network. An N-k security analysis for

$k> 1$ is perceived as being impossible to achieve due to the huge number of cases that need to be investigated. In fact, under the assumption of independence between successive events, it would require checking the impact on the system reserve margins of the loss of every k out of N pieces of equipment, which yields a number of cases to be tested that grows exponentially with N. However, it is clear that this chain of contingencies are dependent on each other due to the protection-system interactions, either directly or indirectly via the changes in the distribution of power through the network or due to the possible multiple impacts of a triggering event, such as lightning or other natural hazards. Consequently, the probability of the occurrence of cascading failures is much higher than the probability of a random (i.e., independent) tripping of k out of N components of the system.

It is also the usual practice in reliability and security analysis to neglect the impact of the protection systems. As a result, cascading failures leading to blackouts or brownouts are not investigated. Until recently, large-scale blackouts were considered to be sufficiently rare events to be disregarded from the analysis. However, at least in the U.S.A., ideas are evolving in this respect, prompted by the increasing number of major incidents that has plagued the U.S. power systems since the mid 1990s. For example, in July 1996, a series of blackouts struck the western part of the U.S.A., leaving 2.2 million customers without electricity. One month later, islanding and blackouts affected 11 U.S. western states and two Canadian provinces.

In December 1998 the San Francisco Bay area experienced a series of blackouts and in July 1999 it was the turn of New York City to suffer from the same type of cascading failures. More recently. California has been struck by rolling blackouts initiated by the utilities to overcome a severe shortage of generation during peak hours. An exhaustive account of these blackouts can be found in the report prepared for the Transmission Reliability Program of the Department of Energy. [31]

Besides the causes of the degradation of the power system reliability, there is the detrimental role played by the protection systems during large disturbances. As revealed by a study undertaken by the North American Electric Reliability Corporation (NERC) over the period 1984 to 1988, in 73.5% of the significant disturbances that were investigated, undetected failures of the protection systems, termed hidden failures (HFs), have aggravated the disturbance by tripping fault-free system components and, thereby, helped the perturbation to propagate further. One peculiarity of hidden relay failures is that they cannot be detected *a priori*, that is, they cannot be exposed before the system is perturbed. In particular, routine maintenance testing may not detect them or, even worse, may induce them by damaging relay components, as was the case in the 1977 New York blackout. Another source of HFs is the bad setting of relays. The present practice favors dependability at the expense of security, in that it ensures the isolation of a fault by allowing the tripping of fault free devices from time to time.

The papers [32,33][describes methodologies together with algorithms that assess the risk of catastrophic failures in electric power networks. A catastrophic failure is here defined as one that results in the outage of a sizable amount of load, say 10% of the peak load. It may be by dynamic instabilities in the system or exhaustion of the reserves in transmission due to a sequence of line tripping leading to voltage collapse. Only the latter case is being considered. The aim of the algorithms is to identify the weak links in the systems, which are defined as those branches of the network that's tripping due to a fault lead to the highest probabilities of a catastrophic failure. Once the weak links are identified, they must be consolidated. To this end, a hidden failure monitoring and control system may be developed to supervise adaptive digital relays located in sensitive spots across the system. These relays may perform dynamic load shedding during an emergency state in conjunction with an adaptive splitting of the system that prevents the cascading failures from spreading throughout the network.

Occasionally, security analysis is employed in some stringent cases. However, it is implemented not via an exhaustive search but rather via a partial assessment of the system reserves over a small portion of the transmission network. An N-k security analysis for k > 1 is perceived as being impossible to achieve due to the huge number of cases that need to be investigated. In fact, under the assumption of independence between successive events, it would require checking the impact on the system reserve margins of the loss of every k out of N pieces of equipment, which yields a number of cases to be tested that grows exponentially with N. However, it is clear that this chain of contingencies are dependent on each other due to the protection-system interactions, either directly or indirectly via the changes in the distribution of power through the network or due to the possible multiple impacts of a triggering event, such as lightning or other natural hazards. Consequently, the probability of the occurrence of cascading failures is much higher than the probability of a random (i.e., independent) tripping of k out of N components of the system.

It is also the usual practice in reliability and security analysis to neglect the impact of the protection systems. As a result, cascading failures leading to blackouts or brownouts are not investigated. Until recently, large-scale blackouts were considered to be sufficiently rare events to be disregarded from the analysis. However, at least in the U.S.A., ideas are evolving in this respect, prompted by the increasing number of major incidents that has plagued the U.S. power systems since the mid 1990s. The frequency of major blackouts, which was about one per decade until 1996, has started to grow at an alarming rate since then. For example, in July 1996, a series of blackouts struck the western part of the U.S.A., leaving 2.2 million customers without electricity. One month later, islanding and blackouts affected 11 U.S. western states and two Canadian provinces. [34]

REFERENCES

[1]   Nuclear Weapon Archive, http://nuclearweaponarhive/org.
[2]   *Weapons of Mass Destruction: Biological, Chemical...*www.odl.state.ok.us/us-info/terrorism/wmd.pdf.
[3]   Global warming - *Wikipedia, the free encyclopedia,*http://en.wiki pedia.org/wiki/Global_warming.
[4]   *Crops for the Future* I Crops for the Future, www.cropsforthefuture.org/ Cached - Similar Catastrophic Events, www.stcms.si.edu/ce/ce.htm.
[5]   *Pieces of Evidence That Suggests Intelligent Alien Life* Exists.www.paranor-malhaze.com/5-pieces-of-evidence-that-suggests-intelli.
[6]   *Asteroid Facts - Explore the Cosmos* I The Planetary Societywww.plane-tary.org/explore/topics/asteroids_and_comets/facts.html
[7]   D'Meira, Th., Christian Theology and extraterrestrial intelligent life, *Theological Study*, 80, 1999.
[8]   *History of the Earth*, Wikipedia, the free encyclopedia.
[9]   Katz J. S., *Indicators for complex innovation systems Research Policy* 35 (2006) 893–909.
[10]   *Report on the accident at the Chernobyl nuclear power station.* Report NUREG-1250 rev. 1, U. S. Government Printing Office, Washington, DC, 1988.
[11]   USSR State Committee on the Utilization of Atomic Energy, 1986: The accident at the Chernobyl nuclear power plant and its consequences.

Information compiled for the IAEA experts' meeting, Vienna, August 25–29, 1986.

[12] 2009_Sayano-Shushenskaya_hydro_accident, http://en.wikipedia.org/wiki/Sayano-Shushenskaya Hydroelectric Power Station Accident,*the Russian Plant Disaster*, www.bbc.co.uk:80/go/blq/mast/home/-/

[13] Sputh D.L., Mann M.K., Herr R.D., *Life cycle Assessment of Coal Fired Power Production*, NREL/TP- 570-25119,2009.

[14] D. Hasler, W. Rosenquist, R. Gaiward, *Coal fired Power Plant,*Sangernt& Lundy, Jan.2009.

[15] Anxary A. *Solar Cycles and Earth Weakening Magnetic Field*, www.nexus-magazine.com.

[16] Kappenman, John G. (1996). Geomagnetic Storms and Impacts on Power Systems: Lessons Learned from Solar Cycle 22 and Outlook for Solar Cycle 23. *Minnesota Power Electric*. Retrieved November 26, 2001, from www.mpelectric.com/storms/

[17] *History of Geomagnetic Effects*. (1998). Natural Resources, Canada.

[18] Water Vulnerability for Existing Coal-fired Power Plant, DOE-NETL – 2010/129, Aug. 2010November 26, 2001, http://en.wikipedia.org/wiki/2009_

[19] Begic, F., Hadjiabdic M., Wind Energy : Basic conversion, Environment protection, economy, Publication (in Bosnian) "Svjetloststampad.o.o." Sarajevo, 2004.

[20] J.Ribrant, L.M. Bertling, Survey of failures in wind power systems with focus on Swedish wind power plants during 1997-2005,*IEEE Transaction of Energy Conversion*, Vol.22, No. 1, pp 167-173,2007.

[21] Control and Data Acquisition (SCADA) *Systems, Office of Manager of National Communication System*, Oct. 2004.

[22] M. Entezami, S. Hillmansen, P. Weston and M. Papaelias, Fault detection and diagnosis within a wind turbine mechanical braking system, *Renewable Energy*, Vol7, pp.175-183,2012.

[23] *Summary of Wind Turbine Accident data to 31 March 2012,*URLwww.caithnesswindfarms.co.uk.

[24] M.Boghem, *Safety* of *WindSystems,*https://netfiles.uiuc.edu/.../NPRE Wind...

[25] *Supervisory Control and Data Acquisition (SCADA) Systems*, National Communications System, Oct. 2004.

[26] Th. Esbensen and Ch. Sloth,*Fault Diagnosis and Fault-Tolerant Control*

of Wind Turbine, Faculty of Engineering, Science and Medicine, Aalborg University, Denmark, 2005.

[27] J.A.S.A Hylkema, Offshore Wind Farm, Wind Energy: Facts and Fiction,2005.

[28] Alexandra Von Meier,*Electric Power Systems: A Conceptual Introduction* IEEE Press, ISBN13: 9780470036402,2003.

[29] K. Ioannis, and O Konstantinos, *An Analysis of Blackouts for Electric Power Transmission Systems,* World Academy of Science, Engineering and Technology 12, 2005.

[30] *U.S. Department of Energy Office of Electricity Delivery and Energy Reliability:* Transmission Reliability Program USA, 2005.

[31] L. Mili, Q. Qiu, A.G. Phadke, Risk assessment of catastrophic failures in electric power systems.*J. Critical Infrastructures,* Vol. 1, No. 1, 2004. Ming Ding Summary of research on hidden failures in protection systems, Electrical Machines and Systems, 2008. ICEMS 2008. *International Conference,* Oct 17-20,2008, Sch. of Electr. Eng. &Autom., Hefei Univ. of Technol., Hefei.

[32] Jaime De La Ree, Yilu Liu, LamineMili, Arun G. Phadke, An Luiz-Dasilva, *Catastrophic Failures in Power Systems: Causes, Analyses, and Countermeasures Proceedings of the IEEA,* Vol. 93, No. 5, May 2005.

[33] P. Batra E.,Ioannides, Electric Accidents In The Production Transmission, And Distribution of Electric Energy: A Review of the Literature, *International journal of occupational safety and ergonomics* 2001, vol. 7, no. 3, 285–307.

CHAPTER 3

RESILIENCE CONCEPT

The concept of resilience provides a new and useful framework of analysis and understanding on how individuals, communities, organizations, and ecosystems cope in a changing world facing many uncertainties and challenges. [1] Sometimes change is gradual and things move forward in continuous and predictable ways; but sometimes change is sudden, disorganizing, and turbulent. The resilience approach focuses on the interaction between periods of gradual and sudden change, and provides better understanding on how society should respond to disruptive events and accommodate change. Resilience is an area of research under rapid development with major policy implications for sustainable development. Following definitions for the resilience are used in the science and technical literature [2]

- *Threats and events.* Resilience is seen as the ability to accommodate abnormal threats and events, be they enemy actions, perturbations from climate change, natural disasters such as earthquakes or floods, or economic shocks
- *Positive outcomes.* All definitions of resilience refer to a positive outcome, be it the ability of a material to absorb and release energy and return to its original state; the ability of an individual, group, or organization to continue in existence in the face of some sort of surprise; the ability to recover from or adjust easily to misfortune or sustained

life stress; or the capacity of a system to absorb disturbance and still retain essentially the same function

- *Being prepared.* Resilience involves the ability or capacity to absorb and then recover from an abnormal event. This capacity may be built formally and deliberately by developing plans, standards, and operational procedures, or by developing physical, economic, and/or human capital. It may also evolve informally through the development of social capital or it may exist naturally through the properties of the material being used. Individuals, communities, organizations, and, indeed, nations that are prepared and ready for an abnormal event tend to be more resilient.

- *Desire/commitment to survive.* Survival is a basic human instinct, and individuals who demonstrate the strongest will to remain alive are able to accept extreme and abnormal conditions and recover from traumatic events. Similarly, groups, communities, and organizations with a unity of purpose and a collective commitment to survive are more likely to succeed.

- *Adaptability.* We live in a world that is constantly evolving, in some cases through natural processes and in others through the intervention of mankind. There is common agreement in the literature that systems, organizations, and people who are able and willing to adapt tend to be more resilient.

- *Gaining experience.* The ability and willingness to learn is often linked to adaptability and being prepared. The learning may come from personal experience or by studying the lessons of others in a formal manner: by gathering and evaluating data; by conducting research in an objective, independent, and balanced manner; and by communicating the findings, conclusions, and recommendations.

- *Collective and coordinated response—interdependency.* As society becomes more complex and interconnected and the impact of global factors becomes more immediate and apparent, we find ourselves more vulnerable to disruptive events. In facing such interconnected threats, resilient communities and organizations and, indeed, nations tend to be those that are well coordinated and share common values and beliefs.

3.1. Sustainable Development in a Risky Environment

Sustainability is a notion that comprises the multicriteria validation of the system. Sustainability is the metrics of thequality of human life. It includes social, economic, technological, and environmental validation. It is understood that no generation will be in debt of any commodity of future generations. Sustainability is not the end state of the system but an attribute of thedynamic and adaptive system.

Definitions of sustainability most often cited are:

- To the World Commission on Environment and Development (Brundtland Commission) [3] it is "development that meets the needs of the present without compromising the ability of future generation to meet their own needs."

- To the United Nations Conference on Environment and Development, Agenda 21, Chapter 35, [4] "development requires taking long-term perspectives, integrating local and regional effects of global change into the development process, and using the best scientific and traditional knowledge available."

- To the Council of Academies of Engineering and Technological Sciences, Declaration of the Council Engineering and Technological Sciences, 1995, [5] sustainability "means the balancing of economic, social, environmental and technological consideration, as well as the incorporation of a set of ethic values."

- According to the Franciscan Center of Environmental Studies (The Earth Chapter, 1995), [6] "The protection of the environment is essential for human well-being and the enjoyment of fundamental rights, and as such requires the exercise of corresponding fundamental duties."

- On March 4, 1801, Thomas Jefferson said, "Then I say the earth belongs to each generation during its course, fully and in its right no generation can contract debts greater than may be paid during the course of its existence." (Jenkinson, 1987) [7]

Sustainable development encompasses economic, ecological, technological, and social perspectives of conservation and change. In correspondence with the WCED (World Commission of Economic Development), as mentioned, it is generally defined as the "development that meets the needs of the present without compromising the ability of future generations to meet their own needs." [8] This definition is based on ethical imperative of equity within and between generations. Moreover, apart from meeting basic needs of all, sustainable development implies sustaining the natural life-support systems on earth, and extending to all the opportunity to satisfy their aspirations for a better life. Hence, sustainable development is more precisely defined as "a process of change in which the exploitation of resources, the direction of investments, the orientation of technological development, and institutional changes are all in harmony and enhance both current and future potential to meet human needs and aspirations."

Sustainability provides a framework for integrating economic, environmental, technological, and social interests into an effective strategy. For those who have recognized the need to embrace sustainable development, the first step is to understand how to implement it. Putting this concept into operation requires identifying practical indicators of sustainability and understanding how they can be measured over time to determine if progress is made.

Climate change projections indicate that extreme weather events such as floods and droughts are likely to become more frequent and intense, and that poor and marginalized groups will be most vulnerable to risks presented by these phenomena (e.g., water insecurity, changes in the food supply, adverse health impacts, etc.)

Policies and actions that help to develop resilient socioeconomic systems—that is, socioeconomic systems that are able to resist and/or "bounce back" from shocks such as natural disasters and longer-term stresses (for example changes in water availability)—should receive greater attention in national and international dialog. Investments in the "hardware" needed for climate adaptation are widely understood, while investments in the "software"—the changes in behavior, governance, engagement, and empowerment of multiple stakeholders—have not been sufficiently addressed.

The capacity to resist initial shocks and, over time, to self-organize and to adapt to changing conditions will be increasingly important.

For the purposes of resilience analysis, the following applies:

1. Assessment of whether socioeconomic systems are becoming more, or less, resilient
2. Comparison of resilience (focusing on adaptive capacity) across countries

Folke [8] defined the concept of resilience as something that "shifts policies from those that aspire to control change in systems assumed to be stable, to managing the capacity of social-ecological systems to cope with, adapt to, and shape change."

Resilience in its original ecological sense has been defined in two different ways in the ecological literature. [9] There is no right or wrong use of the term. Rather, the different usage emphasizes two distinct stability properties.

The first definition concentrates on stability near an equilibrium steady state, where the rate and speed of return to preexisting conditions after a disturbance event are used to measure the property. [10] Resilience is then defined as the time required for a system to return to a steady state following a disturbance. This definition matches the etymological meaning of the term *resilience*.

The second definition (2) emphasizes conditions far from any equilibrium steady state, where instabilities can shift a system to another basin of attraction which is controlled by a different set of variables and characterized by a different structure. Resilience, understood in this way, is the "magnitude of disturbance that can be absorbed before the system changes its structure by changing the variables and processes that control behavior." [11–16]

In the recent predictions or forecasts of the potential impacts of future shocks with different "resilience" investments are a way of focusing attention of high-level policy and decision makers toward the need for explicit investments in resilience and also to support policy and decision making. However, the extent to which any of the above is possible or feasible depends on the analytical power behind the concept.

Resource efficiency was identified as a key sustainability challenge for regions. This conclusion was based on the environmental pressures implied (both in terms of resources needed and pollution and waste generated) by meeting current and future socioeconomic needs of the regional population (based on current economic growth patterns).

Since the 2005 report [17], and as oil prices crossed the $100/barrel mark, the connection between resource use patterns and economic viability has become increasingly apparent. Given the relatively low per capita natural resource endowments in Asia and the Pacific, the region can be considered vulnerable to fluctuations in changes in supply and price of differenttypes of resources.

The discussion on developing low-carbon economies refers to the promotion of energy-use efficiency at the macroeconomic level. For the purposes of the resource-efficiency analysis may provide the following:

- Assessments of resource-use efficiency and identification of trends
- Predictions/forecasts of levels of resource use and waste created
- Predictions/forecasts of the potential impacts of future shocks with different policy investments and resource use (as a way of focusing attention of high-level policy and decision makers of the need for explicit investments in resource-efficiency and also to support policy and decision making.

In broad terms, sustainability refers to the quality of a process that allows it to continue indefinitely. Consequently, the term *environmental sustainability*, which refers to the capacity of socioeconomic processes to operate while ensuring that renewable natural resources are not depleted faster than they can be regenerated, and that ecological systems remain viable for habitation. In other words, the flow of ecosystem services must remain capable of meeting both socioeconomic and ecological needs.

Based on their relevance to the Asian and Pacific development and sustainability context, and the increased risks that integrated social ecological–economic systems are likely to encounter in the future, three foci for examining the sustainability of integrated social–ecological–economic systems have been identified: (1) staying within limits; (2) system resilience; and (3) focusing on subsystem linkages.

The notion of limits or thresholds is an important concept in sustainability. Environmental pressures must be maintained within their limits to avoid sudden ecological change that can drastically reduce the flow of ecosystem services and, thereby, increase pressures on the social and economic subsystems.

Ensuring that social–ecological–economic systems can adapt (in a positive sense) to a significant disturbance or shock is equally as important as maintaining pressures within sustainable limits. A system can no longer be considered sustainable if a sudden shock is capable of permanently pushing its functions or feedbacks outside an acceptable range of performance. System resilience is therefore an important criterion for the sustainability of any system, particularly one that faces increased risk.

Resilience enables a country or region to cope with the array of shocks that occur over time, including those associated with climate change. Building climate-resilient economies and societies is an increasingly important objective for policy and decision makers. The projected rate and magnitude of climate change and the likely impact of this change is far beyond the adaptive capacity of many (especially the poorest) communities in Asia and the Pacific. These shocks include but are not limited to: decreased air quality in cities, contamination of water supply, flooding, permanent erosion and submersion of land, and disruption of settlement patterns.

Social, economic, and environmental systems are so intimately connected that, in reality, socio–ecological–economic subsystems are only sustainable if the relationships between the subsystems enable the permanent co-evolution of each subsystem.

The outline of social, ecological, and economic systems show how they are linked. Each arrow indicates a specific type of interaction between activities or entities within the interrelated systems. As shown, the connections between the subsystems mainly lie in the patterns of production and consumption, infrastructure development and the use of ecosystem goods and services.

Thus in the face of a drought, a socioeconomic system that uses water in an efficient way, or uses only a small proportion of the available water resources, will suffer less disturbance than a socioeconomic system that is highly dependent on hydrological inputs. Resource efficiency is therefore integral to maintaining pressures within limits and promoting system resilience, and by consequence, promoting sustainability.

Reducing population growth and promoting technological innovation are some of the other actions that can be taken to maintain pressures within limits. Although transnational environmental linkages and the global nature of trade have made long-term prospects for sustainability increasingly dependent on what happens outside of a country's borders, we will forgo a discussion of transnational sustainability here.

Patterns of resource use also define the nature of the linkage between the socioeconomic and ecological subsystems. [17] The relationships between subsystems determine the extent to which changes in one subsystem impact on changes in another. The sustainable development work of the OECD, UNESCAP, and other organizations focuses on decoupling socioeconomic development (and related human activities) from their environmental impact. The implicit goal is to minimize the negative impacts of one subsystem on the others. Therefore, the concept of sustainability also implies that decoupling negative relationships is important to overall system stability. However, since social, economic, and ecological subsystems cannot be completely decoupled, building resilience also means increasing the diversity of intersystem relationships. [18] In other words, numerous yet varied connections between subsystems enable the system to better absorb specific shocks and adapt to new conditions.

Resilience can be defined in two ways. The first is a measure of the magnitude of disturbance that can be absorbed before the system changes its structure by changing the variables and processes that control behavior. The second, a more traditional meaning, is as a measure of resistance to disturbance and the speed of return to the equilibrium state of an ecosystem. [19]

Resilience networks aim to provide acceptable service to applications: ability for users and applications to access information when needed, for example, distributed database access, sensor monitoring, situational awareness, and operation of distributed processing and networked storage, for example, the ability for distributed processes to communicate with one another and the ability for processes to read and write networked storage. The sustainability paradigm is a complex idea, which is defined and interpreted as the intergenerational phenomena: the level of scale, multiple domains, social development of societies, and multiple interpretations of sustainable development. In the understanding of sustainability development the major precondition is to highlight the role of the material and energy consumption as a source of unsustainable pattern of the development. The need to balance the economic, environmental, technological, and socialsustainability is the goal forenergy accessibility, availability, and acceptability.

The energy sustainability keys are: energy diversity and energy efficiency, energy infrastructure investment, cost-reflective prices and market-sensitive intervention, supply reliability, regional integration of the energy system, market-based climate change responses, technological innovation and development, and public understanding and trust. [20]

The resilience of a system relates to the magnitude of disturbance required to fundamentally disrupt the system causing a dramatic shift to another state of the system, controlled by a different set of processes. When resilience is lost or significantly decreased, a system is at high risk of shifting into a qualitatively different state. The new state of the system may be undesirable. Restoring a system to its previous state can be complex, expensive, and sometimes even impossible. Research suggests that to restore some systems to their previous state requires a return to conditions well before the point of collapse. [21]

The energy system resilience refers to the capacity of an energy system to withstand perturbations from, for example, climatic, economic, technological, and social causes and to rebuild and renew it afterwards. Loss of resilience can cause loss of valuable energy system services, and may even lead to rapid transitions or shifts into qualitatively different situations and configurations, described, for example, for people, ecosystems, knowledge systems, or whole cultures. In general terms, the vulnerability of a system is assessed according to the concept of resilience, developed in the mathematics of nonlinear differential equations. According to this frame, the opposite to the vulnerability of a system is its stability, its resilience, defined specifically as an attribute of a system. The system is like a net; it consists of a great number of notes, which are interlinked.

Resilience provides a new framework for analyzing economic, ecological, technological, and social systems in a changing world facing many uncertainties and challenges. It represents an area of explorative research under rapid development with major policy implications for sustainable development.

Sometimes change is gradual and things move forward in roughly continuous and predictable ways. At other times change is sudden, disorganized, and turbulent reflected by climate impacts, earth system science challenges, and vulnerable regions. Evidence points out to a situation where periods of such abrupt changes are likely to increase in frequency and magnitude. [22]

3.2. RESILIENCE: INDEX AND MEASUREMENT

The term *resilience* was first applied to ecosystems and, based on this work as well as the work of organizations such as the Resilience Alliance and the Stockholm Resilience Center, resilience has become an important concept in the global dialog on climate action, featuring prominently in successive IPCC (International Panel for Climate Change) reports. [23]

It has been noted that transferring the concept of resilience to social and economic systems can present difficulties, and the concept may be differently appliedin different contexts.

The ability of a social or ecological system to absorb disturbances while retaining the same basic structure and ways of functioning, the capacity for self organization, and the capacity to adapt to stress and changes, the ability to absorb disturbances, to be changed and then to reorganize and still have the same identity and retain the same basic structure and ways of functioning is the essential role in the development of the ability of the system.

However, for thethe IPCC definition of resilience, wherein resilience is reflected by:

1. The amount of change or stress a system can endure while retaining control of its function and structure
2. The system's capacity for adaptation when responding to pressures
3. The system's ability for self-organization in the pursuit of long-term objectives

The first aspect of resilience identified above affects the "vulnerability" of the system, that is, the susceptibility of the system to specific shocks.

The second aspect of resilience identified is often discussed in terms of *adaptive capacity*. Adaptive capacity, as defined by the IPCC in relation to climate change, is "the ability of a system to adjust to climate change (including climate variability and extremes) to moderate potential damages, to take advantage of opportunities, or to cope with the consequences. Thus, adaptive capacity is reflected both is both the ability of a system to recover from shocks and to pursue long-term goals by reforming system functions and feedbacks in order to meet specified objectives." [24]

In discussing economic resilience, notes that resilience is explicitly linked "to the behavior of individuals, markets and the regional macroeconomy," and can therefore be manifested at the micro-, mesa-, and macro-economic levels. Prices, by influencing behavior at all levels, can guide resource allocation when a system disturbance or disaster occurs, although the need to ensure that principles of equity in market allocations are reflected by interventions such as income or material transfers to those in need. Another author uses the concept of resilience to explain why a number of inherently vulnerable countries have attained relatively high levels of GDP per capita.

Levels of poverty and inclusiveness of economic growth are important determinants of socioeconomic resilience. Those who are poor, or who are otherwise marginalized orexcluded from the opportunity, have fewer options and can be easily faced with the choice of having to sell productive assets in the face of a crisis. This, in turn, reduces future options and lowers adaptive capacity is the primary goal of the development.

The 2008 Human Development Report (HDR) [24] describes how climate change impacts on a range of impoverished communities and on overall human development. It concludes that limited options for individuals and social groups lowers their ability to adapt to climate change (and so lowers their resilience). Inclusive economic growth, on the other hand, allows knowledge and flexibility to be integrated into the institutions that sustain "human well-being in the face of complexity and change." Different groups in society (e.g., those in urban settings, those living in rural areas, etc.) can be described as having different levels of resilience and as being more or less resilient to different kinds of shocks. Similarly, they can play different roles in building resilient socioeconomic systems.

Investment strategies should also target human, social, natural, and finance capital to promote the robustness, redundancy and resourcefulness of the linked subsystems. The development of resilient socioeconomic systems is supported by aspects of the "green growth" policy focus as it relates to eco-efficiency, sustainable infrastructure development, and sustainable consumption and production. The concept of resilience also strengthens the case for investment in some of the basic tenets of sustainable development, such as stakeholder involvement, use of traditional knowledge, community empowerment, and management of natural resources.

Based on various studies of resilience, the following factors that build resilience in any system can be identified.

- *Robustness*: The ability of a system to withstand a perturbation without significant loss of performance.
- *Redundancy*: The extent to which systems and system elements can satisfy the same functional requirements. A diversity of pathways (or potential for creating a diversity of pathways) for achieving the same goal.
- *Resourcefulness*: The ability to diagnose, prioritize, and initiate solutions to problems; the capacity for self-organization, where internal feedback influences development; the ability to combine different types of knowledge in order to cope with change and uncertainty.

Furthermore, it reinforces the "benefits" side of the cost-benefit analysis of investments in renewable energy and distributed energy systems, recycling, and other "sustainability" interventions. Finally, it provides forward-thinking governments justification for investments in monitoring, knowledge management, early warning, networking, and identification of solutions as a risk management strategy.

3.3. DEVELOPING RESILIENCE INDEX

Most methodologies are applied to limited geographical and time scales and quantitative approaches have been largely based on valuation. While resilience is defined by the resilience community in specific terms, resilience measures are not always coherent with these definitions and rely on parameters that reflect resilience, rather than measure resilience directly.

As can be expected, all assessments are constrained by complexity of socioeconomic and ecological systems, and the availability of data. Regardless, two approaches for assessing resilience at different scales—(1) the development of a resilience index to compare resilience across countries, and (2) case study or series of case studies—are discussed in the following sections.

Although certain studies construct indices that attempt to provide an indication of the relative subsystem resilience (either social, ecological, or economic), there is no index of resilience for unified social–ecological–economic systems. Developing a unified systems index would fill an important gap left by available indices insofar as it would consider shocks that are transmitted across and feedback into subsystems, which affects the resilience of each subsystem. Folke et al. argue that resilience measures must focus on the variables that underlie the capacity of environmental systems to provide ecological services to socioeconomic systems.

The construction of a resilience index from an integrated systems perspective may beconsidered. One approach for creating a resilience index for linked social–ecological–economic systems would be to develop a conceptual basis for the selection and weighting of indicators that measure the resilience of each subsystem and to combine them to capture the adaptive capacity of the integrated system. Taking, for example, climate change shocks, a resilience index would support policy decision making by identifying the potential impacts of climate change and strategies to safeguard the socioeconomic and environmental systems from these impacts. Indeed, the 2007/2008 Human Development Report identifies the five areas of climate change impact as (1) agricultural productivity, (2) water security, (3) increased human health risks, (4) increased exposure to extreme weather events, and (5) the collapse of ecosystems.

Thus, useful indicators for assessing social, ecological, and environmental resilience in light of the shocks that are likely to accompany climate change in each of the five domains could be identified (using a framework such as suggested by Table 3.1), assessed, weighted (if appropriate), and then combined to provide an index of resilience to climate change. [25]

Table 3.1. Resilience Index:
Potential Framework for a Resilience Index

	Robustness	Redundancy	Resource-fullness
Economic Resilience			
Ecologic Resilience			
Social Resilience			

3.3.1. Application of a Case Study or Series of Case Studies

In its quantitative analysis, the approach is based on work by Loucks and Gladwell [26], which quantifies resilience by defining indicators of system performance and establishing a range that constitutes acceptable performance,. Loucks and Gladwell then track these parameters over time to determine how often the system fails (i.e., indicators fall outside the predefined acceptable limits) and how long it takes for the system to return to a state of acceptable performance. Thus, they assess resilience by measuring the "speed of recovery" from unsatisfactory performance and vulnerability by measuring the extent of system failure in response to a shock. However, since the time to return to acceptable limits would depend on the "degree" of shock experienced, a better indication of resilience may be obtained if the time taken to return can be related to the degree of shock experienced. Some examples of types of shock arising from climate change are shown in Table 3.2.

Table 3.2. Potential Framework for Case-Study Approach

Output	Component of analysis	Parameters specific to proposed analysis
Quantitative analysis of the availability resilience of a specific socioeconomic system based on historical data	Definition of system parameters Definition of shock to be investigated specific sources of shock Identify simple, but important indicators of system disturbance, track over time Relate magnitude of shock to the recovery time to assess resilience	Socioeconomical Key shocks related to climate change and resource Quantitative analysis of the availability resource Quantitative analysis of the availability
Identification of responses to improve resilience	Identify specific factors that may explain evidence for resilience (or lack of resilience) in historical terms	

3.4. RESILIENCE OF ENERGY SYSTEMS

Every system's catastrophic event comprises the resilience metric of the potential hazard of system. [27] It is important to realize that the sudden change of energy system indicators is a resilience parameter for the verification of a catastrophic event.

The energy system's catastrophe depends on the energy resilience. In this respect a group of catastrophic events are called a *power plant catastrophe*, namely, a nuclear plant catastrophe, solar power plant catastrophe, wind power plant catastrophe, fossil fueled power plan catastrophe, and energy transmission.

This chapter explores ways of enhancing the resilience of the energy system to withstand external shocks. The concept of resilience explored and a set of indicators is developed to define quantitatively the characteristics of a resilient energy system. In the paper we systematically test the response of the energy system to hypothetical shocks under different scenarios. We then assess mitigating measures that can help to reduce the impact of these shocks and test their cost effectiveness using an insurance analogy.

Three energy models are usedto conduct this analysis. [28] The first is the MARKAL-MED model, a linear optimization model that covers the entire energy system and can address interactions between different parts of the energy system. The second is the WASP electricity generation planning model originally developed by the International Atomic Energy Agency (IAEA). It is used to explore in more detail the levels of generation investment needed to maintain reliable supplies. It is a cost-minimizing model. The WASP model is fed electricity demand assumptions from MARKAL-MED.

The third model is the geographically explicit combined gas and electricity networks (CGEN) model, which is used to assess where electricity generation capacity should be located and how much gas and electricity infrastructure (wires, pipes, gas storage, and import terminals) should be constructed. It is another cost-minimizing model which is fed results from both MARKAL-MED and WASP.

3.5. CHARACTERIZING RESILIENCE

The advantage of focusing on resilience as the key concept is that it can be seen asan intrinsic characteristic of the energy system. It does not require us to think aboutthe underlying causes of a particular shock, for example, a prolonged interruption ofgas supply.

Drawing heavily on the ecological sciences, the following working definitionof energy system resilience:

"Resilience is the capacity of an energy system to tolerate disturbance and to continue to deliver affordable energy services to consumers. A resilient energy system can speedily recover from shocks and can provide alternative means of satisfying energy service needs in the event of changed external circumstances."

The following quantified indicators of resilience were arrived at by assessing their practical feasibility and by conducting a variety of sensitivity analyses using the MARKAL-MED model.

Energy demand and imports. It has set *a* constraint that final energy demand should fall by about 3.2% per annum relative to GDP, or about 1% per annum in absolute terms, from 2010 onwards. Different levels of demand reduction were benchmarked against bottom-up estimates of the potential impact of energy efficiency measures up to 2020 made by Government in the most recent carbon and energy projections available at the time the analysis was conducted. Our assumptions about constrained final energy demand correspond roughly to the assumption of a high impact of energy efficiency measures up to 2020. We then assume that the same pace of improvement will continue thereafter. This constraint is therefore at the upper end of the plausible range in terms of energy demand reduction.

*Primary energy demand.*It has constrained primary energy demand so that no single energy source (e.g., natural gas, oil) gains more than a 40% market share. The constraint on maximum share for primary energy supply ensured supply diversity in the economy as a whole.

Electricity generation. I have constrained the electricity generation mix so that no single energy source gains more than a 40% market share. Generation mix was constrained because the electricity sector was found to play a key role in shifting the overall primary energy mix.

With these constraints applied, the "resilient" and "low carbon resilient" scenarios differ considerably from the "reference" and "low carbon" scenarios.[29] The low carbon scenario is dominated by rapid decarburization on the supply side, especially in the electricity sector. The sector is virtually decarbonized by 2030 and electricity enters new markets through electric and plug-in hybrid vehicles and heat pumps in the residential sector. In the resilient scenario, electricity decarbonization takes place only slowly. In the low carbon resilient scenario, the electricity system decarbonizes by 2050 but the pace of decarbonization is about 10–15 years behind the low carbon scenario.

The main theme in the resilient scenarios is the driving down of energy demand. Thisis reflected mainly in the residential sector and in demand for gas. The reduction ingas demand leads directly to lower levels of imports. We have hypothesized a set of shocks to the gas system and investigated the impacts. There is a system response that adds to costs, but with the most severe shocks supply curtailments are inevitable. The model predicts the following sequence of responses: (a) invoking interruptible gas contracts with industry, (b) redispatching the electrical generators to use less gas, (c) use of backup distillate oil at CCGTs, and (d)

The costs associated with the shocks were much lower in the resilient and low carbon resilient scenarios. This is because gas demand is so much lower. This is because these two scenarios are characterized by lower levels of residential gas demand, which is strongly seasonal. The system can cope better when demand is less "peaky." Demand reduction demonstrably contributes to energy system resilience.

The imputed value of unnerved energy (in billions of $) is an order of magnitude larger than the changed system costs. System costs generally rise as more expensive gas is sourced and coal substitutes for gas in electricity generation. However, this does not take account of the response in energy spot markets that would be expected following such events, which would tend to increase costs.

The patterns of response are complex because the facilities play different roles in the gas network. In none of the scenarios is it necessary to curtail electricity supplies. Response is taken up entirely by exercising interruptible gas contracts, redispatch of electricity generators, use of distillate oil at certain CCGTs, and noncontracted industrial gas interruptions.

The effectiveness of a set of infrastructure investments, over and above those required to meet reliability standards is in mitigating the hypothesized shocks. These included gas storage, LNG terminals, new gas interconnectors, and storage of distillate oil backup at a CCGT plant.

The most severe shock, for a 40-day period and assessed the impact of these mitigating investments was in the low carbon scenario. The biggest impact in terms of reducing the volume of energy unserved came from the expansion of import facilities by new LNG terminals or a new interconnector. Dedicated gas storage and 40 days' distillate storage have half to two thirds the impact of more import facilities. The effectiveness of gas storage is critically dependent on how much gas is in store at the time of the shock. If a storage facility is kept completely full for emergencies it will be much more effective in mitigating shocks.

Making a mitigating investment can be regarded as taking out insurance against theeventuality of adverse events. If a rate of return of 10% real is required on investment in two LNG terminals, then the 40-day outage would need to take place more than once every 35 years to pay off. Given the severity of the event, and the improbability of its happening as frequently as this, it is almost impossible to conceive of this as a good investment in a market context.

On the other hand, investment in mitigating measures could be regarded as being in the public interest for strategic reasons. At a rate of return on investment of only 3.5% real, the Treasury "social" discount rate, investing in LNG terminals might still pay off if the event were to occur as infrequently as once in 100 years.

There are costs and benefits associated with moving from the low carbon to the low carbon resilient scenario. Most of these are associated with the macro-indicators of resilience, especially bearing down on final energy demand. Energy system costs are6 $ billion lower in 2025 simply because the energy system is smaller. However, there isan implied loss of welfare of 18 $ billion associated with the loss of consumer surplus asconsumers respond to higher energy prices.

In practice, it may be possible to mitigate some or even all of these welfare losses. If25% of the demand reduction is achieved through low cost conservation measures the welfare loss is reduced by 2,7 $ billion. We also explored a scenario where people voluntarily reduce their energy use as a result of social and cultural change. This mayinvolve no welfare loss at all—and it reduces the energy system cost by 42 $billion in 2025.

The costs of ensuring electricity system reliability and reinforcing gas infrastructure are orders of magnitude less than the costs associated with driving the macrostructure of the energy system in different directions. Enhanced electricity reliability appears to cost around $10–15 per household per year while additional investment in gas storage or import facilities appears to run at around $2 per household.

Achieving the macro goals of reduced imports and greater supply diversity can be achieved through the vigorous pursuit of fairly conventional policy instruments. The key is a very strong emphasis on policies to improve energy efficiency in buildings and transport. The emphasis on the demand side needs to be much stronger than in a pure low carbon scenario. Keeping up the pace of investment in renewables and nuclear will also contribute.

As regards reliability and redundancy, in the electricity system current policy is to deliver an adequate capacity margin by having a licensing obligation on power companies to meet energy demands, and then relying on markets, through price signals, to deliver capacity that may only be rarely used. There is now a widespread view that current market arrangements may not be sufficient to guarantee reliable energy supply while ambitious low carbon targets and renewable energy goals are pursued.

This report suggests that there is potentially a case for investment in further "strategic" gas infrastructure beyond that which the market would deliver if we pursue the supply-led energy strategy embodied in the low carbon scenario. By itself, that investment would be relatively modest and would add little to consumer costs. There are three possible models for stimulating such investment: government provides the appropriate framework for the market to make the investment; the regulator permits the investment through price reviews, but the investment is provided by the regulated companies; or government carries out the investment itself. The third model appears unlikely. The key policy question is whether the benefits of driving this investment through rate-of-return regulation outweigh the disadvantages of driving out investment made on a purely market basis.

In recent years, particularly after the catastrophe of Hurricane Katrina [30] in August 2005, resilience has gained prominence as a topic in the field of disaster research, supplanting the concept of disaster resistance.

Disaster resistance emphasizes the importance of predisaster mitigation measures that enhance the performance of structures, infrastructure elements, and institutions in reducing losses from a disaster. Resilience reflects a concern for improving the capacity of physical and human systems to respond to and recover from extreme events.

For the past seven years, researchers affiliated with the Multidisciplinary Center for Earthquake Engineering Research (MCEER), sponsored by the National Science Foundation and headquartered at the University at Buffalo, have collaborated on studies to conceptualize and measure disaster resilience. The resilience-related projects have involved researchers from a range of disciplines, including civil, structural, and lifeline engineering; sociology, economics, and regional science; policy research and decision science. The goals of the multiyear effort were to define disaster resilience, develop measures appropriate for assessing resilience, and then demonstrate the utility of the concept through empirical research.

To develop a framework, the MCEER research team drew on various literatures and research traditions that focused on resilience and related concepts, including ecology, economics, engineering, organizational research, and psychology. The literature revealed consistent cross-disciplinary treatments in which resilience was viewed as both inherent strength and the ability to be flexible and adaptable after environmental shocks and disruptive events.

MCEER researchers defined disaster resilience as "the ability of social units (e.g., organizations, communities) to mitigate hazards, contain the effects of disasters when they occur, and carry out recovery activities in ways that minimize social disruption and mitigate the effects of future disasters."

Critical infrastructure systems—including transportation and utility lifeline systems—play an essential role in communitywide disaster mitigation, response, and recovery and therefore are high-priority targets for resilience enhancement. Resilient systems reduce the probabilities of failure; the consequences of failure, such as deaths and injuries, physical damage, and negative economic and social effects; and the time for recovery. Resilience can be measured by the functionality of an infrastructure system after a disaster and also by the time it takes for a system to return to predisaster levels of performance.

Resilience-enhancing measures aim at reducing the size of the resilience triangle through strategies that improve the infrastructure's functionality and performance (the vertical axis) and that decrease the time to full recovery (the horizontal axis). For example, mitigation measures can improve both infrastructure performance and time to recovery. The time to recovery can be shortened by improving measures to restore and replace damaged infrastructure. In examining the attributes and determinants of resilience, MCEER investigators developed the R4 framework of resilience:

Resourcefulness reflects the availability of materials, supplies, repair crews, and other resources to restore functionality. Hurricane Katrina was a catastrophe because of the extent and severity of the physical damage and the inability to move critical resources into the disaster-stricken region.

Rapidity is a consequence or outcome of performance of highway bridges and is a major concern after earthquakes and other extreme events. Serious damage can impede critical emergency response, and the failure to detect collapsed bridge spans—particularly during the first few minutes of an earthquake—can result in serious injuries and fatalities.

During the past five years, a group of researchers from the Multidisciplinary Center for Earthquake Engineering Research in Buffalo, New York, has investigated the use of remote sensing technologies to detect urban damage and to assist in emergency response. The research has focused on damage detection, including the development of algorithms for using optical and synthetic aperture radar data to locate highway and building collapses, as well as a mapping scheme to display and disseminate earthquake-related geospatial data.

Another technology is a tiered reconnaissance system, which uses satellite images to determine the location, extent, and severity of building damage after an earthquake; the accompanying photographs offer a schematic representation. Output from the TRS can assist in determining the scale of site visits and of relief efforts and in settingpriorities.

A second major effort in post-disaster damage assessment was completed recently under the Joint Program on Remote Sensing and Spatial Information Technologies of the U.S. Department of Transportation and NASA. As part of the Safety, Hazards, and Disasters Consortium led by the University of New Mexico, ImageCat, Inc. developed innovative methods for near real-time damage assessment of highway bridges. The methods employ remote sensing technology. The products from the research were Bridge Hunter, which produces a catalogue of key bridge attributes and images from a range of airborne and satellite sensors, and Bridge Doctor, which assesses the damage state of bridges by evaluating changes between images acquired before and after an earthquake.

The slow pace of restoration and recovery in the Gulf Region after Hurricane Katrina indicates low levels of resilience throughout the area. At the same time, some states, communities, and infrastructure systems have proved more resilient than others.

The literature and the MCEER research consider resilience to comprise both inherent and adaptive properties. Inherent resilience refers to an entity's ability to function well during noncrisis times. [31] Adaptive resilience refers to an entity's demonstrated flexibility during and after disasters: the ability to adapt behavior and exercise creativity in addressing disaster-induced problems. These two properties of resilience may be correlated; entities with inherent resilience also may be better able to develop and implement adaptive coping strategies.

3.6 RESILIENCE DOMAINS AND METRICS

MCEER [32] investigators identified four dimensions or domains of resilience: the technical, organizational, social, and economic (TOSE):

The technicaldomain refers primarily to the physical properties of systems, including the ability to resist damage and loss of function and to fail gracefully. The technical domain also includes the physical components that add redundancy.

Organizationalresilience relates to the organizations and institutions that manage the physical components of the systems. This domain encompasses measures of organizational capacity, planning, training, leadership, experience, and information management that improve disaster-related organizational performance and problem solving. The resilience of an emergency management system, therefore, is based on both the physical components of the system—such as emergency operations centers, communications technology, and emergency vehicles—and on the properties of the emergency management organization.

The socialdimension encompasses population and community characteristics that render social groups either more vulnerable or more adaptable to hazards and disasters. Social vulnerability indicators include poverty, low levels of education, linguistic isolation, and a lack of access to resources for protective action, such as evacuation.

*Local and regional economies*and business firms exhibit different levels of resilience. Economic resilience has been analyzed both in terms of the inherent properties of local economies—such as the ability of firms to make adjustments and adaptations during nondisaster times—and in terms of their capacity for post-disaster improvisation, innovation, and resource substitution. In general, social and economic resilience relate to the ability to identify and access a range of options for coping with a disaster—the more limited the options of individuals and social groups, the lower their resiliency.

Understanding the attributes and dimensions of resilience provides guidance for defining and achieving acceptable levels of loss, disruption, and system performance. The R4 approach highlights the multiple paths to resilience. Investments can improve all four resilience components—robustness, redundancy, resourcefulness, and rapidity. The TOSE framework emphasizes a holistic approach to community and societal resilience, looking beyond physical and organizational systems to the impact of the disruptions on social and economic systems.

The MCEER perspective suggests a range of approaches to enhance resilience, including mitigation-based strategies, the development of a robust organizational and community capacity to respond to disasters, and improving the coping capabilities of households and businesses. In conjunction with disaster loss estimation techniques and other types of decision support tools, the MCEER resilience framework can help community officials, transportation and utility lifeline service organizations, and other stakeholders to explore the outcomes and tradeoffs associated with different resilience-enhancing strategies. As part of the conceptualization of a framework to enhance the seismic resilience of communities, seismic resilience has been defined as the ability of a system to reduce the chances of a shock, to absorb such a shock if it occurs (abrupt reduction of performance), and to recover quickly after a shock (reestablish normal performance). More specifically, a resilient system is one that shows:

- Reduced failure probabilities
- Reduced consequences from failures, in terms of lives lost, damage, and negative economic and social consequences
- Reduced time to recovery (restoration of a specific system or set of systems to their "normal" level of functional performance)

Resilience concept.

A broad measure of resilience that captures these key features can be expressed, ingeneral terms, by the concepts illustrated in Figure 3.2 based on the notion that a measure, $Q(t)$, which varies with time, can be defined to represent the quality of the infrastructure of a community. Specifically, performance can range from 0% to 100%, where 100% means no degradation in quality and 0% means total loss. If an earthquake or other disaster occurs at time t_0, it could cause sufficient damage to the infrastructure such that the quality measure, $Q(t)$, is immediately reduced (from 100% to 50%,.. Restoration of the infrastructure is expected to occur over time, as indicated in that figure, until time t_1 when it is completely repaired and functional (indicated by a quality of 100%). Hence, community earthquake loss of resilience, R, with respect to that specific earthquake, can be measured by the size of the expected degradation in quality (probability of failure), over time (that is, time to recovery).

Much research is needed to quantify resilience, particularly for some type of critical facilities. For critical systems for which the deliverable is not a simple engineering unit, such as for the case of acute care facilities, the vertical axis is harder to define, not to mention quantify. This paper presents concepts developed in attempts to quantify the seismic resilience of facilities. The engineering tools that could result from an implementation of the concepts presented here could contribute and be integrated into decision support tools, which in turn could be used for the formulation of strategies and policies at a higher level.

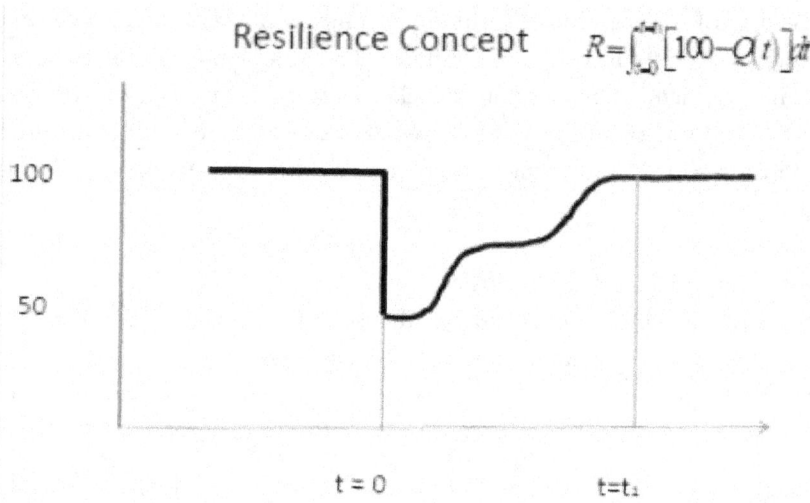

Figure 3.1. Tracking system performance and resilience.

As such, the vertical and horizontal axes in Figure 3.1 address the ends of resilience, namely robustness and rapidity. However, Figure 3.2 can be expanded in 3D to capture the means of resilience, namely resourcefulness and redundancy. This is illustrated in Figure 3.2. In theory, if infinite resources were available, time to recovery would asymptotically approach zero. Practically, even in the presence of enormous financial and labor capabilities, human limitations will dictate a practical minimum time to recovery.

3.7. CONCEPTUALIZING AND MEASURING RESILIENCE

In recent years, particularly after the catastrophe of Hurricane Katrina in August 2005 [32], resilience has gained prominence as a topic in the field of disaster research, supplanting the concept of disaster resistance.

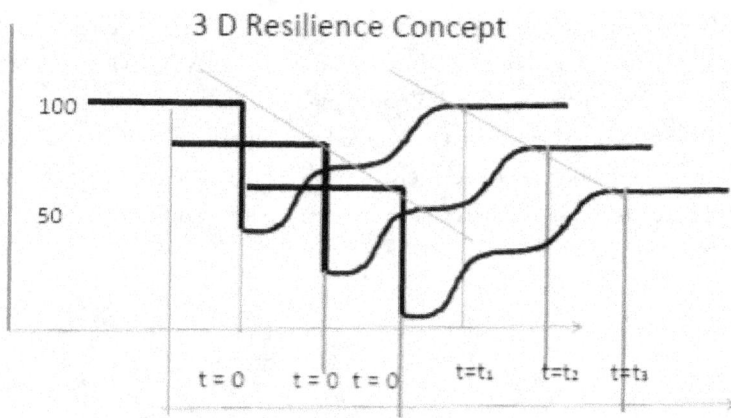

Figure 3.2. 3D Resilience Concept.

Disaster resistance emphasizes the importance of predisaster mitigation measures that enhance the performance of structures, infrastructure elements, and institutions in reducing losses from a disaster.

Resilience reflects a concern for improving the capacity of physical and human systems to respond to and recover from extreme events.

For the past seven years, researchers affiliated with the Multidisciplinary Center for Earthquake Engineering Research (MCEER), sponsored by the National Science Foundation and headquartered at the University at Buffalo, have collaborated on studies to conceptualize and measure disaster resilience. The resilience-related projects have involved researchers from a range of disciplines, including civil, structural, and lifeline engineering; sociology, economics, and regional science; policy research; and decision science. The goals of the multiyear effort were to define disaster resilience, develop measures appropriate for assessing resilience, and then demonstrate the utility of the concept through empirical research.

To develop a framework, the MCEER research team drew on various literatures and research traditions that have focused on resilience and related concepts, including ecology, economics, engineering, organizational research, and psychology. The literature revealed consistent cross-disciplinary treatments in which resilience was viewed as both inherent strength and the ability to be flexible and adaptable after environmental shocks and disruptive events. frastructure systems have proved more resilient than others

The literature and the MCEER research consider resilience to comprise both inherent and adaptive properties (2–3). Inherent resilience refers to an entity's ability to function well during noncrisis times. Adaptive resilience refers to an entity's demonstrated flexibility during and after disasters— the ability to adapt behavior and exercise creativity in addressing disaster-induced problems.

These two properties of resilience may be correlated; entities with inherent resilience also may be better able to develop and implement adaptive coping strategies.

3.7.1. Resilience Domains

MCEER investigators identified four dimensions or domains of resilience: The Technical, Organizational, Social, and Economic (TOSE):

The technicaldomain refers primarily to the physical properties of systems, including the ability to resist damage and loss of function and to fail gracefully. The technical domain also includes the physical components that add redundancy.

Organizational resilience relates to the organizations and institutions that manage the physical components of the systems. This domain encompasses measures of organizational capacity, planning, training, leadership, experience, and information management that improve disaster-related organizational performance and problem solving. The resilience of an emergency management system, therefore, is based on both the physical components of the system—such as emergency operations centers, communications technology, and emergency vehicles—and on the properties of the emergency management organization such as the quality of the disaster plans, the ability to incorporate lessons learned from past disasters, and the training and experience of emergency management personnel.

The socialdimension encompasses population and community characteristics that render social groups either more vulnerable or more adaptable to hazards and disasters. Social vulnerability indicators include poverty, low levels of education, linguistic isolation, and a lack of access to resources for protective action, such as evacuation.

Local and regional economiesand business firms exhibit different levels of resilience. Economic resilience has been analyzed both in terms of the inherent properties of local economies—such as the ability of firms to make adjustments and adaptations during nondisaster times—and in terms of their capacity for post-disaster improvisation, innovation, and resource substitution In general, social and economic resilience relate to the ability to identify and access a range of options for coping with a disaster— the more limited the options of individuals and social groups, the lower their resiliency.

Understanding the attributes and dimensions of essence provides guidance for defining and achieving acceptable levels of loss, disruption, and system performance. The R4 approach highlights the multiple paths to resilience. Investments can improve all four resilience components—robustness, redundancy, resourcefulness, and rapidity. The TOSE framework emphasizes a holistic approach to community and societal resilience, looking beyond physical and organizational systems to the impact of the disruptions on social and economic systems.

The MCEER perspective suggests a range of approaches to enhance resilience, including mitigation- based strategies, the development of a robust organizational and community capacity to respond to disasters, and improving the coping capabilities of households and businesses. In conjunction with disaster loss estimation techniques and other types of decision support tools, the MCEER resilience framework can help community officials, transportation and utility lifeline service organizations, and other stakeholders to explore the outcomes and tradeoffs associated with different resilience-enhancing strategies.

3.7.2. R4 Framework

MCEER researchers defined disaster resilience as the ability of social units (e.g., organizations, communities) to mitigate hazards, contain the effects of disasters when they occur, and carry out recovery activities in ways that minimize social disruption and mitigate the effects of future disasters.

Critical infrastructure systems—including transportation and utility lifeline systems—play an essential role in communitywide disaster mitigation, response, and recovery and therefore are high-priority targets for resilience enhancement.

Resilient systems reduce the probabilities of failure; the consequences of failure—such as deaths and injuries, physical damage, and negative economic and social effects; and the time for recovery.

Resilience can be measured by the functionality of an infrastructure system after a disaster and also by the time it takes for a system to return to predisaster levels of performance.

Resilience-enhancing measures aim at reducing the size of the resilience triangle through strategies that improve the infrastructure's functionality and performance (the vertical axis in the figure) and that decrease the time to full recovery (the horizontal axis). For example, mitigation measures can improve both infrastructure performance and time to recovery.

The time to recovery can be shortened by improving measures to restore and replace damaged infrastructure. In examining the attributes and determinants of resilience, MCEER investigators developed the R4 framework of resilience:

- Robustness—the ability of systems, system elements, and other units of analysis to withstand disaster forces without significant degradation or loss of performance;
- Redundancy—the extent to which systems, system elements, or other units are substitutable, that is, capable of satisfying functional requirements, if significant degradation or loss of functionality occurs;
- Resourcefulness—the ability to diagnose and prioritize problems and to initiate solutions by identifying and mobilizing material, monetary, informational, technological, and human resources; and
- Rapidity—the capacity to restore functionality in a timely way, containing losses and avoiding disruptions. In transportation systems, robustness reflects the ability of the entire system—including the most critical elements—to withstand disaster-induced damage and disruption.

Redundancy can be measured by the extent that alternative routes and modes of transportation can be employed if some elements lose function. After the 1989 Loma Prieta earthquake, for example, expanded use of the Bay Area Rapid Transit system and the trans-Bay ferries overcame to some extent the loss of the San Francisco Bay Bridge.

Resourcefulness reflects the availability of materials, supplies, repair crews, and other resources to restore functionality. Hurricane Katrina was a catastrophe because of the extent and severity of the physical damage and the inability to move critical resources into the disaster-stricken region.

Rapidity is a consequence or outcome of improvements in robustness, redundancy, and resourcefulness. The slow pace of restoration and recovery in the Gulf Region after Hurricane Katrina indicates low levels of resilience throughout the area.

REFERENCES

[1]   Afgan N.H., *Sustainable Resilience of Energy System*, 2010, Nova Science Publisher, Inc. New York, ISBN: 978-1-61668-483-9.

[2]   *Report of The United Nations Conference on Environment and Development*, Rio de Janeiro, Brazil, Vol. 1, Chapter 7, (June 1992.

[3]   Agenda 21, Chapter 35, 1992 *Science for Sustainable Development*, United Nations Conference on Environment and Development.

[4]   *The Role of Technology in Environmentally Sustainable Development, Declaration of the Council of Academies of Engineering and Technological Sciences*,Kiruna, Sweden, June 21,1995.

[5]   *The Earth Chapter: A Contribution Toward Its Realization*, Franciscan Center of Environmental Studies, Rome, Italy (1995),www.globalsustainability.org.

[6]   Jenkinson C.S., *The Quality of Thomas Jefferson's Soul*, White House Library, 1987.

[7]   WCED (WorldCommission Of Economic Development.

[8]   Folke, C., et al., 2000. The value of nature and the nature of value. *Science* 289, 395–396.

[9]   Hollnagel, E. & Woods, D. (2005). *Joint Cognitive Systems: An Introduction to Cognitive Systems Engineering*. Taylor & Francis.

[10] Holling, C. S. (1973). "Resilience and stability of ecological systems." *Annual Review of Ecology and Systematic*. 4: 1–23.

[11] Hollnagel E., Woods D., Levesen N., *Resilience Engineering: Concepts and Percepts*,Ashgate Publishing Limited, 2005.

[12] Hollnagel F., Nemet, Dokker P. S., *Resilience Engineering Perspective*,Ashgate, June 2008.

[13] Gunderson, L. H., Holling, C. S., Pritchard Jr., L. and Peterson, G. D. (2002). "Resilience of Large-Scale Resource Systems". Gunderson, L. H. and Pritchard Jr., L. (Eds.) *Resilience and the Behaviour of Large-Scale Systems*. Washington DC, Island Press. Pp 3–18.

[14] Gruenn H.R.,*Resilience and its Application to Energy System*, Springer Berlin/Heidelberg, 2006.

[15] Hollnagel, E., Woods, D. D. and Leveson, N. (Eds.) (2006). *Resilience Engineering: Concepts and Precepts.*Ashgate Publishing Ltd, Aldershot, England.

[16] Pimm, S.L., 1991. *The Balance of Nature? Ecological Issues in the Conser-*

vation of Species and Communities. University of Chicago Press, Chicago.

[17] Folke, C. (2006). "Resilience: The Emergency of a Perspective for So-cial-Ecological Systems Analyses". *Global Environmental Change.* 16(3): 253–267.

[18] Walker, B.H., Holling, C.S., Carpenter, S.R., Kinzig, A.P., 2004.Re-silience, adaptability and transformability in social–ecologicalsystems. *Ecology and SocietyURL* http://www. Ecology andsociety.org/vol9/iss 2/art5/.

[19] Luhmann Hans-Jochen; Manfred F.; Otto Schallaböck Karl,*Vulnerability of the energy system in the age of man made global change,* Wuppertal In-stitute,, 42103,2003, Wuppertal, Germany

[20] Walker, B.H., Holling, C.S., Carpenter, S.R., Kinzig, A.P., 2004. *Re-silience, adaptability and transformability in social–ecological systems. Ecology and Society* URL www. Ecology andsociety.org/vol9/iss2/artSpecial Re-port on Renewable Energy Sources and Climate Change Mitigation (SRREN), IPPC 2011.

[21] *Jim Skea Building A Resilient Energy System,* UKERC Energy 2050 Proj-ect, www.ukerc.ac.uk.

[22] Loucks D., Gladwell J., *Sustainability Criteria for Water Resources Systems,* Cambridge Press, ISBN 0-521-056044-6, 199.

[23] Afgan N., Veziroglu A. Sustainable resilience of hydrogen energy sys-tem, *International Journal of Hydrogen Energy,*Volume 37, Issue 7, April 2012, Pages 5461–5467.

[24] Ander Kraak, Karen Press, HSRC, *The 2008 Human Development Report (HDR),* Press, ISBN 978-0-7969-2203-8, 2008.

[25] Briguglio, L. "Economic Vulnerability and Resilience: Concepts and Measurements." In LinoBriguglio and Eliawony J Kisanga eds., *Eco-nomic Vulnerability and Resilience of Small States, Islands and Small States Institute and Commonwealth Secretariat.* (2004).

[26] Loucks D., Gladwell J., Sustainability Criteria for Water Resource Sys-tems (1999), International Hydrology Series, Cambridge University press, 1999.

[27] K.J. Horowitz and M.A. Planting, *Concepts and Methods of the Input-Out-put Accounts,* Bureau of Economic Analysis, U.S. Department of Com-merce, September 2006 (April 2009).

[28] *MARKAL-MED model runs of long term carbon reduction targets in the U.K.,* AEA Energy and Environment, 2008.

[29]   *A low carbon and resilient urban future,*ISBN 978-1921298-81-3, www.ag.
       gov.au/cca.

[30]   Binu Jacob, Anthony R. Mawson, Marinelle Payton, John C. Guignard,
       Disaster Mythology and Fact:Hurricane Katrina and Social, *Public
       Health Reports* / September–October 2008 / Volume 12.

[31]   *Multidisciplinary Center for Earthquake Engineering Research (MCEER),*
       mceer.buffalo.edu.

CHAPTER 4

ENERGY SYSTEM RESILIENCE

4.1. INTRODUCTION

The energy resilience is the ability of energy system to provide and maintain an acceptable level of service in the face of various to normal operation.

Resilience can be defined in two ways. The first is a measure of the magnitude of disturbance that can be absorbed before the system changes its structure by changing the variables and processes that control behavior. The second, a more traditional meaning, is as a measure of resistance to disturbance and the speed of return to the equilibrium state of an ecosystem.

Resilience networks aim to provide acceptable service to applications: ability for users and applications to access information when needed, e.g. distributed database access, sensor monitoring, situational awareness and operation of distributed processing and networked storage, e.g.: ability for distributed processes to communicate with one another, ability for processes to read and write networked storage.Note that resilience is a superset of survivability [1].

The sustainability paradigm is a complex idea, which is defined and interpreted as the intergenerational phenomena, as the level of scale, multiple domains, social development of societies and multiple interpretations of sustainable development. In the understanding of sustainability development the major precondition is to highlight the role of the material and energy consumption as a source of unsustainable pattern of the development. The need to balanceeconomic, environmental, technological and socialsustainability is the goal forenergy accessibility, availability and acceptability [2].

The energy sustainability keys are: energy diversity and energy efficiency, energy infrastructure investment, cost-reflective prices and market-sensitive intervention, supply reliability, regional integration of the energy system, market-based climate change responses, technological innovation and development and public understanding and trust [3].

Sustainable development encompasses economic, ecological, technological and social perspectives of conservation and change. In correspondence with the WCED (World Commission for Economic Development), it is generally defined as the "development that meets the needs of the present without compromising the ability of future generations to meet their own needs" [4]. This definition is based on ethical imperative of equity within and between generations. Moreover, apart from meeting basic needs of all, sustainable development implies sustaining the natural life-support systems on earth, and extending to all the opportunity to satisfy their aspirations for a better life. Hence, sustainable development is more precisely defined as 'a process of change in which the exploitationof resources, the direction of investments, the orientation of technological development, and institutional changes are all in harmony and enhance both current and future potential to meet human needs and aspirations.

Sustainability provides a framework for integrating economic, environmental, technological and social interests into an effective strategy. For the life support systems, that have recognized the need to embrace sustainable development, the first step is to understand how to implement it. Putting this concept into operation requires identifying practical indicators of sustainability and to understand how they can be measured over time to determine if progress is made.

The energy system can be visualized in different scales, domains, societies, and verified with multiple indicators.

With regard to the scale, the energy system can be local, regional, state or global. Each of these scales will lead to different implications reflecting specific characteristics to be as the attribute for its definition.

The energy system domain will quantify the energy demand in every energy system scale. This will imply the specification of energy consumption in different forms needed by society within the defined energy system.

The resilience of a system relates to the magnitude of disturbance required to fundamentally disrupt the system causing a dramatic shift to another state of the system, controlled by a different set of processes. When resilience is lost or significantly decreased, a system is at high risk of shifting into a qualitatively different state. The new state of the system may be undesirable. Restoring a system to it's previous state can be complex, expensive, and sometimes even impossible. Research suggests that to restore some systems to their previous state requires a return to conditions well before the point of collapse.

The energy system resilience refers to the capacity of energy system to withstand perturbations from e.g. climatic, economic, technological and social causes and to rebuild and renew it afterwards [5]. Loss of resilience can cause the loss of valuable energy system services, and may even lead to rapid transitions or shifts into qualitatively different situations and configurations, described for e.g. people, ecosystems, knowledge systems, or whole cultures. In general terms, the vulnerability of a system is assessed according to the concept of resilience, developed in the mathematics of non-linear differential equations. According to this frame, the opposite to the vulnerability of a system is its stability, its resilience, defined specifically as an attribute of a system. The system is like a net; it consists of a great number of nodes, which are interlinked.

Resilience provides a new framework for analyzing economic, ecological, technological and social systems in a changing world facing many uncertainties and challenges. It represents an area of explorative research under rapid development with major policy implications for sustainable development.

Sometimes change is gradual and things move forward in roughly continuous and predictable ways. In other times, change is sudden, disorganized and turbulent reflected by climate impacts, earth system science challenges and vulnerable regions. Evidence points out to a situation where periods of such abrupt changes are likely to increase in frequency and magnitude [6].

Sustainability comprises complex system approach in the evaluation of the system state. By its definition sustainability includes the definition of quality merits without compromising among different aspects of system complexity. It is of paramount importance for any system as the complex system to quantify elements of complexity taking into consideration various degrees of complexity. As regards complexity, the system can be codified as the specific structure system reflecting different.

Any process is characterized by the entropy production as the measure of the reversibility of the processes within the system. So, the complexity element of the system reflecting internal parameter interaction can be defined by the entropy production in the system. In the complexity definition of the system, one of the elements is entropy generation of the system or exergy losses in the process [7]

Complexity elements of the economic indicators structured in different levels are intrinsic to the specific levels and are measured in different scales. In the classical evaluation of a system the economic merits are of primary interest. Since the economic quality is reflecting an optimization function imposing minimum final product cost, there are a number of parameters, which are of interest to be taken into consideration in the mathematical model for the determination of the optimized values required for its evaluation.

Mutual interaction between the system and its surrounding is imminent for any life support system. As it is known, the system takes material resources from the surrounding and disposes residuals to the environment. Among those residuals, the most important are those, which are in gaseous form and are dissipated into the environment. Also, most of the energy system is disposing low entropy heat to the environment

The social aspect of complexity is property of the complex systemreflecting the social aspects of the system are the risk of environmental change as well as health and nuclear hazards; these may have to deal with a compound of complexity at different levels. Also, under social constrain reflecting social aspects of complexity of energy system are added values, which improve the quality of human life, Figure 4.1.

The technological quality of the system is defined and qualified as the potential upgrading of theindividual part of the system and also as the interrelation among the different aspects. In the language of complex systems, this property can be understood as the inherent creativity of the spontaneous appearance of a novel structure. Thermodynamically, information introduced in the system is the neg-entropy as the result of the change in the structure of the system leading to better performance.

The safety of anenergy system is the immanent property to any system. It reflects the quantitative measure of degradation of the may be seen as the potential property predicting total degradation of the system. It is commonly known that any degradation of the system proceeds with changes of the main properties of the system. Since the sustainability index is a complex property of the system it will lead to the possibility to define those rates of change, which may have different consequences [8].

The resilience of energy system is defined as the capacity of an energy system to withstand perturbations from e.g. climatic, economic, technological and social causes and to rebuild and renew itself afterwards. In this respect, quantification of the resilience capacity can be used as the merit for withstanding differing events leading to potential damaging consequences. So, the change of resilience of an energy system can be used in the assessment of the system behavior and the potential for its malfunction development. As the sustainability index definition we have used specific quality indicators reflecting corresponding criteria, it is possible to use the sustainability index as the resilience metric parameter.

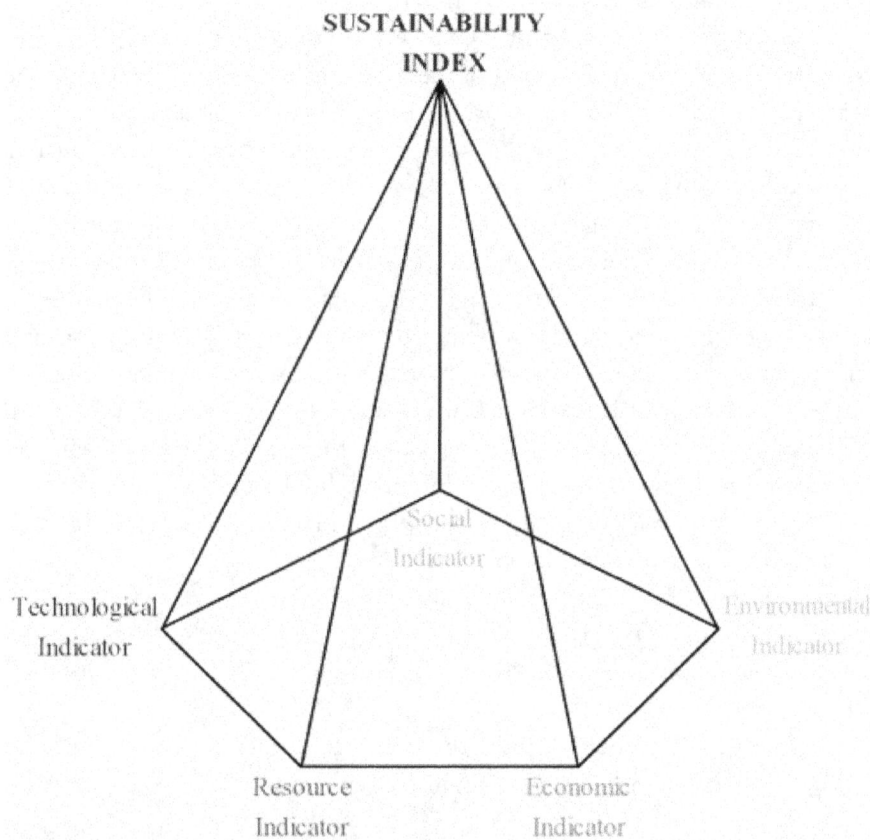

Figure 4.1. Sustainability Index Structure.

The change of the economic indicator is intrinsic to the specific characteristic to be measured in the time scale. The time change of the economic indicators is common to the classical evaluation of a system. Any crises of the economic system are preceded with corresponding changes in the economic indicators of the system. Qualitative measurement of the indicator changes may lead to the forecast of the economic crises, which is only one element of the potential disastrous changes of the system affecting its safety [9].

The mutual interaction between the system and its surrounding is imminent for any system. The changes in interaction rate will affect the safety of the system. If these processes are in steady state, it can be considered that the system is safe. As good example for this type of changes of indicator is the interaction of system and its surrounding in the case of radioactive leaks from nuclear facilities, which may lead to hazardous consequences.

The change of social element of complexity of the system is a property of the complex system. The social aspect of thesystem includes the risk of changes as health hazards and may have to deal with a compounding of complexity at different levels. It is of interest to notice that some of the social changes are an inherent characteristic of the system. As an example we can take any strike, which is the result of the economic changes of the system. A similar example can be seen if there is a sudden change in the environment, which will lead to social disturbances.

If it is assumed that the Sustainability index is a linear agglomeration function of products between indicators and corresponding weighting coefficients, we can write the aggregation function, which is presented in the form of additive convolution. If it is adapted, which means that each of the criteria is weighted by the respective factor, the sum of thecriteria multiplied with the corresponding factor will lead to the Sustainability Index [10].

For the case under consideration, the Sustainability Index Q(q,) will lead to the following mathematical function

$$Q(t) = \sum_n \omega_n q_n(t) \tag{4.1}$$

where

n – weighting coefficient for the n-th specific indicator

q_n – n-th criterion for sustainability assessment.

4.2 RESILIENCE INDEX OF ENERGY SYSTEM

The Resilience Index is integral of the Sustainability Index between thetime of the sudden change in the respective indicator and thetime when it resumesa steady state value, Figure 4.2. The resilience index for an energy system is composed of the following elements: economic, environmental, technological and social.

$$R_j = \sum_{i=1}^{k} w_i \int_{t_0}^{t_1} \left[1 - q_i(t) \right]$$

(4.2)

where

j – resilience index

q_i –indicator

w_i- weight coefficient

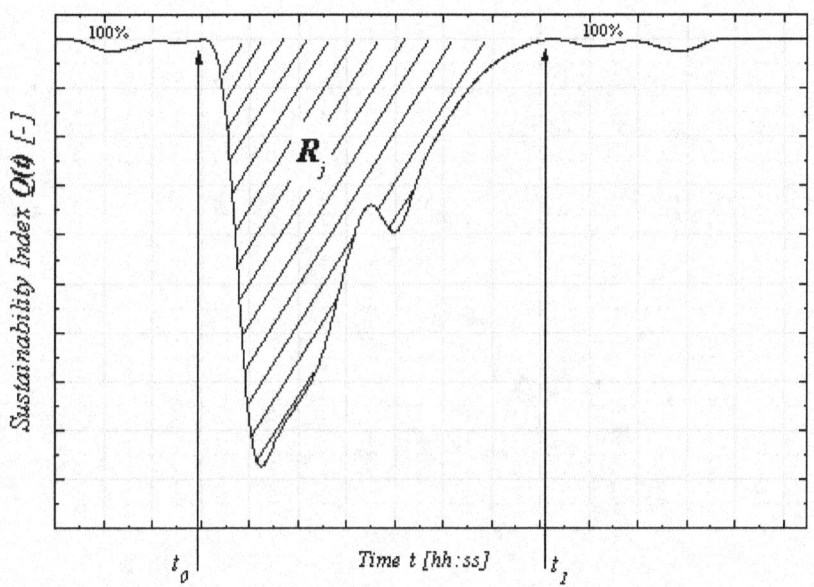

Figure 4.2. Graphical presentation of Resilience Index.

The resilienceindex is composed of sub-indicators. In the same way the economic,environmental, technological and social resilience element could be obtained, as follows. Under theassumption that the sudden indicator change resumes is a linear function of time, then we can write

$$R_j = \frac{1}{2} w_i \left(\Delta q_i \Delta t \right)$$

$$(4.3)$$

If it is assumed that the time interval for resuming starting state is equal for all indicators than the Resilience Index for the individual case is

$$R_j = \frac{\Delta t_o}{2} w_i \Delta q_i$$

$$(4.4)$$

The total Resilience Index is an additive function of all resilienceIndexes as follows

$$R_{total} = R_{econ} + R_{env} + R_{soc} + R_{tech} + R_{rc}$$

$$(4.5)$$

Generic monitoring and analysis flow chart for the Resilience Index monitoring is shown on Figure 4.3

Schematic Structure of Monitoring and Analysis System

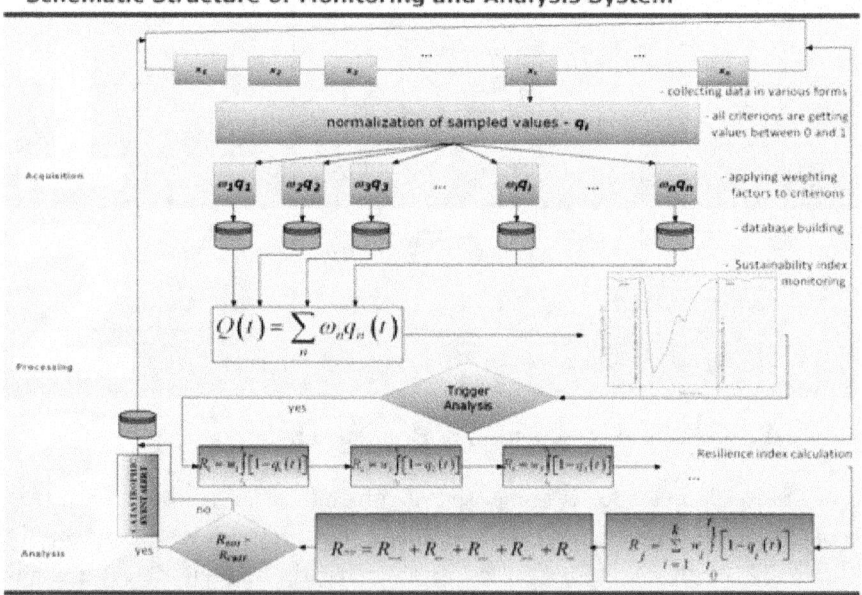

Figure 4.3. Generic Monitoring and Analysis System Flowchart.

This exercise is aimed to demonstrate the potential to use of resilience index in the assessment of thesafety of the selected energy system.

In this analysis, we will consider a coal fired power plant of 300 MW in condensed regimes Figure 4.4. [11,12]. Due to the limited availability of data, this exercise will be limited to the economic, environmental, technological and social aspects of the respective criteria. As it was defined, the Sustainability Index time derivative is the measure of the Resilience Index. In this respect, the sudden change of indicators is scaled in the single scale, and the time of integration for all indicators is the same. The Resilience Index of power plant under consideration will be defined under specific constrains, namely, the sudden change of specific indicators with other indicators being constant. This approach will give us the possibility to validate the change of indicators on the safety of the energy system under specific constrain.

Options

The following options of energy system resiliencewere taken into a consideration. It is of interest to notethat the design of individual options is linked to the complexity of energy system exposed by the different potential fluctuation of the individual characteristic parameters of the system. Since the characteristic parameters of the energy system reflect specific features of the system, it is important to notice that every fluctuation of the characteristic indicators should be investigated under multi-variable change. In this respect, this analysis focused on the Resilience Index resulting due to multi-variable fluctuations.

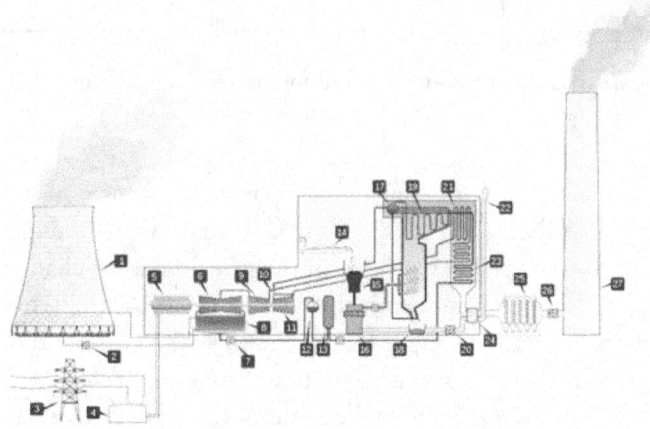

Typical diagram of a coal-fired thermal power station

1. Cooling tower	10. Steam Control valve	19. Superheater
2. Cooling waterpump	11. High pressure steam turbine	20. Forced draught (draft) fan
3. transmission line (3-phase)	12. Deaerator	21. Reheater
4. Step-up transformer (3-phase)	13. Feedwater heater	22. Combustion air intake
5. Electrical generator (3-phase)	14. Coal conveyor	23. Economiser
6. Low pressure steam turbine	15. Coal hopper	24. Air preheater
7. Condensate pump	16. Coal pulverizer	25. Precipitator
8. Surface condenser	17. Boiler steam drum	26. Induced draught (draft) fan
9. Intermediate pressure steam turbine	18. Bottom ash hopper	27. Flue gas stack

Figure 4.4. Coal fired power plant in condensing regime [source: Wikipedia].

Option A

The design of Option A is based on the assumption to introduce the Economic Indicator change of 0 cEuro/kWh [13], with an Environmental Indicator change of 100 gr/kWh [14], a Technological Indicator change of 130 Euro/kW [15] and a social indicator change of 1.75 Jobs/kW [16] defined within the same time increment (see also Table 4.1). The validation of the indicator changes is made for Option A with the calculation of the General Sustainability Index change for individual cases reflecting respective constrains. In particular, attention is focused on the introduction of constrains on the mutual relation between options under consideration. Using selected data the resilience value is determined for every case reflecting changes of the indicators. It should be emphasized that the resilience index reflects the essential parameter of the energy system under consideration.

Option B

Option B comprises the environmental change with the assumption of 0 gr/kWh, while other indicator values are 0.015cEuro/kWh, 260 Euro/kW, and 3.3 Jobs/kW, respectively Table 4.2. The option with the zero change of the environmental indicator represents the case with the Resilience Index changes resulting from the changes introduced by respective change of other indicators. In the determination of the change of indicators for this option, it is anticipated that these changes are reflecting the same time change of other indicators. It is of interest to notice that this option is also reflecting the same time increment.

Option C

Option C represents the technology change equal to 0 Euro/kW and the other indicators defined with the following characteristic values: an economic indicator change of 0.023, an environmental indicator change of 200 gr/kWh, and a social indicator change of 6.6 Jobs/kW, Table 4.1. This option comprises the fluctuation imposed by the multi-variable indicator change expressed by numerical values of the time change of individual indicators.

Option D

Option D - Social Change is designed under the assumption that the social Indicator change is 0, the economic indicator change of 0.046 cEuro/kWh, the environmental indicator change is 400 gr/kWh, the technological Indicator change is 520 Euro/kW,Table 4.1).The social indicator change option equal to zero is the option characterized with the other indicators having maximum indicators change. This means that the fluctuations introduced are the maximum potential change of the indicators.

In this analysis, the characteristic indicators used the following change indicators.

Indicator normalization is obtained by the selection of the maximum and minimum value for every indicator and expressed in following mathematical form.

Table 4.1. Resilience Indicators

	Economic Indicator Change cEuro/kWh	Environmental Indicator Change gr/kWh	Technological Indicator Change x 106 Euro/kW	Social Indicator Change Jobs/kW
Option A	0	100	130	1.75
Option B	0.0115	0	260	3.3
Option C	0.023	200	0	6.6
Option D	0.046	400	520	0

The Resilience Index of energy system is a characteristic parameter, which is used for the assessment of the energy system resilience. The multi-criteria assessment method is used for the evaluation of options under consideration [10].

The demonstration of assessment is presented by the analysis of thefollowing cases.Figure 4.5, Figure 4.6, Figure 4.7.

CASE 1

Priority given to the following criteria: EnIC>EcIC = TIC = SIC

Weighting Coefficient

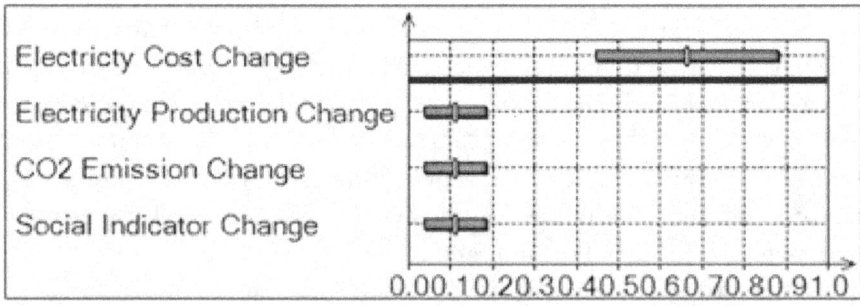

Resilience Index

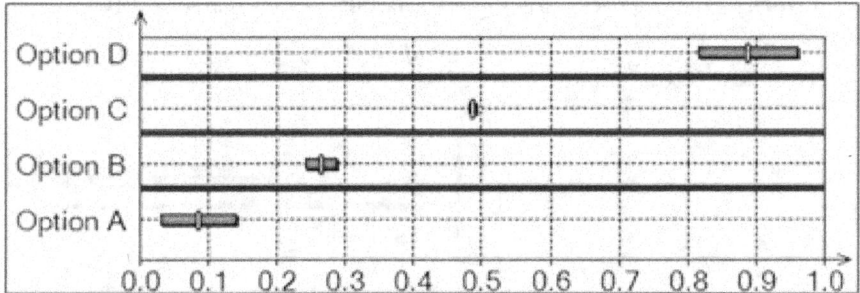

Figure 4.5. Weight Coefficient and Resilience index for Case 1.

CASE 2

Priority given to the following criteria: TIC >EcIC = EnIC = = SIC

Weighting Coefficient

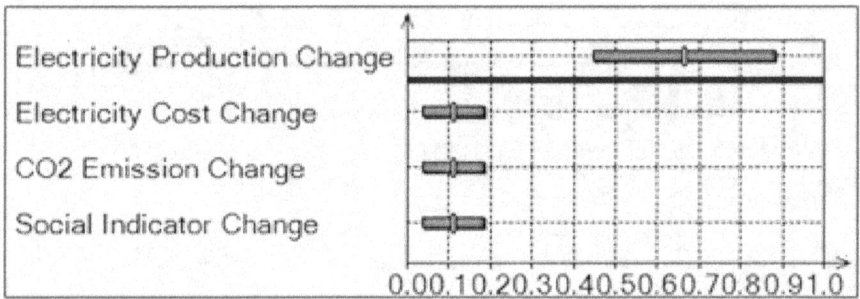

Resilience Index

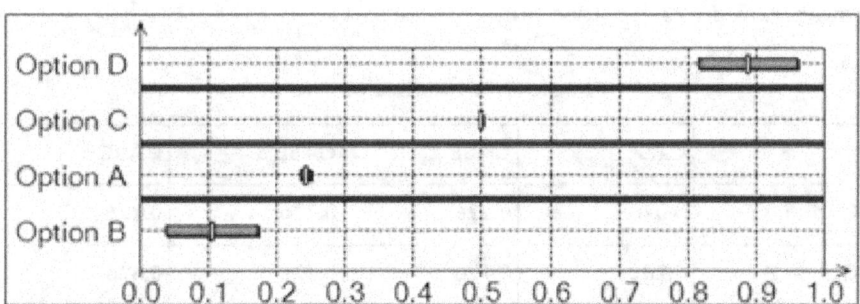

Figure 4.6. Weight Coefficient and Resilience index for Case 2.

CASE 3

Priority given to the following criteria: SIC>EcIC>EnIC = TIC

Weighting Coefficient

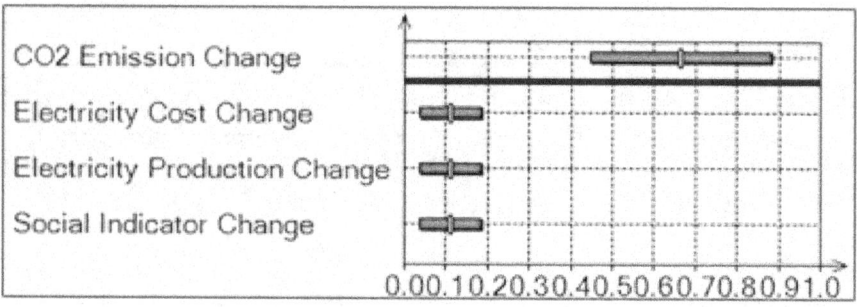

Resilience Index

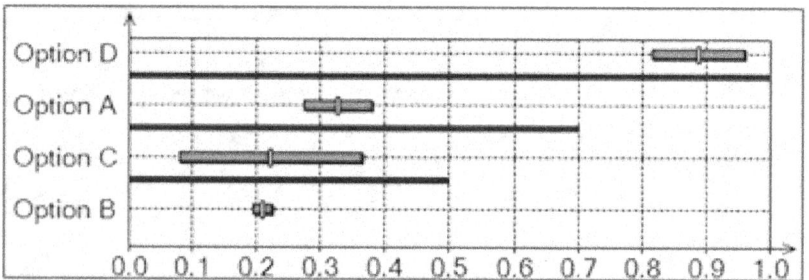

Figure 4.7. Weight Coefficient and Resilience index for Case 3.

The results are expressed in the value of agglomerated indicator for the power plant under consideration, Table 4.2.

Table 4.2. Resilience Index

	CASE I	CASE 2	CASE 3	CASE 4
Option A	0.0765	0.226	0.226	0.236
Option B	0.282	0.126	0.426	0.426
Option C	0.500	0.500	0.20	0.800
Option D	0.900	0.900	0.90	0.300

The Resilience Index is the measure of thepotential ability of anenergy system to recover after changes introduced by the respective indicator change. In this exercise, four indicators were used for the evaluation of the system. In designing specific cases, individual casesare anticipated with single indicator change equal tozero and other indicator changes as specified in Table 4.2.

Results obtained by this analysis are presented as the agglomerated indicators reflecting constrains introduced for every case. It is of interest to notice specific cases.

Case 1 is reflecting a situation, which imposes zero Economic Indicator Change while other indicators have values as specified in Table 4.2. Regarding obtained results for this case it reveals thatthe agglomerated indicator rating with the priority to Option 4 -Social Indicator Change with other options rated as shown in Table 2. It is of interest to notice that this case is designed with the aim to show the effect of economic indicator change on the ability to avoid, minimize, withstand, and recover from the effects of adversity, whether natural or man-made, under all circumstances of use on the system under consideration.

Case 2 describesa situation where the Environment indicator is taken with zero value change and other indicator changes are specified with numerical values as shown in Table 3. Results obtained for this case are presented as the rating of agglomerated indicator of Options under consideration.As it can be noticed the obtained results are not substantial different in comparison with Case 1. The Resilience Index rating for this Case is different in the position of Option A on the rating List.

Case 3 shows a substantial change in the rating list among options. Even Option- Social Change is in the first place in the rating list the position of other options is changed. Option B is moved in the second place of the List and Option C has exchanged position on the List. The Resilience Index change is aresult of the strong effect of social change on the energy system.

Case 4 shows the effect of the technological change on the Resilience Index. This means the introduction of technology on the ability of an energy system to withstand fluctuation of social parameters on the energy system behavior. It is obvious that there are potentially different effects on the resilience of theenergy system.

Resilience Index, as the parameter of an energy system, is the quantification of the elasticity of the system. If the instant change of a single parameter is introduced, it leads to the Resilience Index defined with the exponential time change. Multi-indicators changesrequire a respective definition of the Resilience Index, which include agglomerated indicator as the measuring resilience parameter of the system.

The Resilience Index of an energy system expressed in the form of agglomerated indicators, gives the opportunity to assess a complex system complied with potential malfunction of the energy system. It is of special interest to learn about the relation among the indicators leading to the degradation of the energy system. In this respect, the behavior of an energy system is vulnerable with the complex degradation.

It is of interest to establish an appropriate methodology for the energy system resilience measurement as a tool for the quantitative verification of the system. In particular, there is a need for the resilience quantification as a safety assessment parameter. The Energy system, as a complex system,has an imminent need for safety assessment and evaluation during operation.

4.3 RESILIENCE OF WIND POWER PLANT

The total amount of economically extractable power available from the wind is considerably more than present human power use from all sources [17]. An estimated 72 TW of wind power on the Earth potentially can be commercially viable, compared to about 15 TW average global power consumption from all sources in 2005.

The insurance market thought it had a bad 12 months with Australian fires and floods, plus the New Zealand Earthquake. Then Japan happened. The world is still reeling from the horrific damage and loss of life due to the March earthquake and tsunami. Governments, businesses, nuclear-plant operators, and renewable-energy companies are reviewing the risk profiles and models now associated with catastrophe losses. Meanwhile, insurers—and perhaps more importantly the global reinsurance market—are undertaking in-depth reviews of their exposure to loss from natural disasters and asking: How could we get it so wrong, again? It seems an appropriate time to look at how these events may affect modern grid-connected wind farms.

Contrary to popular belief, average wind speeds along coastal areas in many parts of the world, particularly the U.S. Gulf Coast, are often lower than in inland areas. As a result, most wind farms have been built away from coastlines. However, turbines have steadily improved with new designs letting them capture more energy from low wind regimes than previously possible. This makes coastal development an increasingly attractive alternative, yet also increases turbine exposure to hurricane damage.

Project developers are looking closely at sites such as the U.S. Gulf and East Coast, the Caribbean, Philippines, Taiwan, Pakistan other parts of the Far East. Insurers classify all these locations as High-Risk Zones for the peril of windstorm and other national catastrophe, "Nat Cat," events such as earthquake and flood. As a result, insurers usually establish a sublimit of liability on their coverage based on the likelihood of events happening over a given period of time using modeling tools. This means to more fully protect the project assets, an owner must purchase "catastrophe" coverage, above that provided in their basic property coverage.

a) Windstorm Loss History

A number of global windstorm losses have affected wind-farm coverage. In September 2008, Hurricane Ike passed near Jamaica where a $28 million wind project had just reached full operation. The site was affected by winds estimated to have exceeded 140 mph. Its turbine rotors feathered as designed upon power loss, and yaw systems locked in place. Nearly all nacelle covers were lost. Fortunately, damage was limited to a number of electrical components and feathered blades where high winds struck their flat sides. Wind-driven flexing damaged blade roots.

More recently with Katrina, significant flooding (wind-driven water) damaged a wind farm under construction in the Gulf Coast. To date, these events have been limited, but if thewind industry continues to expand and seek new locations— especially along coastal areas—project debt and equity will require adequate protection.

Wind-farm flood exposures are relatively rare because most turbines are generally installed on ridge lines, mesas, or mountain slopes—areas rarely affected by floods. However, heavy rains on project sites can erode access roads and scour earth from around turbine foundations. Recent events in the U.S. have resulted in complete turbine collapse.

Knowing that a project's basic Operating All Risk insurance policy will generally include a sublimit for catastrophe cover, the question becomes: How much additional catastrophe cover should a project owner buy.

It is almost a given that the cost of purchasing catastrophic insurance to the full replacement value of a project in a highly exposed area will be far too costly. As a general rule, most projects work to 30 to 50% of their asset value but also give some consideration for debt service.

Another complicating factor is that these costs can vary widely from year to year because the cost of catastrophic coverage in any year is highly dependent on the market's loss history during the previous several. In 2005, after the worst year for insured catastrophe losses with Katrina, Rita, and other storms, insurers were required to establish stronger financial reserves to maintain financial ratings. Consequently, after a year of significant losses, insurers will move quickly to reestablish financial strength and their ratings.

b) Wind Power Plant Resilience Index

Resilience of the wind power plant is the capacity of the system to withstand changes of the following parameters: wind velocity, mechanical energy conversion into electricity, electricity transmission efficiency and electricity cost. Resilience index comprise following indicators: change in wind velocity, change in mechanical energy conversion efficiency, change in conversion factor, and change in transmission efficiency end change in electricity cost.

The demonstration ofresilience index monitoring is presented by using following indicators, namely: average wind velocity, power production, efficiency of electricity production, and power-frequency change in evaluation of the resilience index of wind power plant special attention is devoted to the determination of the resilience index for situation with priority given to individual indicators.

State-of-the-art wind power plants use large spinning blades to capture the kinetic energy in moving wind, which then is transferred to rotors that produce electricity [17]. At the best wind sites, wind plants today are nearly competitive with the conventional natural gas-fired combined-cycle plants — even when natural gas prices have recently been at historically low levels. Regions where average wind speeds exceed 12 miles per hour are currently the best wind power plant sites [18].

Current costs of wind-generated electricity at prime sites approach the costs of a new coal-fired power plant. Wind power is the lowest-cost renewable energy technology available on the market today. Costs of wind power are projected to continue to fall and may rank the cheapest electricity source of all options by 2020.

The strength of wind varies, and an average value for a given location does not alone indicate the amount of energy a wind turbine could produce there. To assess the frequency of wind speeds at a particular location, a probability distribution function is often fit to the observed data. Different locations will have different wind speed distributions. The Rayleigh model closely mirrors the actual distribution of hourly wind speeds at many locations [19].

Because so much power is generated by higher wind speed, much of the energy comes in short bursts. The consequence is that wind energy from a particular turbine or wind farm does not have as consistent an output as fuel-fired power plants; utilities that use wind power provide power from starting existing generation for times when the wind is weak thus wind power is primarily a fuel saver rather than a capacity saver. Making wind power more consistent requires that various existing technologies and methods be extended in particular the use of stronger inter regional transmission to link widely distributed wind farms since the average variability is much less; the use of hydro storage and demand-side energy management [20]. The Earth is unevenly heated by the sun resulting in the poles receiving less energy from the sun than the equator does. Also, the dry land heats up (and cools down) more quickly than the seas do. The differential heating drives a global atmospheric convection system reaching from the Earth's surface to the stratosphere which acts as a virtual ceiling. Most of the energy stored in these wind movements can be found at high altitudes where continuous wind speeds of over 160 km/h occur. Eventually, the wind energy is converted through friction into diffuse heat throughout the Earth's surface and the atmosphere.

The total amount of economically extractable power available from the wind is considerably more than present human power use from all sources.[21] An estimated 72 TW of wind power on the Earth potentially can be commercially viable,[22] compared to about 15 TW average global power consumption from all sources in 2005.

The strength of wind varies, and an average value for a given location does not alone indicate the amount of energy a wind turbine could produce there. To assess the frequency of wind speeds at a particular location, a probability distribution function is often fit to the observed data. Different locations will have different wind speed distributions. The Rayleigh mode closely mirrors the actual distribution of hourly wind speeds at many locations.Rayleigh flow refers to diabetic flow through a constant area duct where the effect of heat addition or rejection is considered. Compressibility effects often come into consideration, although the Rayleigh flow model certainly also applies to in-compressible flow. For this model, the duct area remains constant and no mass is added within the duct.

Wind power density (WPD) is a calculation relating to the effective force of the wind at a particular location, frequently expressed in terms of the elevation above ground level over a period of time. It further takes into account wind velocity and mass. Figure 4.8.

Since wind speed is not constant, a wind farm's annual energy production is never as much as the sum of the generator nameplate ratings multiplied by the total hours in a year. The ratio of actual productivity in a year to this theoretical maximum is called the capacity factor. Typical capacity factors are 20-40%, with values at the upper end of the range in particularly favorable sites. For example, a 1 megawatt turbine with a capacity factor of 35% will not produce 8,760 megawatt-hours in a year (1x24x365), but only 1x0.35x24x365 = 3,066 MWh, averaging to 0.35 MW. Online data is available for some locations and the capacity factor can be calculated from the yearly output [23].

Unlike fueled generating plants, the capacity factor is limited by the inherent properties of wind. Capacity factors of other types of power plant are based mostly on fuel cost, with a small amount of downtime for maintenance. Nuclear plants have low incremental fuel cost, and so are run at full output and achieve a 90% capacity factor. Plants with higher fuel cost are throttled back to follow load. Gas turbine plants using natural gas as fuel may be very expensive to operate and may be run only to meet peak power demand. A gas turbine plant may have an annual capacity factor of 5-25% due to relatively high energy production cost.

According to a 2007 Stanford University study published in the Journal of Applied Meteorology and Climatology, interconnecting ten or more wind farms can allow an average of 33% of the total energy produced to be used as reliable, baseload electric power, as long as minimum criteria are met for wind speed and turbine height (Figure 9).

The best way of measuring wind speeds at a prospective wind turbine site is to fit an anemometer to the top of a mast which has the same height as the expected hub height of the wind turbine to be used. This way one avoids the uncertainty involved in recalculating the wind speeds to a different height.

By fitting the anemometer to the top of the mast one minimizes the disturbances of airflows from the mast itself. If anemometers are placed on the side of the mast it is essential to place them in the prevailing wind direction in order to minimize the wind shade from the tower.

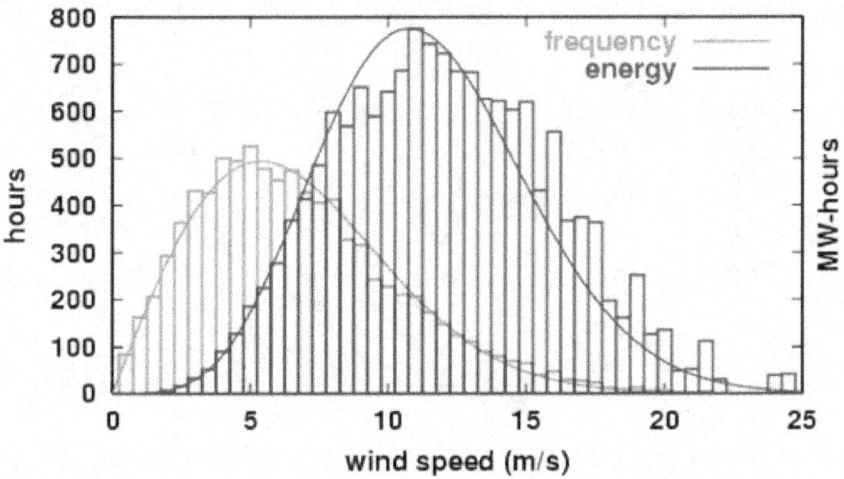

Figure 4.8. Frequency and energy probability.

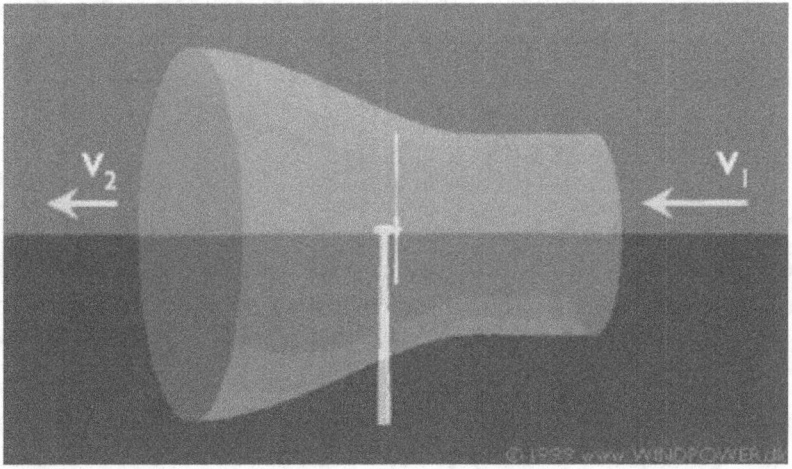

Figure 4.9. Wind Power Model.

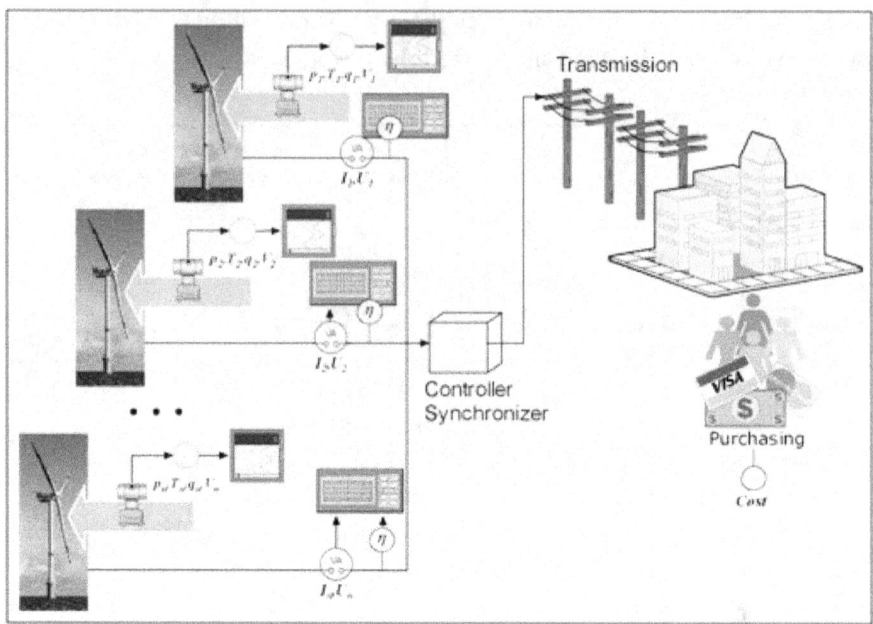

Figure 4.10. Schematic Presentation of Wind Power Plant.

Calculation the energy available in the wind [24] relies on knowledge of basic geometry and physics behind kinetic energy. Kinetic energy of collection of objects KK with total mass M and velocity V is given by expression

$$KE = \frac{1}{2} \cdot M \cdot V^2 \qquad (4.6)$$

In order to define kinetic energy of the molecules of air we can define volume of the air particles in the shape of a huge hockey pack with thickness D that has geometry of collection of air molecules passing through the A plane of a wind turbine blade over a given time.

The volume of the pack is determined by

$$Vol = A \cdot D$$
$$if = M / Vol$$

Then we can write that

$$KE = \frac{1}{2} \cdot V^3 \cdot A \cdot T \qquad (4.7)$$

If the kinetic energy is divided by time, T, the power available from air parcel can be expressed as

$$Pwr = \frac{1}{2} \cdot V^3 \cdot A$$

If the Pwr is divided by the cross section of parcel, A, then we can obtain expression

$$Pwr / A = \frac{1}{2} \cdot V^3 \qquad (4.8)$$

This term is called the "Wind Power Density". It can be noticed that the WPD depends the density of air and the wind speed and size, the efficiency wind power plant.

The wind speed is defined with average wind velocity obtained by the geometry of blade and its local position.

The average wind velocity is characterized by two parameters: wind frequency and wind speed. Since both of these parameters are time dependent their measurement will require respective models for their evaluations to be used in the monitoring of WPD.

The monitoring of wind power plant is based on the number of indicators. The definition of each indicator is specified by the respective wind power model as presented in following description:

c) Wind Power Density

These evaluations lead us to the definition of the tree parameters to be as the monitoring of the Wind Power Density, namely: pressure and temperature of the air, average wind velocity and frequency of the wind.

d) Efficiency of Wind Power Plant

Mechanical energy obtained by the wind energy is converted to the electricity by the electric generator with respective efficiency defined respective efficiency defined by

$$= WDP \cdot A / E_{power} \qquad (4.9)$$

Monitoring parameters are: WDP and E_{power}

e)Power Frequency

Power frequency is parameter needed for the wind power plant synchronization. Together with electric power measured by the electric currency in amperes and grid voltage in volt, it is stability constrain for the connection to the grid. It is required monitoring of following parameters: frequency fluctuation and voltage fluctuation in the grid.

f) ElectricityCost

Cost of the electricity produced by the wind power plant is defined as the total amount of plant expenses divided by power produced. The expenses are defined by the cost of manpower and maintenance cost.

Resilience Index Monitoring of Wind Power Plant

On Figure 4.10 are shown schematic structure of monitoring position. Monitoring system for the wind energy power plant comprise measurement individual parameters as they are shown on thw monitoring scheme, Figure 4.11.

Data processing is organized with the appropriate definition of the Sustainability Index. As shown on Figure 4.11 the first step in data processing is the data normalization with the aim to obtain specific indicators to be agglomerated in the Sustainability Index.It is assumed that the Sustainability index is a linear agglomeration function of products between specific indicators and corresponding weighting coefficients, in the form of additive convolution. If it will be adapted that each of the specific indicator is weighted by the respective weighting coefficient.

Schematic Structure of Monitoring and Analysis System

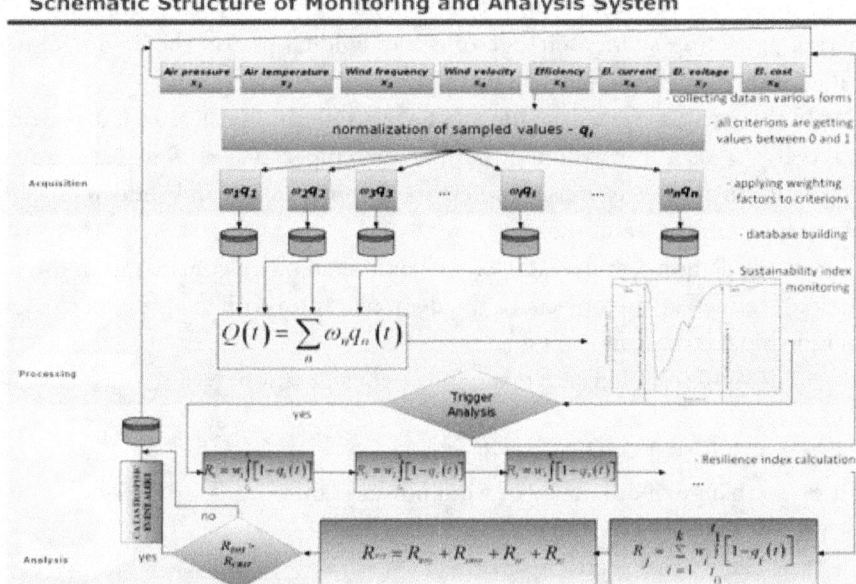

Figure 4.11. Monitoring and Analysis System Flowchart of Wind Power Plant.

The evaluation of wind energy system as the complex system is the prestigious goal of modern approach to the validation of the energy system. In this context it is introduced notion of the Resilience Index as the agglomerated indicator for the measurement of the wind energy system quality [24,25]. Resilience Index is the property of wind energy system based on the assumption that the wind energy system is a complex system with time change of main system parameters. The integral value of the Sustainability Index recovery after sudden change leads to the definition of Resilience Index.

The second step in the data processing is the determination of the resilience index component corresponding to the sudden change of the specific indicators. It is anticipated the total Resiliency Index is the sum of the resiliency index components.

The monitoring of individual indicators is performed by the respective instrument. It is anticipated that instruments are calibrated to appropriate scale for individual unites. Signal processing includes a following operation: instrument calibration, signal digitalisation and signal acquisition within the respective time increment and calculation of the resilience indicator.

Following determination of the resilience index in the appropriate time period reflecting sudden change of the individual period the agglomerated value of the total resilience will be monitored.

In this exercise we will assume that every indicator is measured in the time interval t_0. Also, it is assumed that the air temperature and air pressure are constant during this exercise. Indicators nominal values and sudden changes are as given in the Table 4.3.

In this demonstration exercise we have taken into a consideration the situations defined as the objects of the demonstration with the sudden changes of individual indicators.

Following situations are taken into a consideration:

- Change of wind power density
- Change of efficiency of wind power plant
- Change of frequency
- Change of electricity cost

The total Resilience Index is an additive function of all resilienceIndexes as follows

$$R_{TOT} = R_{WPD} + R_{EWPP} + R_{PF} + R_{EC} \tag{4.10}$$

where

$$
\begin{aligned}
&R_{TOT} && - \text{total resilience index} \\
&R_{WPD} && - \text{wind power density} \\
&R_{EWPP} && - \text{efficiency of wind power plant} \\
&PF && - \text{power frequency} \\
&R_{EC} && - \text{electricity cost}
\end{aligned}
$$

In the design of the Objects under consideration it is introduced assumption that the sudden change of indicators is triggered at the same moment for all indicators. Also, the change of indicators are normalised and the maximum change for each of the indicator expressed in normalised value. It is of particular interest for this demonstration to have each object defined as the composition simulations sudden changes of all indicators as shown on Table 4.3.

Table 4.3.

Objects	Wind power density, WPD	Efficiency of wind power plant, EWPP	Power frequency EF	Electricity cost EC
	Δm/sec	Δ %	Δ Ampere	Δ€/kWh
Object 1	4/20	2.5	1.25	0
Object 2	2	5/100	2.5	1.25
Object 3	1	1.25	5/50	2.5
Object 4	0	0	0	5/20

The Total Resilience Index is determined for following cases.

Case 1 - WPD > EWPP = PF = EC
Case 2 - EWPP > WPD = PF =EC
Case 3 - PF > WPE = EWPP = EC
Case 4 - EC > WPPD = EWPP = PF

The results obtained for these cases are shown in Table 4.4.

Table 4.4.

Cases	Resilience Index
Case 1	0.755
Case 2	0.866
Case 3	0.612
Case 4	0.647

The Resilience Index is the stability parameter of any system and can be used as the measuring parameter for the assessment of the potential hazard events. As regards the wind power plant analysis it prove that the most stable case in sudden change of the indicators is the Case 2 when the priority of the indicators is given to the Efficiency Wind Power plant.

In particular, it is of interest to mention that the Resilience Index is the parameter of the system which can be used as the diagnostic tool in the assessment of the potential hazard event of the system. As regards wind energy power plant hazard events can lead to mal function of the wind power plant elements.

4.4 RESILIENCE OF SOLAR POWER PLANT

There is a range of solar energy applications instead the inworld-wide for electricity production. The WEC highlights the role of photovoltaic (PV) panels and solar thermal power plants such as concentrated solar power (CSP) for the global electricity supply. It indicates the most promising areas for CSP are the Southwest of the US, Central and South America, Africa, the Middle East, the Mediterranean countries of Europe, South Asia, certain countries of the Former Soviet Union, China and Australia. However there are major barriers which shell need to be overcome before solar energy can compete with fossil fuel energy [26,27].

These barriers are higher production costs, a lack of adequate Research and Development (R&D) and a lack of favorable policies. Neverthelesscosts for solar power could be more comprehensive in many places if fossil fuel subsidies would be reduced. In addition, generation costs for solar energy are significantly below the generation costs for fossil fuels as energy from the sun is for free and no fuel has to be purchased. However the up-front costs for solar energy are high and are a prohibitive factor for individual consumers as well as for investors.

There are two major ways in which climate change and intensified disaster risks can affect the solar power sector. First, solar power generation depends on the availability of solar radiation. Climatic changes which off cloud cover and solar radiation can have negative off effects on solar power generation.

Second, solar equipment could be impacted by changing disaster risks such as storms, floods, heavy precipitation on events and other extreme weather events. Both points are elaborated in more detail below. It is argued a changing climate might affect solar energy product on due to changing cloud covers and increasing temperatures which might reduce the electric output. PV cells can operate even on cloudy days, however mirror-based solar thermal applications such as CSP need direct sunlight.

However the key issue is the impact of climate change on disaster risks. An increase in the frequency and severity of cyclones and storms could increase the risk of destruct on of solar energy infrastructure. Sea-level rise and flooding could also impact solar energy equipment. Nevertheless, there are many uncertainties and more research is needed into the changing disaster risks for solar energy.

Solar power plant is designed to convert solar energy in the electricity. PV plants are composed of following elements, namely: Solar collector, DC convertor, Transmission element. Safety of PV plant depend the potential changes of the behaviors of the plant elements. In order to keep control of the PV plant it is of great importance to validate potential changes of the power plant indicators.

Sustainability index of PV plant is defined by the number of indicators specified to reflect respective quality of the system. Among those indicators are: Local insulation, Collector conversion efficiency, DC conversion efficiency, Environment precipitation and Maintenance Cost. The change of sustainability index is result of the changes of the individual parameters of the system.

Resilience of the Photo-voltaic power plant is the capacities of the plant to withstand sadden changes of the indicators. In this analysis we will present application of the resiliency index to monitor the stability of the PV plant system. This analysis will be based on the monitoring of following indicator changes: Local insulation change, Collector efficiency change, DC conversion efficiency change, Environment precipitation and Maintenance change.

The photovoltaic effect is the basic physical process through which a PV cell converts sunlight into electricity. Sunlight is composed of photons (like energy accumulations), or particles of solar energy. These photons contain various amounts of energy corresponding to the different wavelengths of the solar spectrum when photons hit the PV electricity. When this happens, the energy of the photon is transferred to an electron in an atom of the cell (usually silicon atoms). The electron is able to escape from its normal position associated in the atom to become part of the current in an electrical circuit [28,29].

To produce the electric field within a PV cell, the manufacturers create a junction of two different semiconductors (types P and N). The most common way of making P or N type silicon material is adding an element that has an extra electron or has a deficit of an electron. Silicon is the most common material used in manufacturing process of photovoltaic cells. Silicon atoms have 14 electrons, where the four electrons in the last layer are called valence electrons.

In a crystal solid, each silicon atom normally shares one of its four valence electrons in a covalent junction with another silicon atom. The silicon crystal molecule is formed of 5 silicon atoms in a covalent junction [30].

The process of doping introduces an atom of another element into the silicon crystal to alter its electrical properties. The element used for doping has three or five valence electrons.

The PV industry is rapidly maturing because of worldwide environmental concerns and its energy production potential due to the widely available free solar resource. The industry is in a race to achieve grid parity (PV energy costs equal to conventional utility costs) and increase competitiveness in the energy markets.

a) Photo-modules

A number of solar cells electrically connected to each other and mounted in a support structure are called a photovoltaic module. Modules are designed to supply electricity at a certain DC voltages such as 12, 24 or 48 volts. The current produced is directly dependent on how much light hits the module. Multiple modules can be wired together to form an array. A larger area of a module or array will produce more electricity. PV modules are rated on the basis of the power delivered under Standard Testing.

Conditions (STC) of 1 kW/m² of sunlight and a PV cell temperature of 25 degrees Celsius (°C). Their output measured under STC is expressed in terms of "peak Watt" or Wp nominal capacity. A typical crystalline silicon module consists of a series circuit of 36 cells, encapsulated in a glass and plastic package for protection from the environment. Although PV modules are warranted for power output for periods from 10-25 years, they can be expected to deliver amounts of energy (voltage and current)for periods of 40 to 50 years.

b) Invertors

Inverters have the task of DC/AC conversion. There are two main categories of grid-tied inverters. Line-commutated inverters derive their switching signals directly from the grid line currents. The low switching frequencies produce harmonic currents that need to be filtered out. In the case of small single-phase inverters the bulky and expensive filtering networks are not practical. In the case of large three phase-inverters, multiple units could be connected through a multi-phase isolation transformer at the utility output to filter any unwanted currents; the transformers should be rated to withstand additional heating due to harmonic current copper losses. Self-commutated inverters derive their switching frequencies from internal control units as they monitor grid conditions, in particular frequency and voltage.

The resilience of a system relates to the magnitude of disturbance required to fundamentally disrupt the system causing a dramatic shift to another state of the system, controlled by a different set of processes [31]. When resilience is lost or significantly decreased, a system is at high risk of shifting into a qualitatively different state. The new state of the system may be undesirable.

Restoring a system to it's previous state can be complex, expensive, and sometimes even impossible. Research suggests that to restore some systems to their previous state requires a return to conditions well before the point of collapse.

The energy system resilience refers to the capacity of an energy system to withstand perturbations from e.g. climatic, economic, technological and social causes and to rebuild and renew itself afterwards. Loss of resilience can cause loss of valuable energy system services, and may even lead to rapid transitions or shifts into qualitatively different situations and configurations, described for e.g. people, ecosystems, knowledge systems, or whole cultures. In general terms, the vulnerability of a system is assessed according to the concept of resilience, developed in the mathematics of non-linear differential equations. According to this frame, the opposite to the vulnerability of a system is its stability, its resilience, defined specifically as an attribute of a system. The system is like a net; it consists of a great number of nods, which are interlinked.

Resilience provides a new framework for analyzing economic, ecological, technological and social systems in a changing world facing many uncertainties and challenges. It represents an area of explorative research under rapid development with major policy implications for sustainable development.

Resilience Matrix for Photo-voltaic Power Plant

Quality of the photo-voltaic plant can be defined by the sustainability index, including economic, environment and social indicators. Economic indicator will include energy cost and energy production sub-indicators. Energy production indicator will reflect total energy production by the photo-voltaic plant.

Environment indicator will comprise CO_2 emission and particle emission. CO_2 emission measurement will reflect potential gain in the decease of CO_2 emission with subsidizing coal fired power plant with the photo-voltaic power plant. Social indicator will include maintenance cost which is from the need for cleaning photo modules.

On Figure 4.12 are shown schematic structure of Photo-voltaic Power Plant. Monitoring system for the Photo-voltaic power plant comprise measurement individual parameters as they are shown on the monitoring scheme, Figure 4.13.

Resilience index is formed by the Sustainability Index expressed as the linear function of quality indicators multiplied with respective weighting coefficients.

Sustainability Index composition reflects the quality indicators of the system under consideration. Its integral value in time scale after sudden change is the stability merits of the system. If it is assumed that the Sustainability Index change of individual indicators can be approximated with linear function then the change of indicator multiplied by the time increment for return to the starting value is the Resilience Index and is measure of the stability of the system. Also, with numerical integration of indicators in the time scale Resilience Index can be obtained in the real time scale of the system.

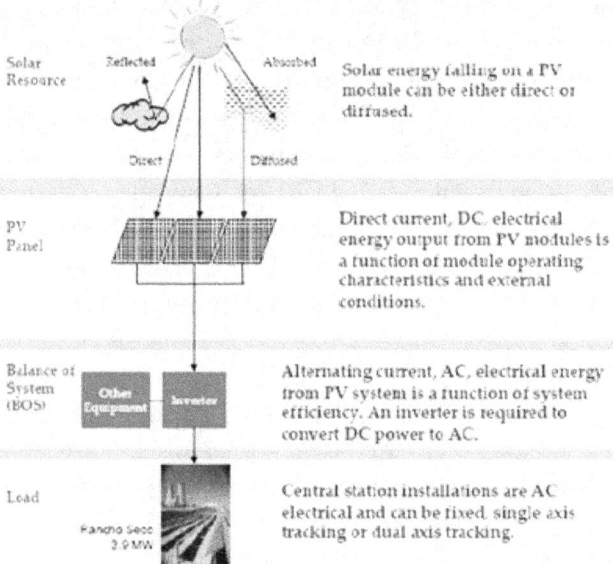

Figure 4.12. Photo-voltaic Power Plant.

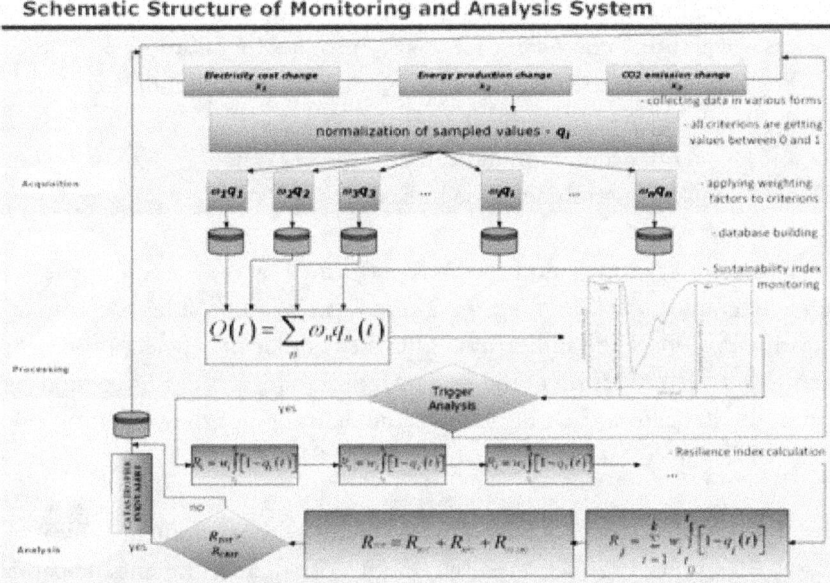

Figure 4.13. Monitoring and Analysis System Flowchart for Photo-Voltaic Power Plant.

In the evaluation of the Photo-voltaic power plant a following indicators will be taken into a consideration.

Economic Indicator – Electricity cost – 0.23 Euro/kWh
Maximum change 0.023 Euro/kWh

Energy Production Indicator – Electricity Production – 80 kWh/day
Maximum change – 8 kWh/day

Environment Indicator – CO_2 emission decrease – 220 gr/kWh
Maximum change – 20 gr/kWh

Sustainability Index based on the indicators as shown can be defined with following expression

$$Q(t) = \varphi_1 q_1(t) + \varphi_2 q_2(t) + \varphi_3 q_3(t) \qquad (4.11)$$

where

φ_1 - weighting coefficient for electricity cost indicator
φ_2 - weighting coefficient for energy production indicator
φ_3 - weighting coefficient for CO_2 emission decease indicator
$q_1(t)$ - electricity cost indicator- Euro/kWh
$q_2(t)$ - energy production indicator – cEuro/kWh
$q_3(t)$ - CO_2 emission decrease indicator – gr/kWh

Sustainability Index monitoring is performed by the measurement of the individual indicators. The first step in the Sustainability Index determination is normalization of the indicators. This means that the special procedure is adapted for the formation of the Sustainability Index as the aggregation function of the indicators. The next step is the definition of the weighting coefficient constrains. In our analysis we have used following cases:

Case 1 Electricity Cost > Electricity Production = Environment Indicator
Case 2 Electricity Production > Electricity Cost = Environment Indicator
Case 3 Environment Indicator > Electricity Cost = Energy Production

The Resilience Index for photo-voltaic is defined as

$$R = \left(\varphi_1 \Delta q_1 + \varphi_2 \Delta q_2 + \varphi_3 \Delta q_3 \right) \Delta t \tag{4.12}$$

where
q_1 - Electricity Cost Change
q_2 - Energy Production Change
q_3 - CO_2 Emission Change

In order determine specific value of the Resilience Index for the individual cases following options are taken into a consideration. The design of options is based on the on the priority given to the change of individual indicators. Each option is defined with maximum change of specific indicator and changes other indicators are introduced as specified in Table 4.5.

Table.4.5.

	Electricity Cost Change	Electricity Production Change	CO_2 Emission-Change
	Euro/kWh	kWh/day	gr/kWh
Option A	0.023	4	0
Option B	0.0115	8	10
Option C	0	0	20

Case 1 Electricity Cost Change = Energy Production = Environment Indicator
Case 2 Electricity Cost Change > Energy Production = Environment Indicator
Case 3 Energy Production >Electricity Cost Change = Environment Indicator
Case 4 Environment Indicator > Electricity Cost Change = Energy Production

The Resilience Index will be determined as the sum of all indicators sudden change multiplied with time period for their recovery. Resilience Index rating for each case will be obtains in the numerical form corresponding to constrains as specified for each case. For each case the maximum value Resilience Index will be determined and presented as the rating among the cases under consideration.

It is of interest to notice that the case 2 has the maximum value of Resilience Index. This imply that under this constrain the photo-voltaic power plant has highest capacity to sustain sudden change of the indicators as specified in this analysis.

In general, it can be stated that this demonstration shows the catastrophic event depends on all potential sudden change of the indicators. It is a toll for the assessment of the potential of hazard event and stability evaluation. Photovoltaic power plants require time dependent control in order to have constant justification of the potential catastrophic events. In particular the appropriate selection of the indicators may be very important for the qualitative validation of the Resilience Index for the assessment of the photovoltaic power plant system.

It should be emphasizedthat the principle idea in resilience engineering stem from the recognition that failure does not always stem from malfunction or poor design. Instead, many adverse effects stem from the network interaction and adaption that are often necessary for complex systems to be in "real world".

Energy resilience is the ability of the energysystem to provide and maintain an acceptable level of servicein the face of various faults and challenges to normal operation.

The sustainability change in time is defined as the resilience of the system. It describes the safety capacity of the system. With the monitoring of the sustainability change of the system in time, it can be used as the diagnostic parameter of safety the system.

4.5. HIGH VOLTAGE TRANSMISSION SYSTEM RESILIENCE

Energy losses represents nowadays between 2% and 4% (depending of local climatic conditions) of total energy electric power transmission. In Europe, this figure is expected to grow as a result of the expected economic development of Southern and new EU states. For the case of the high voltage transmission sector, the energy losses depend on the temperature of the environment range. The high voltage system is highly vulnerable: central generation creates high value targets, long vulnerable transmission lines, unique high voltage transformers, vulnerable substations [32].

The electricity system currently experiences many disruptions due to natural hazards and human error. Large, costly blackouts occur frequently.

- It is highly vulnerable to human attack. A worst case scenario would be highly destructive.
- Many investments would simultaneously improve reliability& reduce vulnerability or the amount of damage from terrorist attack
- Evaluating the reliability and security benefits together would justify many new investments

In the analysis of the of the energy grid system the existing electricity distribution networks regulatory framework will be taken also into account. A Smart Grids Factor will be formed based on indicators such as grid volume and distributed generation rate. This factor is introducing the effect of the regulation on the system, which is further to the performance-based ratemaking (guaranteed or overall standards). Using also the quality and efficiency factors implemented, a "third pillar" (besides economy and quality) for the regulation will be developed according to the countries existing incentive and quality based regulation [33].

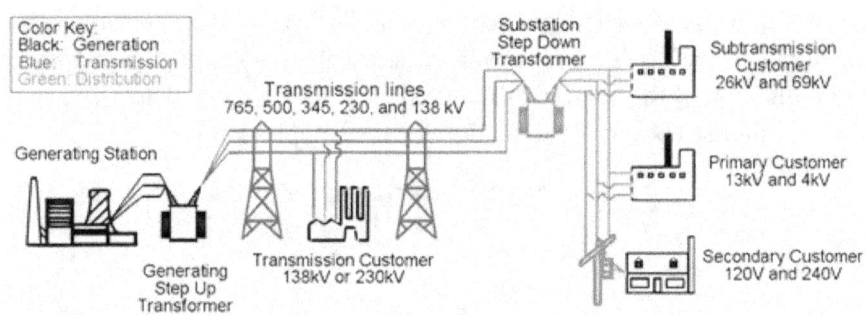

Figure 4.14. High Voltage Transmission System.

This factor should reveal the current state of play, the changes compared to previous years and should allow a future outlook of the trends in network development. As an incentive it should have positive effects directly on the network operators' revenues in case of an improvement of the situation (less grid losses, more distributed generation compared to previous year). In order to measure the performance of each individual network operator and to make results comparable, each regulator should define reference values in advance. Different reference values for the individual operators are foreseen to include structural varieties. If the operator didn't reach the expected level it should consequently reduce its revenues. This would be an efficient method, which gives to network operators a financial incentive to foster network development in line with the approach of a Smart Grids [34].

An electricity blackout causes us to freeze (sweat) in the dark. We find it difficult to: commute (no traffic signals, no trains); get up and down in buildings (no elevator); work (no light, computers, copiers, faxes) ;cook (no microwave, refrigerators, appliances, solid state ignition); get entertainment (no TV, radio, VCR). Almost all modern activities depend on electricity.

The high voltage system is disrupted frequently by natural hazards, human error, andhuman attack.Worst Cases Scenarios: Ice Storm: Quebec and NY in 1998, Hurricanes: Florida in 2004, Earthquake: Bay area, California in 1989, Reactive power: NE in 2003, Hurricane Ivan: Almost occurred in 2004. Since these happened recently, a 500 year worst case would be much, much worse. [35]

Sustainability is the word which is used to create the special meaning for the interaction of the different entities in our world. In its definition sustainability was attributed to the interaction of system with its surrounding, including, social, cultural, environmental, economic and other aspects. More than that, the sustainability has become a quality measure of the system in the assessment and evaluation of the respective system. It has been noticed that the sustainability comprise complexity definition for the complex system.

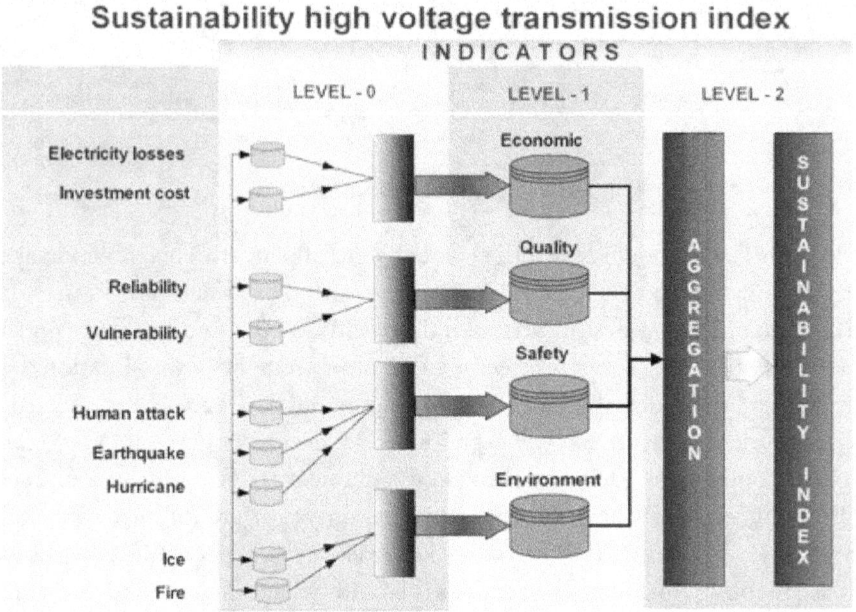

Figure 4.15. Sustainability High Voltage Transmission Index.

The high voltage transmission system comprise a number of elements which functionality is defined in accordance with is role in the system. The complex system of high voltage transmission system is characterized with the specific number of the indicators reflecting individual properties of the system, as shown on Figure 4.15.

The sudden change of the indicator and its return to the primary state is the measurement of the capacity of the respective system to withstand the changes of the system. There are several potential changes of every system which may result in the eventual catastrophic event. It is of interest to visualize characteristic behavior following the sudden change of the indicator. Integral value of the indicator in the time scale until it reaches the steady state is the measuring parameter of the resiliency index.

Since the every sudden indicator may be contribute to the resilience index is the sum of the individual indicator of the sudden change the resilience index is the value representing the capacity of the system under consideration. For the high voltage transmission system The Resilience Index of the high voltage transmission system is the agglomeration of the capacity of the system reflecting the total change of the resilience capacity of the system [36,37].

Figure 4.16 shows the Resilience Index monitoring scheme with procedure for the indicator agglomeration and presentation.

Schematic Structure of Monitoring and Analysis System

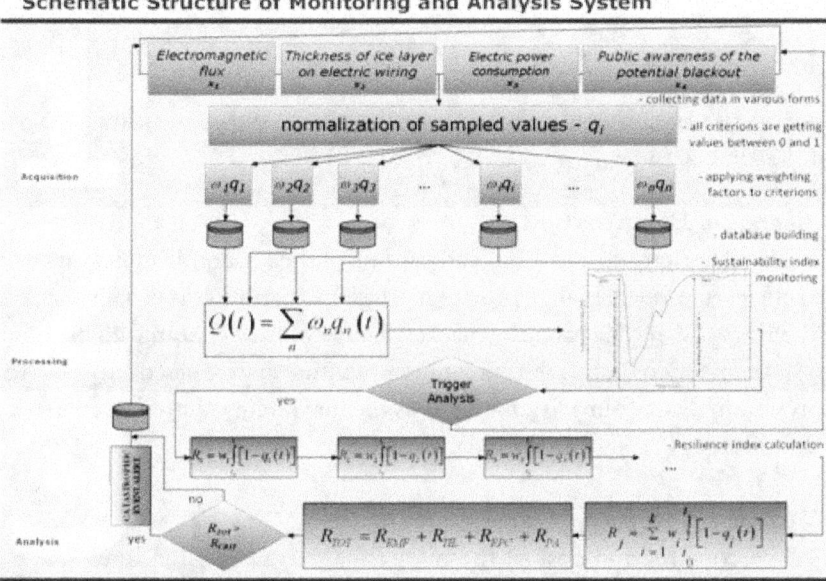

Figure 4.16. Resilience Index Monitoring for Power Transmission System.

Resilience engineering is applied in a number of systems in order to justify potential stability limits which may lead to the catastrophic events. The resilience of the high voltage transmission system is the capacity of the system to withstand the sudden change of the internal or external parameters of the system. It reflects the quality of the system measured by the appropriate changes of the indicators. The potential possibility of the high voltage transmission system is to reach limits leading to the catastrophic events require the investigation of the cases which might be the qualitative measure of the stability of the system. As regards the high voltage transmission system a number of parameters is taken as the specific indicators for the definition of the potential changes to be used for the verification of the individual cases.

In this analysis of the Resilience Index of High Voltage Transmission System a following indicators are take into a consideration, as shown on Figure 4.17.

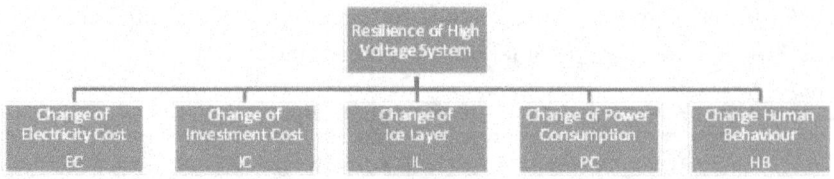

Figure 4.17. Agglomeration Scheme of the High Voltage Transmission System Resilience Index.

a) Change of ElectricityCost

The electricity cost sub-indicator is one of the economic indicators which are subject to sudden changes due to market fluctuation. It is usually expressed in the Euro/kWh reflecting the market change of the economic environment. It is anticipated to design the maximum potential change electricity cost to be expressed in Euro/Euro. In this analysis the maximum value of electricity cost sub-indicator is 20% of the standard electricity cost.

b) Change of InvestmentCost

The construction cost of the high voltage transmission lines is subject to time change due to the increase of the material, manpower and capital cost. These changes are followed by the expenses expressed in Euro/Investment cost. These expenses are normalised by the maximum change of the capital cost.

c) Change of Ice Layer

Due tot o adverse climate in the vicinity of the high voltage transmission line there is potential possibility for the formation of the ice layer on the power line wires. This ice formation will have adverse effect on the power transmission. There is potential development of the ice layer. The change of the thickness ice layer leads to the increase the weight of the ice which may cause fracture of the power line. In the design of the power line special precautions is made to preserve safety of the power lines. In this respect the design of power line include the maximum thickness as of the ice layer as the limit to prevent eventual catastrophic events.

d) Change of Power Consumption

The change of power consumption is an immanent problem for any high voltage transmission line. There is possibility to have sudden increase of the power demand in some urban regions leading to the potential critical state of the power transmission. It is of interest to notify that the change in power consumption and its maximum value may result in the catastrophic event.

e) Change in HumanBehaviors

The social aspect of the potential sudden change of the electric power consumption may lead to the diverse reaction of the human behavior. In particular, the prediction of the human behaviors is important issue which may lead to the catastrophic events. The human dwellings are designed with the respective communication space in order to make possible human movement within the dwelling under a severe power shortage. In the situation when it happens there is a need for mass communication.

In this exercise a following cases are taken into a consideration:

CASE 1- EC > IL = IC = PC = HB

Case 1 represent situation when the priority is given to the Change of Energy Cost indicator with other indicators having the same value Figure 4.18. It is of interest to notice that if the priority given to the Change of Electricity Cost Indicator the result prove that the relation among the option under consideration the electricity optionis having the highest value of the resilience Index with Investment Cost, Ice Layer, Power Consumption and Human Behavior following.

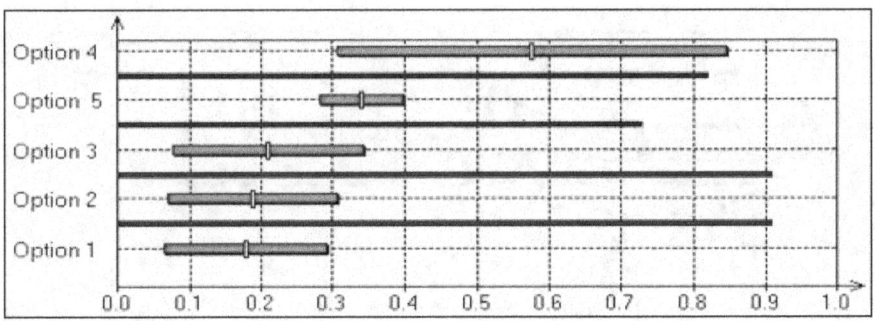

Figure 4.18. Resilience Index for Case 1.

CASE 2- IC > EC = IL = PC = HB

Case 2 imply that the priority is given the Change of Investment Cost indicator with other indicators having equal values Figure 4.19. It is of interest to notice that in this case rating among the options under consideration is smaller difference in resilience index. Also, the mutual relation among the resilience index option less is less pronounced and shows small difference among option.

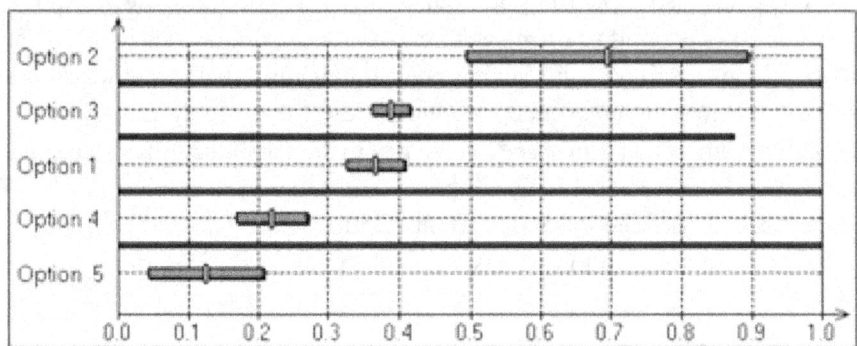

Figure 4.19. Resilience Index for Case 2.

CASE 3 – IL > EC = IC = PC = HB

The case 3 is designed with priority given to Change of Ice Layer Indicator. The relation among the option under consideration shows linear change of the resilience index among options (Figure 4.20).

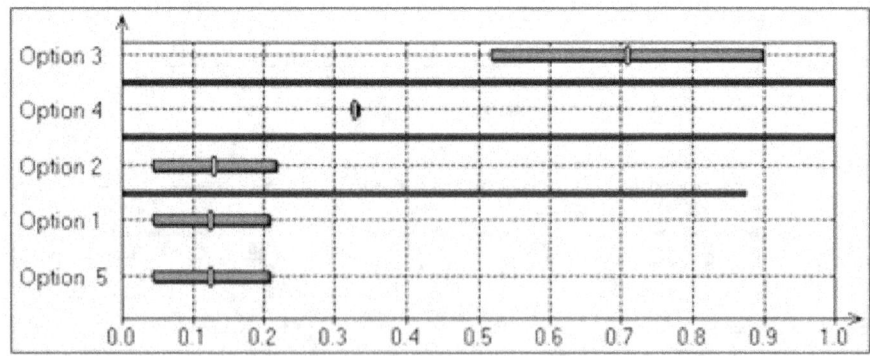

Figure 4.20. Resilience Index for Case 3.

CASE 4 – PC > EC = IC = IL = HB - Figure 4.21

It is of interest to notice that case 4 presents the resilience index relation for the priority given to Change of Power Consumption. The contribution of the other changes to the mutual relation is very similar to the other cases under consideration.

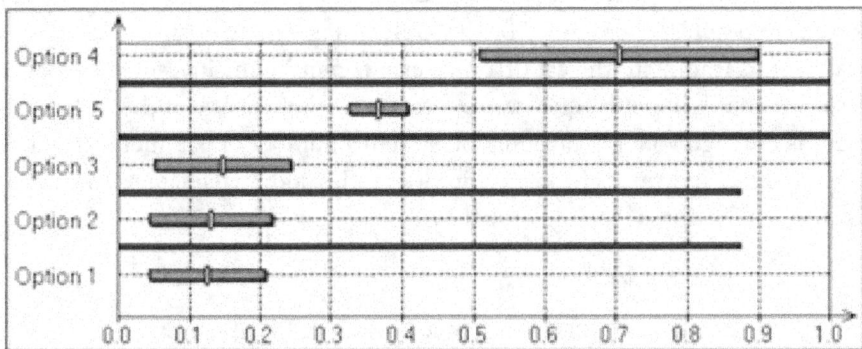

Figure 4.21. Resilience Index for Case 4.

CASE 5 – HB > EC = IC = IL = PC

The change in Human Behavior effect on the rating list among the option is very limited as regard resilience index for the other option Figure 4.22. In this respect it is of interest to verify that the difference of the resilience index value for of Human Behavior, Power Consumption and Ice Layer options are having marginal differences.

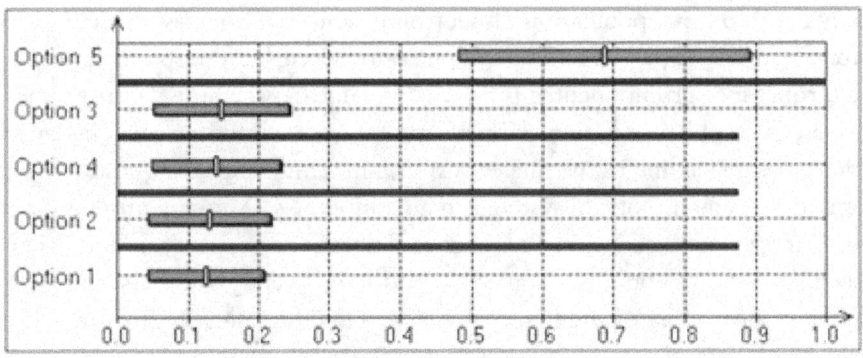

Figure 4.22. Resilience Index for Case 5.

The resilience index of the high voltage transmission system is the capacity to measure the stability of the system. The potential occurrence of the adverse affect is an immanent catastrophic event leading to the disruption of the high voltage structure. There are number of the indicators which can be used for the assessment of the stability of the system. The selection of appropriate indicator is a primary goal in the design of the stability of the system. It reflects the quality of the system measured by the appropriate changes of the indicators. The potential possibility of the high voltage transmission system is to reach limits leading to the catastrophic events require the investigation of the cases which might be the qualitative measure of the stability of the system. As regards the high voltage transmission system a number of parameters is taken as the specific indicators for the definition of the potential changes to be used for the verification of the individual cases.

4.6 RESILIENCE INDEX FOR NUCLEAR POWER PLANT

Today, nuclear energy is used for the electricity production in 40 countries. In 10 countries the electricity production by nuclear power plants is more than 50 %. This implies that the nuclear energy is an important energy source in modern society. Since 1956, when the first nuclear power plant was put in operation, nuclear energy has been promising source of energy to meet future demand. In the years of high expectation the development of different prototypes has open a new era of energy welfare.

The safety of nuclear reactor is an imminent problem of nuclear chain reaction control. Nuclear reactor is controlled by delayed neutrons representing only 2.1 % of total population of neutron produced in the fission chain reactions. The major part of neutron population belongs to the so called prompt neutron. Since prompt neutrons have a zero time between the neutron generations, the number of fission chain reaction is almost infinite producing enormous energy leading to the nuclear explosion. This brings the question if the present man made control system can guaranty the safe energy production in nuclear reactor to be utilized for heat and electricity production. There have been several attempts to design so called the inherently safe nuclear reactor without success. The potential possibility to design a nuclear reactor system with the inherently safe characteristic may open new path for the nuclear energy utilization.

The presently available nuclear energy system is constructed with the engineering design of the control system and is subject to the potential probability to the mail function. The potential hazard event in the present nuclear reactor system has developed a great public concern for the safety of nuclear energy system. The hazard events in Three Mile Island reactor and Chernobyl reactor have developed the public awareness of the potential catastrophic events.

It is important to realize the benefit which has been gained by the utilization of nuclear power systems. In 2006 the total installed nuclear capacity in the world was 370 Gwe, or 15 % of electricity production capacity in the world [38] Nuclear power plants electricity production is contributing to local electricity production in 15 countries. In this moment there are 26 new nuclear power plants are in construction. This will lead to the total nuclear power capacity 390 GW. Presently, by the operation nuclear power plants there is production about 14000 t/year of radioactive waste [39]. Under assumption that the same type of reactor will be utilized in 2050 the total amount of radioactive waste will be about 30000 t/year. The quality of nuclear energy in general terms can be assessed as the opportunity with limited value. Due to the potential hazard, it is be very difficult to visualize the nuclear energy as the reliable source of sustainable energy. In summarizing this evaluation, the nuclear energy can be seen as the temporary solution in the specific geographical region. From this point of view it is obvious that the nuclear energy has a limited property to be introduced as the sustainable option for the medium term energy source. It is of the great importance to accept that the high potential of the nuclear energy is envisaged in the long term energy strategy.

"10 years after Rio" the Johannesburg 2002 Conference [40] was the next UN Conference devoted to Plan of Implementation of the Rio Declaration focused to the elaboration of the concrete measures of the sustainable development The sustainable development encompasses theeconomic, social, and ecological perspectives of conservation and change. In correspondence with the WCED, it is generally defined as "development that meets the needs of the present without compromising the ability of future generations to meet their own needs." This definition is based on the ethical imperative of equity within and between generations. Moreover, apart from the meeting; basic needs of all; sustainable development implies sustaining the natural life-support systems on Earth, and extending to all the opportunity to satisfy their aspirations for a better life. Hence, the sustainable development is more precisely defined as 'a process of change in which the exploitation of resources, the direction of investments, the orientation of technological development, and institutional change are all harmony and enhance both current and future potential tomeet human needs and aspiration.

It was recognized that the complexity of sustainability concept imply the need for the joint actions based on the multi-criteria assessment to provide a framework for integrating economic, environmental and social interest into the effective strategy. For the life support systems that have recognized the need to embrace sustainable development the first step is to understand how to implement it. Putting this concept into operation requires identifying practical indicators of sustainability and understands how it can be measured over time to determine if progress is made.

Potential catastrophic events are immanent to the nuclear power plant design [41].The catastrophic events are based on the probabilistic assessment of the potential accidents leading to the dispersion of the radioactive material in the distant area of the pant. Essential project tool for the assessment of radioactive material dispersion is based on the Loss of Coolant Accident evaluation. This tool comprise number of scenarios which may be leading to the reactor core melt down and radioactive material dispersion. There are number of indicators which are signals for the eventual core melt down accident.

It is recognized that the nuclear power plant beside the catastrophic accident is subject to the sudden change of of the vital parameters of the plant, Figure 4.24. In this respect there are several potential parameters change which potentially exposed to the sudden change of the indicators leading to the accidents or to the resilience monitoring. With the resilience monitoring the nuclear power system is exposed to the control of those indicators which may be relevant for the measurement of the nuclear power system resilience index.

The time integral of the sudden change of individual indicator is the capacity of the system return to the primary value of the indicator and is expressed as the Resilience Index. TheResilience Index is integral of the individual indicator between thetime of the sudden change and thetime when it resumesa steady state value. The resilience index for a nuclear power system is composed of the following elements: economic, environmental, technological and social.

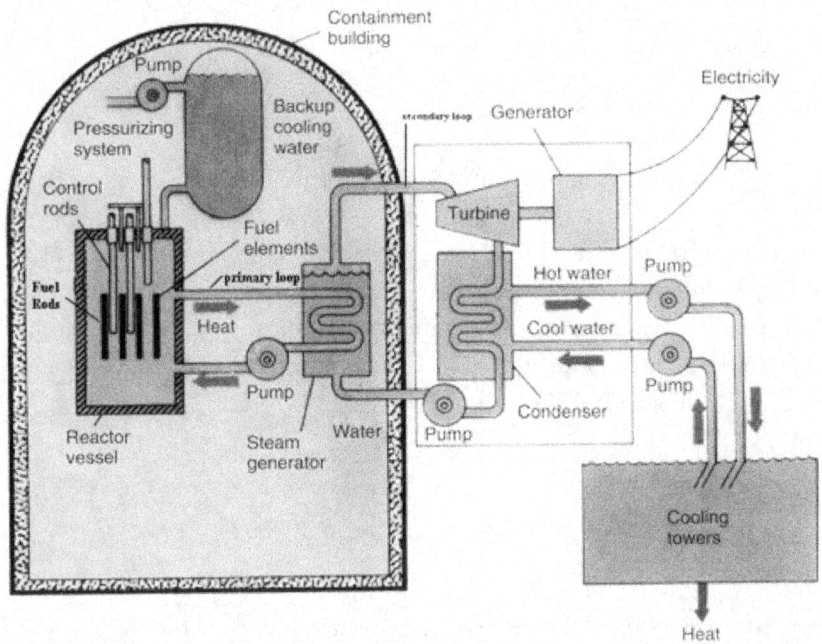

Figure 4.24. Schematic presentation of Nuclear Power Plant.

Single Indicator Change

Resilience indicators for nuclear power plant are defined as the integral of the sudden change of the respective indicator. In our case we will define following indicators:

a) Change of the AverageNeutron Flux
The average thermal neutron flux is parameter which corresponds to the energy produced in the nuclear reactor core. The thermal neutron flux is subject to the time change and is controlled by the nuclear reactor control system. The sudden change of neutron flux is the result of the change of reactor core reactivity. This change may be produced by the control rod system which leads to the increase of the neutron flux in the reactor core. There are potentially different control rods absorption. In this exercise we deal only with one change of neutron flux due to the sudden absorbent insertion.
Resilience Index due to sudden change of neutron flux will be

$$R_{NF} = \int_{t_0}^{t_1} [1 - q_{NF}] dt$$

(4.13)

where q_{NF} – neutron flux change

t_0 – time of sudden change

t_1 – time when neutron flux resume initial value.

In order to demonstrate the determination of numerical value of the Resilience Index due to sudden change of neutron flux it is assumed to have 10 % of the average neutron flux and time interval for the neutron flux recovery t = 60 sec. If we assume to have linear function of the neutron flux change in time the Resilience Index will be

$$R_{NF} = \frac{\Delta t_{NF}}{2} \Delta q_{NF}$$

(4.14)

where

- time interval for the neutron flux change indicator recovery
- neutron flux change indicator sudden change

With this numerical value of the parameters the Resilience index will be R = 30/0.1 = 300 /sec.

b) Change of the Pressure in Primary Cycle

The pressure change in the primary cycle of nuclear reactor is usually result of the reactor. Power change. It is usually the result of the change in the secondary cycle cooling. Any reactor scram is leading to the sudden pressure change in the primary reactor cycle. The recovery of the sudden change in reactor pressure is possible if the change is not large. In this respect only very small change can be by the available resilience capacity of the system. The primary cycle reactor pressure for the water cooled reactor around 160 bars. The resilience capacity for the reactor pressure can be defined as the sudden pressure change divided by the nominal reactor pressure.

Resilience Index due to sudden change of reactor pressure will be

$$R_{RP} = \int_{t_0}^{t_1} [1 - q_{RP}] dt$$

(4.15)

where q_{RP}- reactor pressure

t_0- time of sudden change

t_1 – time when reactor pressure resume initial value.

$$R_{RP} = \frac{\Delta t_{RP}}{2} \Delta q_{RP}$$

(4.16)

where

- time interval for the reactor pressure indicator recovery
- reactor pressure indicator sudden change

In this analysis of the reactor pressure change affect on the Resilience Index is assumed that the maximumvalue of the sudden change of reactor pressureis=10 bars and= 600 sec.

c) Change of the Energy Cost

The change of energy cost indicator reflects potential possibility of the sudden change of energy cost due to the economic crisis in the energy system. It is usually result of the unexpected economic events which are related to the market fluctuation and economic crisis. The Energy Cost Indicator is measured in €/kWh.

Resilience Index due to sudden change of energy cost will be

$$R_{EC} = \int [1 - q_{EC}] dt$$

(4.17)

where

$q_{ENERGY\ COST}$ - energy cost

t_0 – time of sudden change

t_1 – time when energy cost indicator resume initial value

If it is assumed that the sudden change of the energy cost will happen in the time t_o and the energy cost will reach recovered value at the time t_1 then the resilience index will be

$$R_{EC} = \frac{\Delta t_{EC}}{2} \Delta q_{EC}$$

(4.18)

where
> - time interval for the energy cost indicator recovery
> - energy cost indicator sudden change

For the demonstration of the energy cost on the Resilience Index it is assumed to have the maximum change in the energy cost to be 10% of the nominal energy cost. So that =and = 60 sec.

d) Change of the CO$_2$ Compensation

Recent problem with the global warming has introduced the need for the assessment of manmade pollution with the substitution of new energy sources in order to prevent further pollution problems. It was recognized that the nuclear energy may be used as the substitution for non renewable energy sources. So, the compensation of the CO$_2$ produced by the combustion of the non renewableby the nuclear energy is opening potential reduction of the CO$_2$ production. In the normal operation of nuclear power plant there is CO$_2$ compensation of due to substitution

Resilience Index due to sudden change of CO$_2$ compensation will be

$$R_{co_2} = \int_{t_0}^{t_1} [1 - q_{co_2}] dt \qquad (4.19)$$

where
> $q_{COMPONENT\ INDATO}$ — CO$_2$ compensation indicator
> t_0 – time of sudden change
> t_1 – time when CO$_2$ compensation indicator resume initial value.

$$R_{co_2} = \frac{\Delta t_{co_2}}{2} \Delta q_{co_2} \qquad (4.20)$$

where
> - time interval for the CO$_2$ compensation indicator recovery
> - CO$_2$ compensation indicator sudden change

The CO$_2$ compensation is resulting from the use of nuclear energy as the substitution of the non renewable energy. It is proved to be the measuring parameter for the benefit of the nuclear energy to the global warming degradation. As measuring parameter for the resilience index change it is used the total nuclear power measured by the Mwdays within the time interval.

e) Change of the Public Acceptance

The change of public acceptance is result of the public learning system and public information guidance. At the beginning of the nuclear power introduction of the world energy system it was developed very high expectation for the reliable energy source. Unfortunately, due to the unexpected hazard accident on Three Mile Island power plant and Chernobyl power plant the public acceptance has severely changed. In this respect it has become desirable to introduce the resilience index as the additional indicator for the assessment of the safety of the nuclear power plant.

Resilience Index due to sudden change of public acceptance will be

$$R_{PA} = \int_{t_0}^{t_1} [1 - q_{PA}] dt \tag{4.21}$$

where

q_{PA} – public acceptance indicator
t_0 – time of sudden change
t_1 – time when public acceptance indicator resume initial value

$$R_{PA} = \frac{\Delta t_{PA}}{2} \Delta q_{PA} \tag{4.22}$$

Where
- time interval for the public acceptanceindicator recovery
- public acceptanceindicator sudden change

In the measurement of resilience index it is anticipated that the maximum change of acceptance indicator = 7 % with = 360 sec.

Multi-indicator Changes

In order to investigate potential possibility to have several change of indicators in the same time interval It is of interest to demonstrate a number of cases with the different internal relation among the indicator changes. It is anticipated to have following options with the relation among the indicator change as shown in Table 4.6.

Table 4.6. Options for multi-indicator changes

Option	Indicators relation
Option I	NF > RP= EC = CO_2= PA
Option 2	RP > NF = EC = CO_2= PA
Option 3	EC > NF = RP= CO_2= PA
Option 4	CO_2> NF = RP = EC= PA
Option 5	PA > NF = RP = EC = CO_2

Beside the demonstration of resilience index by the specific values of indicator and multi-indicators it is of interest to investigate online monitoring of indicators and their processing into the time dependent resilience index. As the method for the agglomeration multi-indicator it is anticipated to have monitoring structure as the measurement of individual indicator within the time scale for every individual events and formation of the resilience index for every event.

With the agglomeration of the resilience index for individual indicators the total resilience is obtained as linear function of the of the individual resilience indices.In this respect we can write

$$R_{TOT} = \sum_{i=1}^{j} w_n R_n = w_{NF} R_{NF} + w_{RP} R_{RP} + w_{EC} R_{EC} + w_{CO_2} R_{CO_2} + w_{PA} R_{PA} \tag{4.23}$$

where,,,,are weighting coefficients for the respective resilience index.

The procedure for the determination of the weighting coefficient is based on the ASPID method designed to quantify weighting coefficients under specific constrain defined in the verified for every option.

Schematic Structure of Monitoring and Analysis System

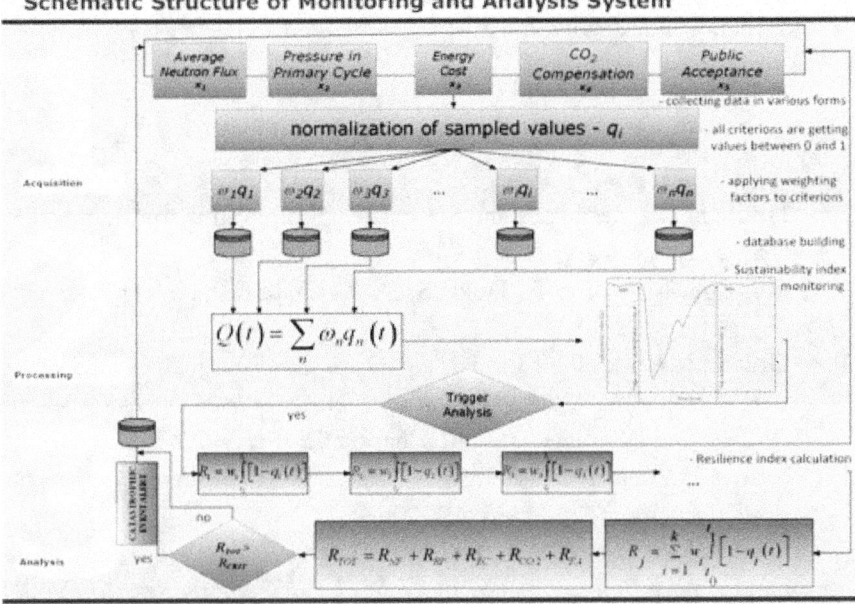

Figure 4.25. Resilience Index Monitoring for Nuclear power plant.

In the procedure for the determination of weighting coefficients there are several steps, namely:

- normalization of indicators,
- determination of the average values for the weighting coefficients for the option which meet specific constrain,
- determination of the total resiliency index for every specific constrain,
- formation of the Rating list among options under consideration.

The graphic presentation of the resilience index is given on the Figure 4.25.

Graphical presentation of Resilience index for nuclear power plant comprises change of indicators within the time scale defined for every indicator. It is anticipated that the change of indicator is defined by t_0 and t_1 respectively. The time for indicators recovery is defined by the time t_2, t_3, t_4 and t_5, respectively.

Taking integral value for every indicator within time of sudden change and time of recovery the respective Resilience Index is obtained. With agglomeration of all Resilience Indexes multiplied with respective weighting coefficient the total Resilience index is obtained.

REFERENCES

[1]   Holling C.S., Resilience and Stability of Ecological System, *Annual Review of Ecology and Systamatics, Vol.*4, pp.1-23, 1973.

[2]   Holbagel F., Nemet P., DokkeS. R, *Resilience Engineering Perspective*, Ashgate, June 2008.

[3]   Gruenn H.R.,Resilience and its Application to Energy System, Springer Berlin/Heidelbrg, *2006 Report of the United Nation Conference on Environment and Development*, Vol.1,Chapter 7,June,1992.

[4]   Kainan H., *Concept and Practices of "Resilience"*, US Agency for International Development, Bangkok, 2006.

[5]   Sanders M.J, Krumdlek, S. Dantas A., *Energy Resilience, Urban Farm and the Associated Risk to Urban Activity, Road and Transport Research*, Vol.15, No. 1 2006

[6]   *Exergy, Energy System Analysis and Optimization*, Edited: Ch. Frangopoulos Encyclopedia of Life Support Systems, 2002.

[7]   Luhman M.J., Fischhedit M., Schalobak K.O., *Vulnerability of Energy System The Age of Manmade Global,*Wuppur Institute, 2003.

[8]   Hollnagel E., Woods D., Levesen N.,*Resience Engineering: Concepts and Percepts,*Ashgate PublishingLimited, 2005.

[9]   Afgan N.H., Carvalho M.G., *Quality, Indicators and Sustainability of Energy Systems,*Begell House Publisher, New York, 2008.

[10]   *power plants,Economic Association "Thermal Power Plants Nikola Tesla"*http://www.eps.rs/Eng/Article.aspx?lista=Sitemap&id=70.

[11]   *Kaplan Melissa ' Collection*, May 4, 2008, Calculating the Cost of Electricity.

[12]   *CO_2Emission,*http://www.iea.org/textbase/work/2008.pdf.

[13]   *Power Plant Development Considerations*, General Electric, May 27, 2005.

[14]   *Power Plant Job Resources,*www.powerplantjobs.com.

[15]   *Energy analysis of power system*, World nuclear association, March (2006), http://world-nuclear.org.

[16]   Ackerman T., SodeL. R, *Wind Energy Technology and Current States: a review, Renewable and Sustainable Energy Reviews,*www.geocities.com/

windenergy.html.

[17] Rahman S., Ahmad A., *Assessment Wind Energy Potential for Cost Location in Saud Arabia*, Energy 2004.

[18] *Rayleigh flow*, http:en.wilipedia.org/wiki/Rayleigh_flow.

[19] Muyeer S.M., at all, Application of Energy Capacitor system to Wind Power Generator, *Wind Energy*, Vol.11, Issue 4,July 2008, pp.336-350.

[20] Wind Power Performance, *General Electric*,http://www.ge-energy.com/wind.

[21] *World Wind Capacity in 2002, Earth Policy Institute*, e2002, http://www.earthpolicy.org/Updaates/update5,htm.

[22] Zlomusica E., The development of the model the optimization of design wind turbines on complex locations, *PhD thesis, Faculty of Mechanical Engineering*,Mostar, 2006., (in Bosnian).

[23] N. Afgan, D. Cvetinovic, *Wind Power Plant Resilience*,Energies (accepted for publication).

[24] Begic F., Hadjiabdic M., 2011, *Wind Energy (in Bosnien) Svtetloststampa*, d.o.o. Sarajevo.

[25] Afgan N., Pilavachi P., *Resilience of Energy Systems*,Energy Policy,2009.

[26] Timilisina G., Kurdgelashvili L. Narbil P., *A Review of Solar Energy*,The World Bank, October 2011.

[27] Multi Year Program Plan 2008-2012, *Solar Energy Program*, US Department of Energy Solar Energy Technology Program, April 2008.

[28] *Photovoltaic Principle*,http://www.our-energy.com.

[29] *Photovoltaic area module design for solar electricity generation system*,United state Patent 6717045, http://freepatentsinline.com/

[30] Photovoltaic Cell Testing, http/solarlight.com/solarcell/

[31] A. Chalmers and F. A. Voorvaat, "High Voltage Transmission System Lines: Proximity, Visibility, and Encum-brabce Effects," *The Appraisal Journal*, 2009, pp. 227-245.

[32] *European Smart Grid*, "Directorate-General for Research Energy System,"EUR 22040, 2006.

[33] *The Smart Grid*, "DOE Smart Grid Pdf,"USA Department of Energy, Litos Strategic Communication, Washington DC, 2008.

[34] L. Lav and J. A. G. Blagin, "Waste Case Electricity Scenario," *CREATE Symposium*, University of South California,Los Angeles, August 1995.

[35] W. N. Adger, *"Vulnerability,"* *Global Environment Change*, Vol. 16, No. 3, 2006, pp. 268-281.

[36] H. Kainan, *"Concept and Practices of 'Resilience',"* US Agency for International Development, Bangkok, 2006.

[37] Nikitin A.B., Andrews A., Holt M., *Management the Nuclear Fuel Cycle*, Congressional Research Center – RL 34234, July, 2009.

[38] Rao K.R., *Radioactive waste: The problem and its management, Current Science*, Vol.81,No.12, Dec.(2001).

[39] Marvin L., *Sustainable Energy from Nuclear Fission Power, National Academy of Engineering*,Vol 32, No.24. Winter (2002).

[40] Nuclear Technology Review 2007, *International Atomic Energy Agency*, Vienna, (2007).

[41] Beckjord E.S., *Future of Nuclear Power*, MIT Study, 2003, ISBN 0-615-12420-8.

CHAPTER 5

EVALUATION OF ENERGY SYSTEM CATASTROPHIC EVENTS

The catastrophic event resilience is a monitoring parameter for the assessment of state of the system [1]. It implies the capacity of the system reflecting the ability of the system to withstand changes of indicators leading to the catastrophe development. The resilience as the integral function of time change of indictor. If there are number of indicators which are potentially leading to a catastrophic eventthey agglomeration will lead to the numerical parameter used for the assessment of the potential catastrophic event.

It is of great importance to verify catastrophe resilience for each case to be analyzed in order to define and to determine respective sudden change of indicators. Also, if there are several potential resilience indexes' of different quality of catastrophic events, their agglomeration will reflect the intensity of catastrophe before the change of system structure will occur.

In every catastrophic event the respective resilience index is merit of the capacity of the system to withstand sudden change of indicators and their return to the state of the system before the change [2]. The integral value of the indicator change before it reaches the steady state of the system is the measuring parameter of the resilience index. Beside the integral value of the indicator change there is a time scale of the system change. With time parameter reflecting the time of sudden change and the time when the system recover from the change of indicator, this time difference will be measuring parameter of the potential disasters if the system.

Every catastrophic event is a result of malfunction of the element of the system. In order to evaluate catastrophic event we will use the resilience index of the system reflecting individual resilience of the system [3,4]. If there are several events reflecting sudden change in the same time interval then the additive function of all resilience indexes. With the additive function of the resilience indexes we will obtain measuring parameter for the evaluation of the system under consideration.

The assessment of the potential catastrophe of the system is evaluated by the agglomeration value of resilience indexesif the agglomeration value will override upper value of the capacity of the system then the catastrophe of the system the result of the evaluation.

In order to establish the methodology to for the evaluation and assessment of the system vulnerability [3] a following steps are adapted:

- selection of indicators of the system for the evaluation of the catastrophe of the system
- define the indicator change for every indicator to be used in the evaluation of the system
- define and measure integral value of the resilience index for every indicator of the system
- determine the agglomerated value of the respective resilience indexes
- compare the agglomerated value of the resilience index with the limiting value of the system under consideration.
- finale assessment of the potential of resilience index in forecasting eventual catastrophic event.

Use of this methodology in the assessment of different system may be a tool for quantitative validation of the safety of the system.

In evolution of the potential catastrophe of the industrial system, it is of paramount importance to introduce a technical instrument for the measurement and acquisition of the indicators value in the time scale of interest for the specific evaluation. Beside the hardware for the acquisition of the respective indicators, it is of the great importance need respective software for the evaluation of the measurement.

In this chapter special attention is devoted to the evaluation of following energy system catastrophic events:

a. Nuclear power system
b. Wind power system
c. Solar power plant system
d. Hydro power system
e. Power transmissionsystem

5.1 NUCLEAR POWER PLANT CATASTROPHE EVALUATION [5,6]

An earthquake of a magnitude of 9.0, the second largest in scientifically observed history, and the accompanying tsunami with a surge of more than 12 meters, hit Tohoku, Japan, on 11 March 2011. It triggered the immediate shutdown of nuclear reactors at the power plants owned by Tokyo Electric Power Company (TEPCO) at Fukushima (6 boiling water reactors, BWRs, at Fukushima No. 1, and 4 BWRs at Fukushima No. 2). However, hydrogen explosions and fuel core meltdowns at the No. 1 reactors occurred within a few days because there was no electricity to drive the pumps to cool them. This catastrophe has generated unknown public costs, symbolized by the emissions of Cesium 137, equivalent to 168 times of release from the detonation of the atomic bomb at Hiroshima, although without the immediate loss of life associated with the nuclear accident. (Most of the more than 20,000 deaths from the tsunami were from drowning.) This nuclear catastrophe has not only generated a global public debate regarding the social costs and benefits of nuclear power generation, but also poses serious engineering and social scientific research questions. In this paper we are concerned with the question of whether theextent of the accident at Fukushimawas an inevitableconsequence ofa natural disaster beyond the"conceivable hypothetical possibilities", as TEPCO claims;orwhether there were inherentcontradictions in thestructure of Japan's nuclear power industry. What kinds of public policies are needed to deal with the economic and social costs of the catastrophe? How should this industry be restructured to be more robust to extreme shocks and to become more innovative? Our theoretical framework is comparative so that our treatment is not only relevant to the Japanese situation, but also has relevance for public risk management, for the regulation of integrated monopolies, for innovation in alternative energy sources, etc. To motivate such a comparative approach, we first highlight briefly the causes and behavioral responses to the emergencies during three major nuclear crises: Three Mile Island, Chernobyl, and Fukushima. Figure 5.1

Figure 5.1. Fokushima nuclear power plant after catastrophe.

The assessment of the potential catastrophe of the nuclear power system [8] is evaluated by the agglomeration value of resilience indexes if the agglomeration value will override upper value of the capacity of the system then the catastrophe of the system the result of the evaluation.

In order to adapt the methodology to for the evaluation and assessment of the NPP system vulnerability a following steps are adapted:

Selection of indicators of the NPP system for the evaluation of the catastrophe of the system.

a) Resilience Index due to sudden change of neutron flux will be

$$R_{NF} = \int\limits_{t_0}^{t_1} [1 - q_{NF}] dt \qquad (5.1)$$

In order to demonstrate the determination of numerical value of the Resilience Index due to sudden change of neutron flux it is assumed to have 10 % of the average neutron flux and time interval for the neutron flux recovery t = 60 sec. If we assume to have linear function of the neutron flux change in time the Resilience Index will be

$$R_{NF} = \frac{\Delta t_{NF}}{2} \Delta q_{NF} \qquad (5.2)$$

where   – time interval for the reactor pressure indicator recovery
                        – reactor pressure indicator sudden change
                        – neutron flux change

With this numerical value of the parameters the Resilience index will be R = 30/0.1 = 300 /sec. Figure 5.2

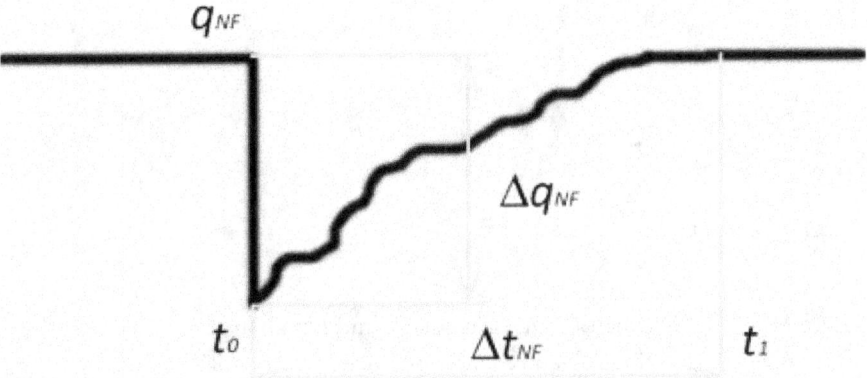

where t_0 – time of sudden change
          t_1 – time when neutron flux resume initial value

Figure 5.2. Graphical presentation of neutron flux change.

b) Resilience Index due to sudden change of reactor pressure will be

$$R_{xp} = \int_{t_i}^{t} [1 - q_{xp}] dt \qquad (5.3)$$

$$R_{xp} = \frac{\Delta t_{xp}}{2} \Delta q_{xp} \qquad (5.4)$$

where   – time interval for the reactor pressure indicator recovery
                    – reactor pressure indicator sudden change
                    – reactor pressure

In this analysis of the reactor pressure change affect on the Resilience Index is assumed that the maximum value of the sudden change of reactor pressure is =10 bars and = 600 sec Figure 5.3.

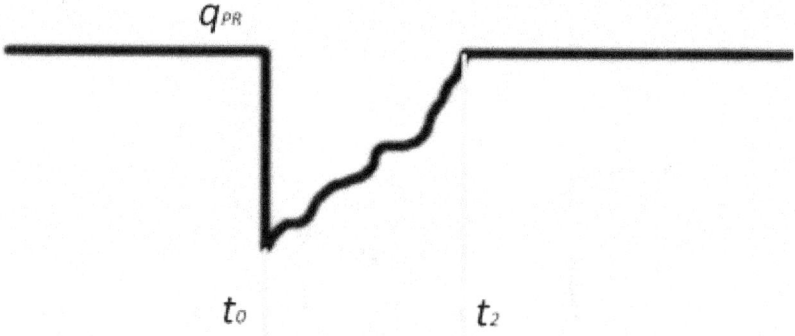

where t_0 – time of reactor pressure sudden change
        t_2 – time when reactor pressure resume initial value

Figure 5.3. Graphical presentation of reactor pressure change.

c) Resilience Index for Change of the Energy Cost
The change of energy Cost indicator reflects potential possibility of the sudden change of energy cost due to the economic crisis in the energy system.

It is usually result of the unexpected economic events which are related to the market fluctuation and economic crisis. The Energy Cost Indicator is measured in €/kWh.

$$R_{\varepsilon c} = \int_{t_0}^{t_1} [1 - q_{\varepsilon c}] dt \qquad (5.5)$$

If it is assumed that the sudden change of the energy cost will happen in the time t_0 and the energy cost will reach recovered value at the time t_1 then the resilience index will be

$$R_{\varepsilon c} = \frac{\Delta t_{\varepsilon c}}{2} \Delta q_{\varepsilon c} \qquad (5.6)$$

where   – time interval for the energy cost indicator recovery
                       – energy cost indicator sudden change
                       – energy cost indicator

For the demonstration of the energy cost on the Resilience Index it is assumed to have the maximum change in the energy cost to be 10% of the nominal energy cost. So that =and = 60 sec Figure 5.4

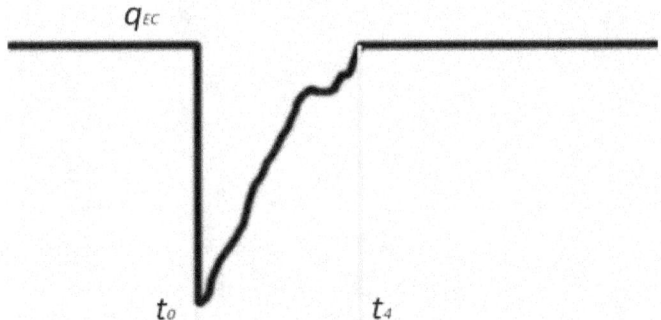

where t_0 – start of energy cost indicator change
                   t_4 – end of energy cost indicator change

Figure 5.4. Graphical presentation of energy cost change.

d) Resilience index for the change of the CO_2 compensation

Recent problem with the global warming has introduced the need for the assessment of manmade pollution with the substitution of new energy sources in order to prevent further pollution problems. It was recognized that the nuclear energy may be used as the substitution for non renewable energy sources. So, the compensation of the CO_2 produced by the combustion of the non renewable by the nuclear energy is opening potential reduction of the CO_2 production. In the normal operation of nuclear power plant there is CO_2 compensation of due to substitutionFigure 5.5

$$R_{co_2} = \int [1 - q_{co_2}]dt$$

(5.7)

$$R_{co_2} = \frac{\Delta t_{co_2}}{2} \Delta q_{co_2}$$

(5.8)

where   – time interval for the CO_2 indicator recovery
                – CO_2 indicator sudden change
                – CO_2 compensation indicator

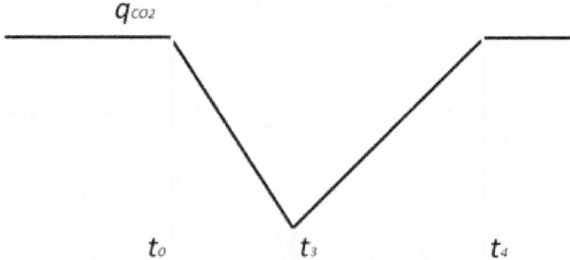

where t_0 – start of CO_2 compensation indicator sudden change indicator change.

                 t_3 – end of CO_2 compensation indicator sudden change.

                 t_4 – end of CO_2 compensation indicator indicator recovery to initial value.

Figure 5.5. Graphical presentation of CO2 change.

The CO_2 compensation is resulting from the use of nuclear energy as the substitution of the non renewable energy. It is proved to be the measuring parameter for the benefit of the nuclear energy to the global warming degradation. As measuring parameter for the resilience index change it is used the total nuclear power measured by the MWdays within the time interval.

e) Resilience index for Change of the of Public Acceptance

The change of public acceptance is result of the public learning system and public information guidance. At the beginning of the nuclear power introduction of the world energy system it was developed very high expectation for the reliable energy source. Unfortunately, due to the unexpected hazard accident on Three Mile Island power plant and Chernobyl power plant the public acceptance has severely changed. In this respect it has become desirable to introduce the resilience index as the additional indicator for the assessment of the safety of the nuclear power plant.

Resilience Index due to sudden change of public acceptance will be

$$R_{z,a} = \int_{t_1}[1 - q_{z,a}]dt \tag{5.9}$$

value

$$R_{z,a} = \frac{\Delta t_{z,a}}{2} \Delta q_{z,a} \tag{5.10}$$

In the measurement of resilience index it is anticipated that the maximum change of acceptance indicator = 7 % with = 360 sec. Figure 5.6

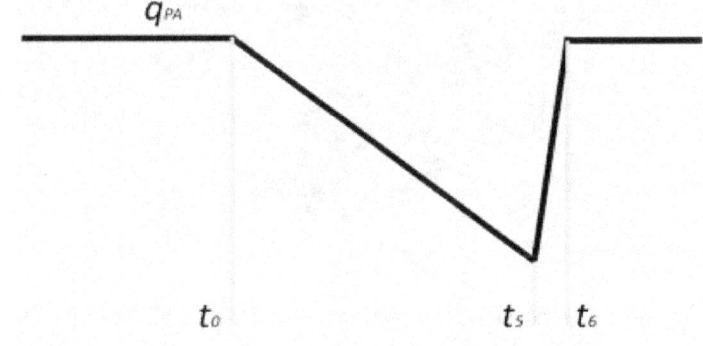

where t_0 – time of public acceptance indicator sudden change

t_5 – end of public acceptance indicator sudden change

t_6 – end of public acceptance indicator resume recovery to initial value

Figure 5.6. Graphical presentation of public acceptance change.

5.2. WIND POWER PLANT CATASTROPHE EVALUATION [8]

Fault is defined as the termination of the capability of an object to complete a function.When a failure occurs inside the wind turbine, e.g. high oil temperature in gearbox, the control unit logs the failure directly or registers the consequences of the fault, and responds referring to the type of the malfunctionFigure 7.Sometimes, in order to avoid safety hazards or main system breakdowns, the turbine has to be shut down. Often they are restarted because of wrong failure detection, which could be caused by noise within the system, and therefore these faults are not considered as crucial problems. If the failure is serious, a visual inspection has to be made which can be carried out by the operators or by authorized personnel.Finally whenever a major failure has happened, a report is documented. This describes the failure reasons, parts involved, and downtime associated with the fault (Figure 5.7 and Figure 5.8). Here are two different examples of various failures that can happen within wind turbines: [9]

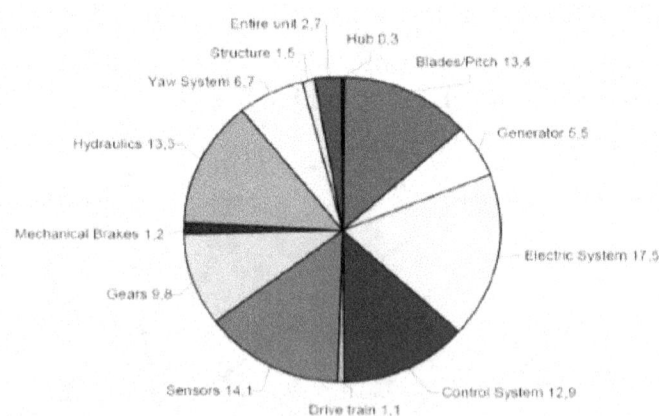

Figure 5.7.Failures of Swedish wind power plant between 2000 and 2004 [10].

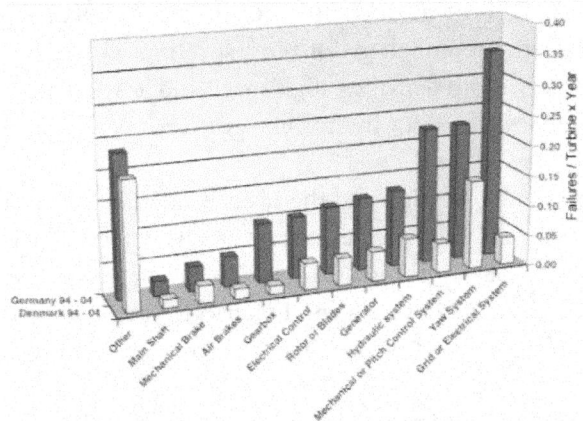

Figure 5.8. Germany and Denmark between 1994 and 2004 [11].

Rotors: Wind turbine rotors are prone to acquire creep and corrosion fatigue, which can be observed as cracks and demolitions in the blades. Moreover, dirt, ice, bird collisions, dampness or manufacturing defects can cause the rotor blades being imbalance and having asymmetric aerodynamic. The roughness in blades will result in loss in energy efficiency which could be caused by erosion, ice, dirt and etc. the techniques that are employed by manufacturer in different situation. For instance, stain gauges has failed to detect the address the problems as it can be affected effects by cross-talk and temperature variations. Moreover, in eddy current inspection for a small shear size, it can take several hours under very difficult working conditions for the human resources.

Figure 5.9. Wind gear tooth damage [12].

Here are some of the most common faults that can occur within the system and the current methodology for the inspection:

Gearbox: Gear tooth damages, high speed and low speed shafts faults are the most common failures in wind turbine gearbox. Typically, vibration measurementFigure 5.9

Generator: Stator, bearing and the rotor inside the generator are subject to failures. Mostly, the faults in generators can be detected by current measurement and Fast Fourier Transformer (FFT)/Spectrum analysis.

Pitch mechanism, Yaw system and Electrical system faults are also can effect on system efficiency and even breakdown. FFT spectrum analysis and Machine Current.

Resilience of the wind power plant is the capacity of the system to withstand changes of the following parameters: wind velocity, mechanical energy conversion into electricity, electricity transmission efficiency and electricity cost. Resilience index comprise following indicators: change in wind velocity, change in mechanical energy conversion efficiency, change in conversion factor, and change in transmission efficiency end change in electricity cost.

Current costs of wind-generated electricity at prime sites approach the costs of a new coal-fired power plant. Wind power is the lowest-cost renewable energy technology available on the market today. Costs of wind power are projected to continue to fall and may rank the cheapest electricity source of all options by 2020.

The strength of wind varies, and an average value for a given location does not alone indicate the amount of energy a wind turbine could produce there. To assess the frequency of wind speeds at a particular location, a probability distribution function is often fit to the observed data. Different locations will have different wind speed distributions because so much power is generated by higher wind speed, much of the energy comes in short bursts. The consequence is that wind energy from a particular turbine or wind farm does not have as consistent an output as fuel-fired power plants; utilities that use wind power provide power from starting existing generation for times when the wind is weak thus wind power is primarily a fuel saver rather than a capacity saver. Making wind power more consistent requires that various existing technologies and methods be extended in particular the use of stronger inter regional transmission to link widely distributed wind farms since the average variability is much less; the use of hydro storage and demand-side energy management. The Earth is unevenly heated by the sun resulting in the poles receiving less energy from the sun than the equator does. Also, the dry land heats up (and cools down) more quickly than the seas do. The differential heating drives a global atmospheric convection system reaching from the Earth's surface to the stratosphere which acts as a virtual ceiling. Most of the energy stored in these wind movements can be found at high altitudes where continuous wind speeds of over 160 km/h (100 mph) occur. Eventually, the wind energy is converted through friction into diffuse heat throughout the Earth's surface and the atmosphere.

The total amount of economically extractable power available from the wind is considerably more than present human power use from all sources. An estimated 72 TW of wind power on the Earth potentially can be commercially viable, compared to about 15 TW average global power consumption from all sources in 2005.

Since wind speed is not constant, a wind farm's annual energy production is never as much as the sum of the generator nameplate ratings multiplied by the total hours in a year. The ratio of actual productivity in a year to this theoretical maximum is called the capacity factor. Typical capacity factors are 20-40%, with values at the upper end of the range in particularly favorable sites. For example, a 1 megawatt turbine with a capacity factor of 35% will not produce 8,760 megawatt-hours in a year (1x24x365), but only 1x0.35x24x365 = 3,066 MWh, averaging to 0.35 MW. Online data is available for some locations and the capacity factor can be calculated from the yearly output.

Unlike fueled generating plants, the capacity factor is limited by the inherent properties of wind. Capacity factors of other types of power plant are based mostly on fuel cost, with a small amount of downtime for maintenance. Nuclear plants have low incremental fuel cost, and so are run at full output and achieve a 90% capacity factor. Plants with higher fuel cost are throttled back to follow load. Gas turbine plants using natural gas as fuel may be very expensive to operate and may be run only to meet peak power demand. A gas turbine plant may have an annual capacity factor of 5-25% due to relatively high energy production cost.

According to a 2007 Stanford University study published in the Journal of Applied Meteorology and Climatology, interconnecting ten or more wind farms can allow an average of 33% of the total energy produced to be used as reliable, baseload electric power, as long as minimum criteria are met for wind speed and turbine height.

The best way of measuring wind speeds at a prospective wind turbine site is to fit an anemometer to the top of a mast which has the same height as the expected hub height of the wind turbine to be used. This way one avoids the uncertainty involved in recalculating the wind speeds to a different height.

By fitting the anemometer to the top of the mast one minimises the disturbances of airflows from the mast itself. If anemometers are placed on the side of the mast it is essential to place them in the prevailing wind direction in order to minimize the wind shade from the tower.

The monitoring of wind power plant is based on the number of indicators. The definition of each indicator is specified by the respective wind power model as presented in following description:

a. Wind Power Density
    These evaluations lead us to the definition of the tree parameters to be as the monitoring of the Wind Power Density, namely: pressure and temperature of the air, average wind velocity and frequency of the wind.
b. Efficiency of wind power plant
    Mechanical energy obtained by the wind energy is converted to the electricity by the electric generator with respective efficiency defined respective efficiency defined by
    Monitoring parameters are: WDP and E_{power}
c. Power frequency
    Power frequency is parameter needed for the wind power plant synchronization. Together with electric power measured by the electric currency in amperes and grid voltage in volt, it is stability constrain for the connection to the grid. I require mentoring of following parameters: frequency fluctuation and voltage fluctuation in the grid.
d. Electricity cost
    Cost of the electricity produced by the wind power plant is defined as the total amount of plant expenses divided by power produced. The expenses are defined by the cost of manpower and maintenance cost.

The monitoring scheme is presented on Figure 5.10.

Data processing is organized with the appropriate definition of the Sustainability Index. As shown on Figure 5.10 the first step in data processing is the data normalization with the aim to obtain specific indicators to be agglomerated in the Sustainability Index. It is assumed that the Sustainability index [9] is a linear agglomeration function of products between specific indicators and corresponding weighting coefficients, in the form of additive convolution. If it will be adapted that each of the specific indicator is weighted by the respective weighting coefficient. The sum of specific indicator multiplied with the corresponding weight coefficient will lead to the Sustainability Index, Q(t), with the following mathematical formulation

$$Q(t) = \sum_n \omega_n q_n(t)$$

(5.11)

Figure 5.10. Schematics Structure of Wind Power Plant Monitoring System.

where

ω_n – weighting coefficient for the n-th specific indicator

q_n – n-th criterion for sustainability assessment.

The evaluation of wind energy system as the complex system is the prestigious goal of modern approach to the validation of the energy system. In this context it is introduced notion of the Resilience Index as the agglomerated indicator for the measurement of the wind energy system quality [13]. Resilience Index is the property of wind energy system based on the assumption that the wind energy system is a complex system with time change of main system parameters. Resilience Index presented on Figure 5.11 is graphical presentation of the sudden Sustainability index change in time and its recovery to the initial state of the system. The integral value of the Sustainability Index recovery after sudden change leads to the definition of Resilience Index.

The second step in the data processing is the determination of the resilience index component corresponding to the sudden change of the specific indicators. It is anticipated the total Resiliency Index is the sum of the resiliency index components.

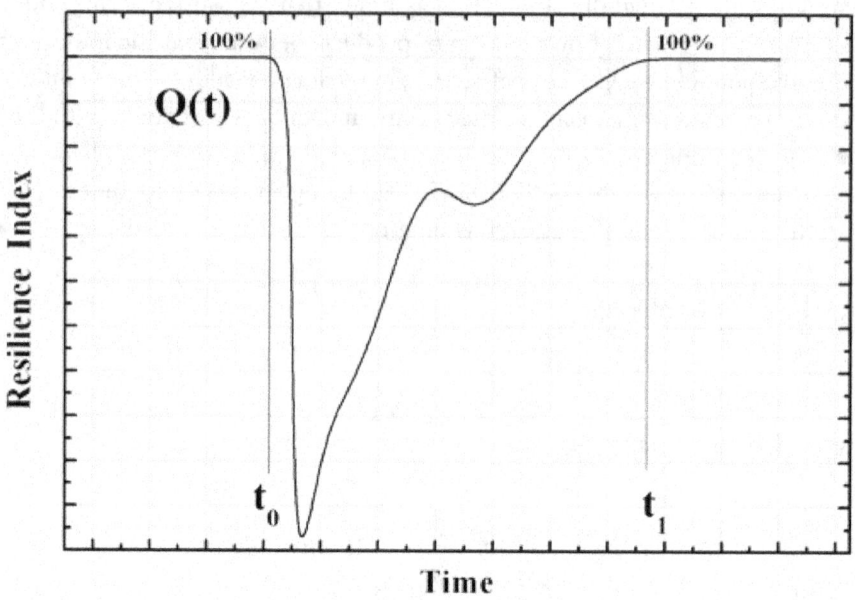

Figure 5.11.Graphical presentation of Resilience Index.

Resilience Index is the variable immanent to the specific potential hazard. This means that Resilience index as the parameter which quantifying the potential probability for the malfunction of the system. Resilience index is expressed with following mathematical formulation

$$R_j = \sum_{i=1}^{k} w_i \int_{t_0}^{t_1} \left[1 - q_i(t) \right] \tag{5.12}$$

In this definition it is anticipated that there is time independent constant for every indicator.

In the processing of the resilience index components a following simplification is introduced. The sudden change of the specific indicator from the initial value will be recovered within the time period t_0. Under theassumption that the sudden indicator change resumes is a linear function of time, then we can write

$$R = \frac{1}{2} w \left(\Delta q \, \Delta t \right) \tag{5.13}$$

If it is assumed that the time interval for resuming starting state is equal for all indicators than and then the Resilience Index for the individual case is

$$R = \frac{\Delta t_0}{2} w \, \Delta q \tag{5.14}$$

The total Resilience Index is an additive function of all resilienceIndexes as follows

The resilienceindex is composed of sub-indicators. In the same way the economic,environmental, technological and social resilience element could be obtained, as follows. Under theassumption that the sudden indicator change resumes is a linear function of time, then we can write

$$R = \frac{\Delta t_0}{2} w \, \Delta q \tag{5.15}$$

If it is assumed that the time interval for resuming starting state is equal for all indicators than and then the Resilience Index for the individual case is

$$R = \frac{\Delta t_0}{2} w \, \Delta q \tag{5.16}$$

The total Resilience Index is an additive function of all resilienceIndexes as follows

$$R_{TOT} = R_{WPD} + R_{EWPP} + R_{PF} + R_{ED} \tag{5.17}$$

where

R_{TOT} – total resilience index

R_{WPD} – wind power density

R_{EWPP} – efficiency of wind power plant

R_{PF} – power frequency

R_{EC} – electricity cost

Catastrophe Demonstration with Resilience Index for Wind Power Plant

In this exercise we will assume that every indicator is measured in the time interval t_0. Also, it is assumed that the air temperature and air pressure are constant during this exercise. Indicators nominal values and sudden changes are as given in the Table 5.1.

In this demonstration exercise we have taken into a consideration the situations defined as the objects of the demonstration with the sudden changes of individual indicators.

Following situations are taken into a consideration:
- Change of wind power density
- Change of efficiency of wind power plant
- Change of frequency
- Change of electricity cost

In the design of the Objects under consideration it is introduced assumption that the sudden change of indicators is triggered at the same moment for all indicators. Also, the change of indicators are normalised and the maximum change for each of the indicator expressed in normalised value. It is of particular interest for this demonstration to have each object defined as the composition simulations sudden changes of all indicators as shown on Table 5.1.

Table 5.1.

Objects	Wind power density WPD	Efficiency of wind power plant EWPP	Power frequency EF	Electricity Cost EC
	Δm/sec	Δ %	Δ Ampere	Δ€/kWh
Object 1	4/20	2.5	1.25	0
Object 2	2	5/100	2.5	1.25
Object 3	1	1.25	5/50	2.5
Object 4	0	0	0	5/20

The Total Resilience Index is determined for following cases:

Case 1 -   WPD > EWPP = PF = EC
Case 2 -   EWPP > WPD = PF =EC
Case 3 -   PF > WPE = EWPP = EC
Case 4 -   EC > WPPD = EWPP = PF

The results obtained for these cases are shown in Table 5.2.

Table 5.2.

CASES	Resilience Index
CASE I	0.755
CASE 2	0.866
CASE 3	0.6I2
CASE 4	0.647

In the evaluation wind power plant catastrophe the comparison cases under consideration the case1- WPD > EWPP = PF = EC is reflecting the Total Resilience Index to be most dangers case in the assessment wind power plant catastrophe.

If the limiting value of the Resilience Index is lower than the Total Resilience index it represents potential situation for the catastrophic event. From this exercise it can be concluded that for every case with lower value of the Total Resilience Index the system will be exposed to the safe mode of the potential catastrophic event.

As the Resilience Index is the stability parameter of any system and it can be used as the measuring parameter for the assessment of the potential hazard events. As regards the wind power plant analysis it prove that the most stable case in sudden change of the indicators is the Case 2 when the priority of the indicators is given to the Efficiency Wind Power plant.

In particular, it is of interest to mention that the Resilience Index is the parameter of the system which can be used as the diagnostic tool in the assessment of the potential catastrophic event of the system. As regards a wind energy power plant the catastrophic events is result of the mal function of the wind power plant elements.

5.3 Solar Power Plant Catastrophe Evaluation

Geomagnetic storms on the scale of the 1859 or 1921 events are very rare, and no one knows when such an event may recur. Huge geomagnetic storms can occur at any portion of the 11-year sunspot cycle, but are most likely within a year of solar maximum. The 1921 event occurred three years after solar maximum, and the 1859 and 1989 events within a year of solar maximum. According to NASA's Bruce Tsurutani, a massive X22+ solar flare event on April 2, 2001, near the peak of the last solar cycle, was even larger than the flare that triggered the 1859 Carrington event. Fortunately, the 2001 flare was not pointed at the Earth, and we escaped a repeat of the Carrington event.

Shortly after midnight on September 2, 1859, campers in the Rocky Mountains were awakened by an "aurorally light, so bright that one could easily read common print. Some of the party insisted that it was daylight and began the preparation of breakfast", according to the Rocky Mountain News. Magnetic observatories world-wide recorded disturbances in Earth's field so extreme that magnetometer traces were driven off scale, and telegraph networks experienced major disruptions and outages. The electricity which attended this beautiful phenomenon took possession of the magnetic wires throughout the country, the Philadelphia Evening Bulletin reported, and there were numerous side displays in the telegraph offices where fantastical and unreadable messages came through the instruments, and where the atmospheric fireworks assumed shape and substance in brilliant sparks. In several locations, operators disconnected their systems from the batteries and sent messages using only the current induced by the aurora. In Havana, Cuba, the sky that night appeared "stained with blood and in a state of general conflagration" and auroras were observed as far south as Hawaii and northern Venezuela. A British amateur astronomer, Richard Carrington, observed an outburst of "two patches of intensely bright and white light" from a large and complex group of sunspots the the center of the Sun's disk the previous day, and so the solar storm of 1859 has been dubbed "the Carrington event". It remains the most severe solar storm to affect the Earth in recorded history.

As the magnetic energy is being released, particles, including electrons, protons, and heavy nuclei, are heated and accelerated in the solar atmosphere. The energy released during a flare is typically on the order of 10^{27} ergs per second. Large flares can emit up to 10^{32} ergs of energy. This energy is ten million times greater than the energy released from a volcanic explosion. On the other hand, it is less than one-tenth of the total energy emitted by the Sun every second.

There are typically three stages to a solar flare, like Figure 12. First is the*precursor*stage, where the release of magnetic energy is triggered. Soft x-ray emission is detected in this stage. In the second or*impulsive*stage, protons and electrons are accelerated to energies exceeding 1MeV. During the impulsive stage, radio waves, hard x-rays, and gamma rays are emitted. The gradual build up and decay of soft x-rays can be detected in the third,*decay*stage. The duration of these stages can be as short as a few seconds or as long as an hour.

Solar flares extend out to the layer of the Sun called the*corona*. The corona is the outermost atmosphere of the Sun, consisting of highly rarefied gas. This gas normally has a temperature of a few million degrees Kelvin. Inside a flare, the temperature typically reaches 10 or 20 million degrees Kelvin, and can be as high as 100 million degrees Kelvin. The corona is visible in soft x-rays, as in the above image. Notice that the corona is not uniformly bright, but is concentrated around the solar equator in loop-shaped features. These bright loops are located within and connect areas of strong*magnetic field*called*active regions*. Sunspots are located within these active regions.

Figure 5.12. Solar flares extend out to the layer of the sun called the*corona*.

Geomagnetic storms on the scale of the 1859 or 1921 events are very rare, and no one knows when such an event may recur. Huge geomagnetic storms can occur at any portion of the 11-year sunspot cycle, but are most likely within a year of solar maximum. The 1921 event occurred three years after solar maximum, and the 1859 and 1989 events within a year of solar maximum. According to NASA's Bruce Tsurutani, a massive X22+ solar flare event on April 2, 2001, near the peak of the last solar cycle, was even larger than the flare that triggered the 1859 Carrington event. Fortunately, the 2001 flare was not pointed at the Earth, and we escaped a repeat of the Carrington event.

Shortly after midnight on September 2, 1859, campers in the Rocky Mountains were awakened by an "auroral light, so bright that one could easily read common print. Some of the party insisted that it was daylight and began the preparation of breakfast", according to the Rocky Mountain News. Magnetic observatories world-wide recorded disturbances in Earth's field so extreme that magnetometer traces were driven off scale, and telegraph networks experienced major disruptions and outages. The electricity which attended this beautiful phenomenon took possession of the magnetic wires throughout the country, the Philadelphia Evening Bulletin reported, and there were numerous side displays in the telegraph offices where fantastical and unreadable messages came through the instruments, and where the atmospheric fireworks assumed shape and substance in brilliant sparks. In several locations, operators disconnected their systems from the batteries and sent messages using only the current induced by the aurora. In Havana, Cuba, the sky that night appeared "stained with blood and in a state of general conflagration" and auroras were observed as far south as Hawaii and northern Venezuela (Figure 1). A British amateur astronomer, Richard Carrington, observed an outburst of "two patches of intensely bright and white light" from a large and complex group of sunspots the the center of the Sun's disk the previous day, and so the solar storm of 1859 has been dubbed "the Carrington event". It remains the most severe solar storm to affect the Earth in recorded history

As the magnetic energy is being released, particles, including electrons, protons, and, are heated and accelerated in the solar atmosphere. The energy released during a flare is typically on the order of 10^{27} ergsper second. Large flares can emit up to 10^{32} ergs of energy. This energy is ten million times greater than the energy released from a volcanic explosion. On the other hand, it is less than one-tenth of the total energy emitted by the Sun every second.

There are typically three stages to a solar flare. First is the *precursor* stage, where the release of magnetic energy is triggered. Soft x-ray emission is detected in this stage. In the second or *impulsive* stage, protons and electrons are accelerated to energies exceeding 1 MeV. During the impulsive stage, radio waves, hard x-rays, and gamma rays are emitted. The gradual build up and decay of soft x-rays can be detected in the third, *decay* stage. The duration of these stages can be as short as a few seconds or as long as an hour.

Solar flares extend out to the layer of the Sun called thecorona. The corona is the outermost atmosphere of the Sun, consisting of highly rarefied gas. This gas normally has a temperature of a few million degrees Kelvin. Inside a flare, the temperature typically reaches 10 or 20 million degrees Kelvin, and can be as high as 100 million degrees Kelvin. The corona is visible in soft x-rays, as in the above image. Notice that the corona is not uniformly bright, but is concentrated around the solar equator in loop-shaped features. These bright loops are located within and connect areas of strongmagnetic field-called *active regions*. Sunspots are located within these active regions. Solar flares occur in active regions.

Gamma-ray burstsare flashes ofgamma raysassociated with extremely energetic explosions that have been observed in distantgalaxies. They are the mostluminouselectromagnetic events known to occur in theuniverse. Bursts can last from ten milliseconds to several minutes, although a typical burst lasts 20–40 seconds. The initial burst is usually followed by a longer-lived "afterglow" emitted at longer wavelengths (X-ray,ultraviolet,optical,infrared,microwaveandradio).

The frequency of flares coincides with the Sun's eleven year cycle. When the solar cycle is at a minimum, active regions are small and rare and few solar flares are detected. These increase in number as the Sun approaches the maximum part of its cycle. The Sun will reach its next maximum in the year 201.

a) The Corona Soft x-raysFlux

Flare is a burst of energy resulting from the nuclear processes on the solar corona. The corona is the outmost atmosphere of the sun. It is the gas at the temperature of few million degrees Centigrade. Radiation from the corona reaching earth surface is composed of different energies. When these energy fluxes reach earth surface it produce adverse effect on the earth surface. Collection of solar energy on the earth is presently done by photo voltaic panels made of different poly-crystal material. Photo voltaic panel are used for electricity production. The intensity of the electricity production depends on the electro-magnetic radiation. Sudden change of electro-magnetic radiation resulting from the flora burst can strongly effect the operation of Photo-voltaic Power Plant which may lead to the catastrophic event (Figure 5.13).

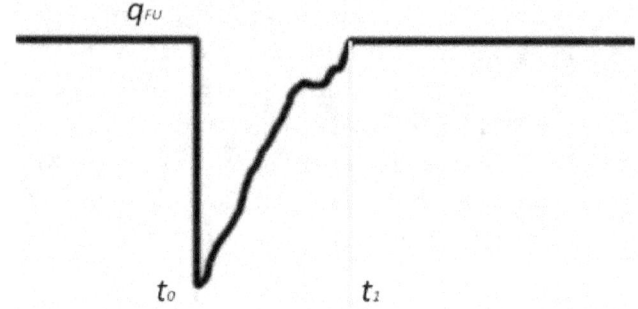

where

q_{FU}	-indicator for flare intensity
t_0	-sudden change of flare indicator
t_1	-flare indicator indicator recovery

Figure 5.13. Graphical presentation of Flare Indicator.

b) Protons and Electrons Radiation with Energies Exceeding 1MeV

The electromagnetic radiation can produce adverse effect in human life. In particular this radiation may disrupt operation of electric transmission system on the earth leading to the hazard events which is affecting human life-Figure 5.14. As the indicator for the effect of solar radiation on the human life we can take the adverse effect of solar radiation on the communication system.

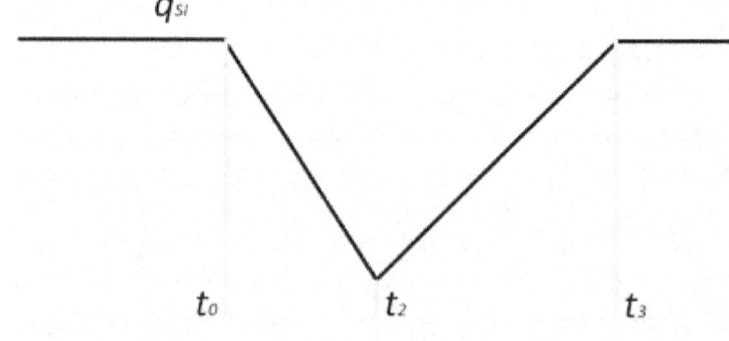

where

q_{SI}	-social indicator
t_0	-start of social indicator
t_2	-end of social indicator change
t_3	-end of recovery time of social indicator

Figure 5.14. Graphical presentation of Social Indicator.

c) Energy Decay Stage

The duration of these stages can be as short as a few seconds or as long as an hour. Figure 5.15

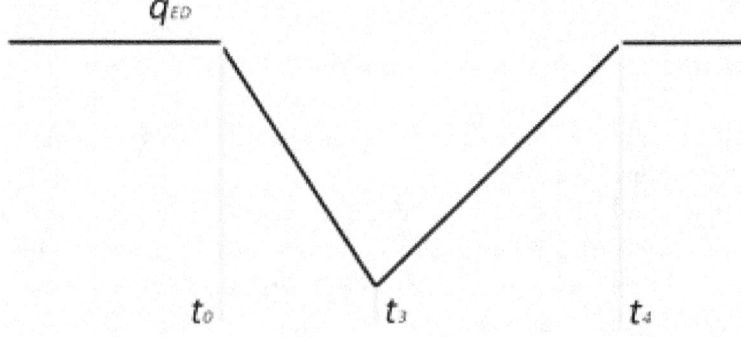

q_{ED} – energy decay
t_0 – start of decay indicator
t_3 – end of energy decay indicator decrease
t_4 – end of recovery time of decay indicator

Figure 5.15. Graphical presentation of energy decay indicator.

5.4 CATASTROPHE OF POWER TRANSMISSION SYSTEM

Power systems are critical infrastructures in the same way as gas and oil networks, water networks, transportation networks, telecommunications and computer systems. These complex networked systems are increasingly inter-dependent on each other, as the digital society matures on a global scale [17,18].

Consequently, their vulnerability and security are raising major concerns worldwide. For instance, the normal operation of water and telecommunication systems is maintained only if there is a steady supply of electrical energy. On the other hand, the generation and delivery of electricity cannot be ensured without provision to the power plants and power networks of fuel, water and various telecommunications and computer services for data transfer and control purposes. These interdependencies are strengthening their grip as the usage of the internet, intranet and other wide area computer networks is becoming prevalent. The strong reliance of critical infrastructures on each other may turn a local disturbance in one of them into a large-scale failure via cascading effects, which may have a catastrophic impact on the whole of society. Unfortunately, the risk of such a disastrous domino effect is growing because of the current trend to operate critical infrastructure systems closer to their stability or capacity limits. One compelling reason for this practice is, of course, economics. Providing these infrastructures with some degree of robustness comes at a price, which entails the achievement of the required level of redundancy in the equipment

A typical example of a critical infrastructure that undergoes rising vulnerability to catastrophic failure is the power transmission network. There are several reasons for such a situation to prevail. Firstly, as witnessed in developed countries, there has been a very slow expansion of the high voltage transmission grid during recent decades due to stringent regulations put forward in response to environmental concerns. Secondly, there are the profound structural reforms that the power industry has embarked on, which are geared towards the emergence and consolidation of competitive energy markets [In these emerging competitive electricity markets, the wholesale market is the first to flourish and expand at a rapid rate, boosted by transmission's open access and the existence of a large variability in electricity prices between the US states. This price discrepancy has resulted in a growing amount of bulk power being transferred over long distances throughout the transmission grid, worsening a shortage of reserve margins in transmission that have prevailed since the mid 1980s. Consequently, blackouts and brownouts in the eastern and western parts of the country have been increasing in number at an alarming rate during recent years [19,20]

In bulk power transmission system planning and operation, the present practice is to carry out an N-1 contingency analysis. Occasionally, an N-2 security analysis is employed in some stringent cases. However, it is implemented not via an exhaustive search but rather via a partial assessment of the system reserves over a small portion of the transmission network. An N-k security analysis for k > 1 is perceived as being impossible to achieve due to the huge number of cases that need to be investigated. In fact, under the assumption of independence between successive events, it would require checking the impact on the system reserve margins of the loss of every k out of N pieces of equipment, which yields a number of cases to be tested that grows exponentially with N. However, it is clear that this chain of contingencies are dependent on each other due to the protection-system interactions, either directly or indirectly via the changes in the distribution of power through the network or due to the possible multiple impacts of a triggering event, such as lightning or other natural hazards. Consequently, the probability of the occurrence of cascading failures is much higher than the probability of a random (i.e. independent) tripping of k out of N components of the system.

It is also the usual practice in reliability and security analysis to neglect the impact of the protection systems. As a result, cascading failures leading to blackouts or brownouts are not investigated. Until recently, large-scale blackouts were considered to be sufficiently rare events to be disregarded from the analysis. However, at least in the USA, ideas are evolving in this respect, prompted by the increasing number of major incidents that has plagued the US power systems since the mid 1990s. The frequency of major blackouts, which was about one per decade until 1996, has started to grow at an alarming rate since then. For example, in July 1996, a series of blackouts struck the western part of the USA, leaving 2.2 million customers without electricity. One month later, islanding and blackouts affected eleven US western states and two Canadian provinces.

In December 1998, the Bay area of San Francisco experienced a series of blackouts and in July 1999, it was the turn of New York City to suffer from the same type of cascading failures. More recently, California has been struck by rolling blackouts initiated by the utilities to overcome a severe shortage of generation during peak hours. An exhaustive account of these blackouts can be found in the report prepared for the Transmission Reliability Program of the Department of Energy [8]. Besides the causes of the degradation of the power system reliability listed previously, there is the detrimental role played by the protection systems during large disturbances. As revealed by the study undertaken by the NERC over the period from 1984 in 73.5% of the significant disturbances that were investigated, undetected failures of the protection systems, termed hidden failures (HFs), have aggravated the disturbance by tripping fault free system components and, thereby, helped the perturbation to propagate further. One peculiarity of hidden relay failures is that they cannot be detected a priori, that is, they cannot be exposed before the system is perturbed. In particular, routine maintenance testing may not detect them or, even worse, may induce them by damaging relay components, as was the case in the 1977 New York blackout. Another source of HFs is the bad setting of relays. The present practice favors dependability at the expense of security, in that it ensures the isolation of a fault by allowing the tripping of fault free devices from time to time.

This paper describes methodologies together with algorithms that assess the risk of catastrophic failures in power networks. It builds on the pioneer work carried out by Thorp, Phadke, Horowitz and Tamronglak [21]. A catastrophic failure is here defined as one that results in the outage of a sizable amount of load, say 10% of the peak load. It may be caused by dynamic instabilities in the system or exhaustion of the reserves in transmission due to a sequence of line tripping leading to voltage collapse. Only the latter case is being considered. The aim of these algorithms is to identify the weak links in the systems, which are defined as those branches of the network that tripping due to a fault lead to the highest probabilities of a catastrophic failure. Once the weak links are identified, they must be consolidated. To this end, a hidden failure monitoring and control system may be developed to supervise adaptive digital relays located in sensitive spots across the system. These relays may perform dynamic load shedding during an emergency state in conjunction with an adaptive splitting of the system that prevents the cascading failures from spreading throughout the network.

5.4.1 Resilience Metrics

The safety of anenergy system is the immanent property to any system. It reflects the quantitative measure of degradation of the system. It may be seen as the potential property predicting total degradation of the system. It is commonly known that any degradation of the system proceeds with changes of the main properties of the system. Since the sustainabilityindex is a complex property of the system it will lead to the possibility to define those rates of change, which may have different consequences

The resilience of an energy system is defined as the capacity of an energy system to withstand perturbations from e.g. climatic, economic, technological and social causes and to rebuild and renew itself afterwards. In this respect, quantification of the resilience capacity can be used as the merit to withstand differing events leading to potential damaging consequences. So, the change of resilience of an energy system can be used in the assessment of the system behavior and the potential for its malfunction development. As the sustainability index definition we have used specific quality indicators reflecting corresponding criteria, it is possible to use the sustainability index as the resilience metric parameter. The change of the economic indicator is intrinsic to the specific characteristic to be measured in the time scale. The time change of the economic indicators is common to the classical evaluation of a system. Any crises of the economic system are preceded with corresponding changes in the economic indicators of the system. Qualitative measurement of the indicator changes may lead to the forecast of the economic crises, which is only one element of the potential disastrous changes of the system affecting its safety [22].

The mutual interaction between the system and its surrounding is imminent for any system. The changes in interaction rate will affect the safety of the system. If these processes are in steady state, it can be considered that the system is safe. As good example for this type of changes of indicator is the interaction of system and its surrounding in the case of radioactive leaks from nuclear facilities, which may lead to hazardous consequences.

The change of social element of complexity of the system is a property of the complex system. The social aspect of thesystem includes the risk of changes as health hazards and may have to deal with a compounding of complexity at different levels. It is of interest to notice that some of the social changes are an inherent characteristic of the system. As an example we can take any strike, which is the result of the economic changes of the system. A similar example can be seen if there is a sudden change in the environment, which will lead to social disturbances.

5.4.2 Mathematical Formulation of Sustainability Index

If it is assumed that the Sustainability index is a linear agglomeration function of products between indicators and corresponding weighting coefficients, we can write the aggregation function, which is presented in the form of an additive convolution. If it is adapted, which means that each of the criteria is weighted by the respective factor, the sum of thecriteria multiplied with the corresponding factor will lead to the Sustainability Index.

For the case under consideration, the sum of specific indicator multiplied with the corresponding weight coefficient will lead to the Sustainability Index, Q(t), with the following mathematical formulation

$$Q(t) = \sum_{n} \omega_n q_n(t) \qquad (5.18)$$

where

W_n– weighting coefficient for the n-th specific indicator

q_n – n-th criterion for sustainability assessment.

Resilience Index, presented in Figure 5.16, is graphical presentation of the sudden Sustainability index change in time and its recovery to the initial state of the system. The integral value of the Sustainability Index recovery after a sudden change leads to the definition of Resilience Index.

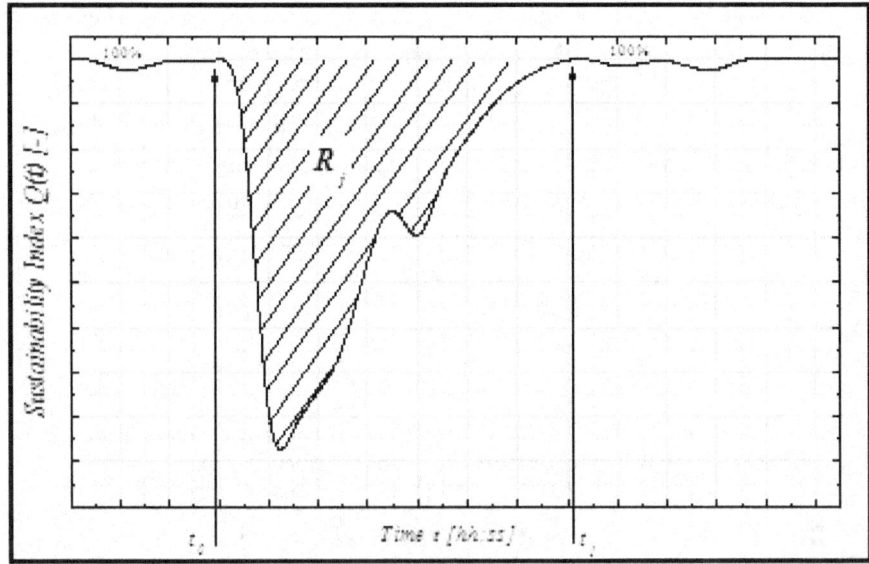

Figure 5.16. Graphical presentation of Resilience Index.

The Resilience Index is integral of the Sustainability Index between the time of the sudden change in the respective indicator and the time when it resumes a steady state value. The resilience index for an energy system is composed of the following elements: economic, environmental, technological and social.

Resilience Index is the variable immanent to the specific potential hazard. This means that Resilience index as the parameter which quantifying the potential probability for the malfunction of the system. Resilience index is expressed with following mathematical formulation: Figure 5.17.

$$R_j = \sum_{i=1}^{k} w_i \int_{t_0}^{t_1} \left[1 - q_i(t) \right]$$

(5.19)

where

$\quad R_j \quad$ – resilienceindex
$\quad q_i \quad$ – indicator
$\quad w_i \quad$ – weight coefficient

In this definition it is anticipated that there is time independent constant for every indicator.

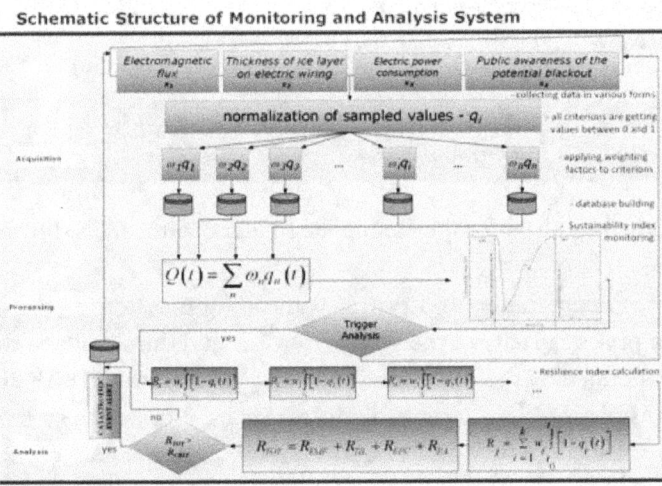

Figure 5.17. Monitoring and analysis of resilience index of a power transmission system.

The resilienceindex is composed of sub-indicators. In the same way the economic,environmental, technological and social resilience element could be obtained, as follows. Under theassumption that the sudden indicator change resumes is a linear function of time, then we can write:

$$R = \frac{1}{2} w \left(\Delta q \, \Delta t \right) \tag{5.20}$$

If it is assumed that the time interval for resuming starting state is equal for all indicators than the Resilience Index for the individual case is:

$$R = \frac{\Delta t_o}{2} w \, \Delta q \tag{5.21}$$

The total Resilience Index is an additive function of all resilienceIndexes as follows:

$$R_{TOT} = \Sigma w \, R = w_1 R_{EMF} + w_2 R_{TIL} + w_3 R_{EPC} + w_4 R_{PA} \tag{5.22}$$

where

R_{TOT} – *total resilience index*
R_{EMF} – *electro-magnetic flux*
R_{TIL} – *thickness of ice layer on electric wiring*
R_{EPC} – *electric power consumption*
R_{PA} – *public awareness of the potential blackout*
w_n – *weighting factor*

Generic flow chart for the Resilience Index monitoring is shown in Figure 5.17.

The resilience index of a power transmission system is the parameter which comprises capacity of the system to withstand the change of the selected indicators defined by the individual indicators [14,15,16,17,18,19,20]. For the power transmission system set of indicators is used to define system capacity reflecting the change of indicators. Among the indicators effecting resilience index are a following sudden change of indicators: electro-magnetic flux, thickness of ice layer on electric wiring, voltage of the power transmission system, electric power consumption, and public awareness of the potential blackout.

5.4.3 Resilience Index Verification

In the evaluation of the Power Transmission System the following indicators are taken into consideration

a) Electro-magneticFlux Indicator

Electromagnetic pulses damage electrical and electronic circuits by inducing voltages and currents that they are not designed to withstand. To understand how this occurs, it is necessary to understand both the characteristics of electromagnetic pulses and the circuits they offend. An electromagnetic pulse is defined by its rise time (measured in volts/second), its electrical field strength (measured in volts/meter (v/m), and its frequency content (measured in Hertz [Hz]).These factors combine to determine the threat electromagnetic pulses pose to a given system. Figure 5.18.It is anticipated that the sudden change electro-magnetic flux indicator is at the time t_0 and will be recovered at the time t_2.

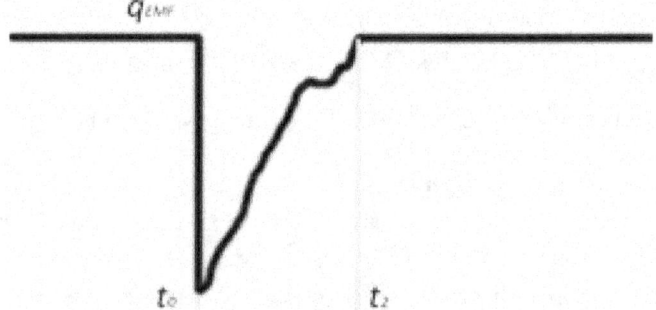

where q_{EMF} – Electro-magnetic flux indicator
  t_o – time of sudden change
  t_2 – recovery time for sudden change

Figure 5.18. Graphical presentation of the electro-magnetic flux indicator.

b) Thickness of Ice Layer on Electric WiringIndicator

It is common that the weather storm with snow is accompanied with the formation of icy layer on the power wiring. This leads to the overweighting of the wiring system. It is usually noticed that the wiring prolongation is visible as the deflection from the primary wiring. The wiring disruption is often notified as the result of snow overweight.

It is appropriate to use as the indicator for thickness of ice layer on electric power wiring the wire prolongation. At the time t_0 wire prolongation start and at the time at the time t_1 it ends, following wire recovery to time t_2. Figure 5.19 shows resilience index change in time scale.

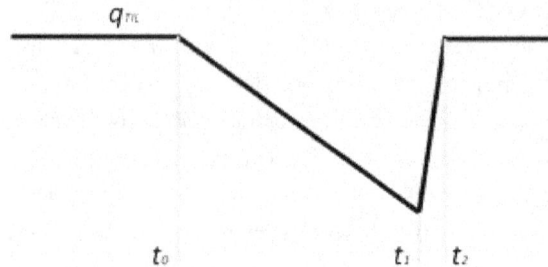

where

q_{TIL} – thickness of icy layer indicator
t_0 – start time of voltage change
t_1 – end of voltage change
t_2 recovery time for voltage change

Figure 5.19. Graphical presentation of the thickness of icy layer indicator.

c) Power ConsumptionIndicator

The power consumption indicator is a measuring parameter of the amount of energy. It reflects the potential change of the electric power consumption. The change of this indicator gives us possibility to determine the resilience index of the power consumption. It is anticipated that the power consumption change start at time t_0 and ends at t_1. It will be recovered at the time t_3 as shown in Figure 5.20.

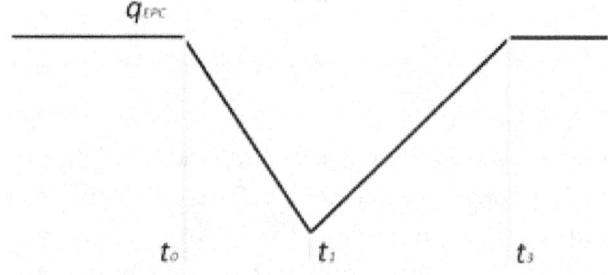

where

q_{EPC}– Electric Power Consumption indicator

t_0– start time of voltage change

t_1– end of voltage change

t_3– recovery time for voltage change

Figure 5.20. Graphical presentation of the electric power consumption indicator.

d)Public Awarenessof the Potential BLACKOUT indicator

The social indicator for the resilience index to be used for the public awareness assessment is the public awareness of the potential blackout. It is assumed that at the time t_0 starts the change of the indicator while it ends at time t_6. It will be recovered at time t_7. The resilience index for the public awareness of the potential blackout is shown on Figure 5.21, while graphical presentation of the resilience index for power transmission system can be seen on Figure 5.22.

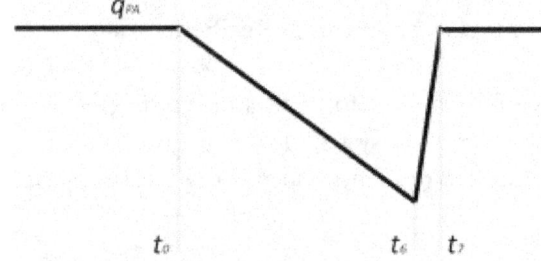

where

q_{PA} – public awareness indicator

t_0 – start time of indicator change

t_6 –end of indicator change

t_7 – recovery time indicator change

Figure 5.21. Graphical presentation of the public awareness indicator.

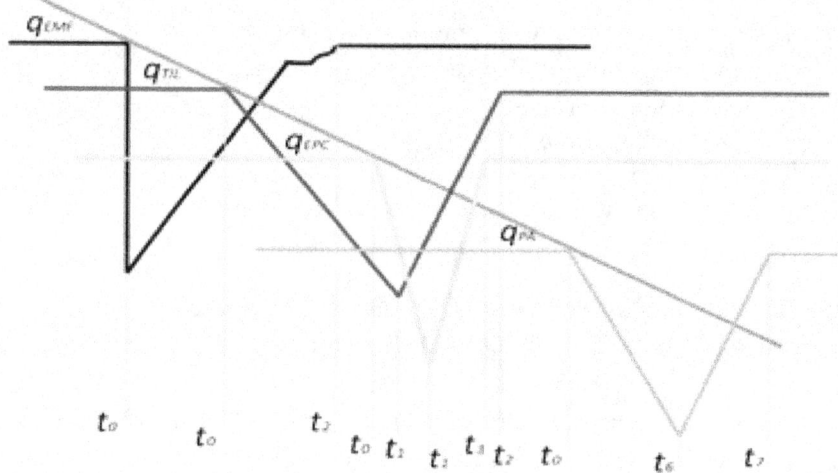

Figure 5.22. Graphical presentation of the Resilience Index for Power Transmission System.

Catastrophic event Assessment with Resilience Index

The capacity of the system to withstand catastrophic event is measured with the resilience index of the system. If the system is subject to the respective change of indicators, the resilience index is the measuring paramour for the assessment of the potential catastrophe of the system.

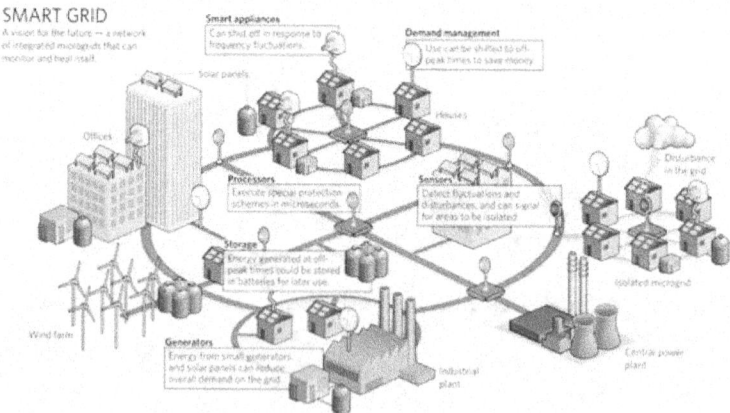

Figure 5.23. Smart Grid.

The impact of GMDs on the grid, Figure 5.23., is aptly described by the North American Electric Reliability Corporation (NERC) as a "high impact, low frequency" event. The "high impact" term is relevant because a significant GMD impacts on a very large area (that is, a band of potential impact around the earth) and can thus impact a large population of utility devices simultaneously. The "low frequency" term is relevant because large GMD events are much less frequent when compared to other utility impacts, such as terrestrial storms. Any utility response to GMDs should thus be taken in the context of both the impact and the probability. An important research goal is thus to develop a risk assessment and mitigation methodology for GMDs which provides a balanced and systematic approach to forecast GMDs, cost-effective hardening of critical assets and quick system restoration.

5.4.4. Agglomeration of the Resilience Index

The Total Residence Index for the evaluation of Power Transmission Systems is a linear function of the resilience indicators for the change of individual indicators.

The critical resilience index for the power system is defined the limiting value for resilience index before the catastrophic event will occur. It means that

$$R_{TOT} < R_{CRIT} \qquad (5.23)$$

It is of special interest, in the evaluation of the catastrophic events, to specify the contribution of the individual resilience index to validate the contribution of the specific resilience indexes. In this respect it is of special interested value to justify the contribution of the specific resilience index to the agglomerated value of the Resilience Index.

In the evaluation of the catastrophe of the power transmission system, the most important parameter to be taken into a consideration is the Resilience Index of Electro-magnetic floury. In particular, it has been taken into a consideration, its effect on the different fields of human interest.

5.5 SOLAR FLARE EFFECTON THE POWER TRANSMISSION SYSTEM

Warning events in 1859, 1921, 1989, and 2003 showed the danger that solar activity can pose to power and distribution systems. Now as we move into another solar maximum, with increased vulnerabilities built into our electrical grid, the danger again looms large.

The greatest danger is to the high-voltage transformers located at power substations along the routes of major transmission lines. An eruptive event on the Sun, known as a coronal mass ejection, sends a powerful flux of charged particles, protons and electrons, into the surrounding space. If the Earth is on a line with the eruption, the charged particles interact with the Earth's radiation belts and geomagnetic field to produce currents in the ionosphere. The power lines which make up the electrical transmission grid act as antennae, to couple these ionospheric currents to the installed transformers which step up the voltage for long-distance transmission.

The ionospheric or auroral currents produced by a powerful solar storm induce strong fluctuating direct currents in the power lines. Known as geomagnetically induced currents (GIC), when they reach the transformers, they piggyback on to the strong alternating current already flowing and cause the iron cores of the transformers to saturate and overheat from hysteresis and reactive resonance effects in the transmission line. This can cause network-wide voltage regulation problems leading to blackouts, or complete transformer burnout.

Because the solar storm threat is greatest to the low-resistance power lines carrying the highest current densities, some of the most vulnerable areas are those of highest population concentration. Metatech estimates that more than 130 million people in the U.S.A. are at high risk for such an event. The highest risk areas are the northern states from the Atlantic seaboard to the Mississippi, coastal states as far south as Georgia, and the northwestern states of Washington, Oregon, and Idaho.

A prolonged lack of electricity in any of these areas would reduce the population to dark age-like conditions. Drinking water supply would break down for lack of pumping, and sewage service would cease shortly thereafter. For lack of refrigeration, the food chain would collapse, and medical supplies would be lost. Fuel could not be pumped, and thus transportation would break down. Heating and air conditioning systems would cease functioning. Communication would be crippled by the lack of electricity as well as from the direct damage to satellites and sensitive electronics which a solar storm produces—perhaps no Internet and no cell phones.

With the appropriate selection of indicators and formation of the respective resilience indexes, it is possible to verify the mail functions of the electricity transmission system. In this respect the verification of potential hazard events is imminent for the prevention of catastrophic event.

The electricity transmission system catastrophe is strongly linked with the respective change of the resilience indexes of the system. The agglomeration of resilience indexes of the sudden change of indicators is parameter which can be used for the determination of critical resilience index for the catastrophic event.

In this exercise four resilience indexes are used for the verification of critical resilience index determining the catastrophic event for the electricity transmission system. In particular attention is focused on the solar flare effect on the Power Transmission System. In the evaluation of catastrophe of the power transmission system it is the most important parameter to be taken into a consideration is Resilience Index of Electro-magnetic flour.

5.6 Hydro Power Plant Catastrophe

Sayano-aShushenskaya is one of the world's biggest hydro power plants. Years of overloading the turbines and inadequate maintenance were probably behind the major accident in 2009. Could greater care have prevented the catastrophe?

On 17 August 2009, a turbine unit was torn out of its anchorage by fluctuating water pressure and catapulted into the air in the Sayano-Shushenskaya hydroelectric power plant in Russia [23,24,25]. Weighing in at around 2,000 tonnes, the turbine destroyed the 27-m-high roof of the turbine hall, as well as several nearby structures and plant parts. Propelled by the pressure of a 200-m water column, an incredible 360 cubic metres of water per second shot through the entire turbine hall, including the lower floors, causing numerous short circuits and immediate failure of the power plant. Those units which were still in operation sustained various degrees of mechanical and electrical damage. All in all, 75 people were killed and many others injured. The damaged turbine unit was extensively overhauled in 2000 and 2005, followed by another minor overhaul in the spring of 2009. At the same time, a new control system was installed so that the hydro power plant could be controlled externally in line with grid requirements. This system was not adapted exactly to the installed turbines.

Figure 5.24. Sayano-Shushenskaya hydroelectric power plant catastrophe.

After the turbine was decommissioned, the vibrations measured in the turbine rotor were only just below the maximum permitted by the manufacturer. However, in the following weeks and months, these vibrations did not stabilize, but instead increased steadily, presumably exceeding the permitted maximum by June 2009. Nevertheless, the turbine remained in operation. Fatigue cracks appeared in the retaining bolts. The bolts sheared as soon as the water pressure was sufficiently high to cause residual forced rupture. The turbine cover with turbine rotor and generator weighing around 2,000 tonnes lost its anchorage in the foundation and led to the accident.

5.6.1 Indicator Selection for Resilience Index

In the evaluation of hydro power plant a following indicators are taken into a consideration.

a) Hydro Power Plant Power Production

One of the potential signals for the hydro power plant failure is lost of the power production. In this respect it is of great importance to be able to verify sudden change of the power production. The sudden change of the electricity production in hydro power plant is the result of the damage of the vital element of the plant. The Control system of HPP is design to close water inlet with maximum speed of closing system. For this indicator it assumed that the change of this indicator in closing step is linear function of time, Figure 5.25. The recovery change of this indicator is anticipated it take between t_2 to t_3.

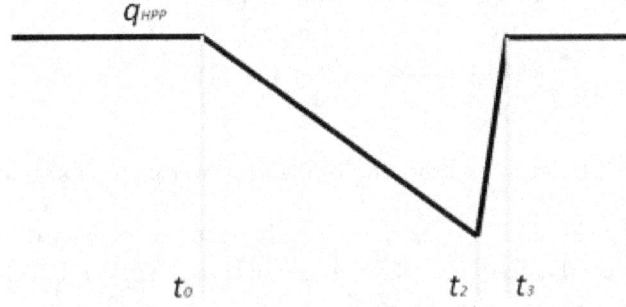

where

q_{hpp} – hydro power plant production indicator.

t_0 – start of power plant production change.

t_2 – end of power plant production change.

t_3 – recovery of power plant production.

Figure 5.25. Graphical presentation of wind power plant production indicator.

b) Turbine Vibration

The essential element hydro power plant is hydro turbine. It represents the main element the water turbine. The potential mal function of hydro turbine is its vibration caused by loss of centricity of the turbine weal. As the first sign of the hazard development is hydro turbine is weal vibration. In this respect the main indicator for the development of the potential catastrophe is measuring eccentricity of the turbine wheel. The development of the vibration process in HPP is slow process and can be activated at appropriate time Figure 5.26

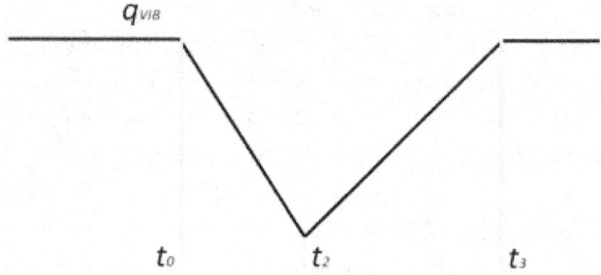

where

q_{VIB} – turbine vibration indicator
t_0 – start of vibration change
t_2 – end of vibration change
t_3 – recovery of vibration

Figure 5.26. Graphical presentation of hydro power plant vibration indicator.

The vibration indicator is represented as the excentricity of the turbine weal. It reflects the decease of the number of rotationsIt is a slow process and it reach minimal value at the time t_0 – start of vibration change and will and up t_2 – end of vibration change andt_3– recovery of vibration.

c) Hydro Power Plant Efficiency

The change of HPP efficiency is a result of the change of hydrodynamic height of the plant. It is usually slow process. It starts at t_0 – start of Power plant efficiency change and t_4 – end of Power plant efficiency change.Timet_5 – recovery of Power plant efficiency meaning that the hydraulic height reaches its maximum value.

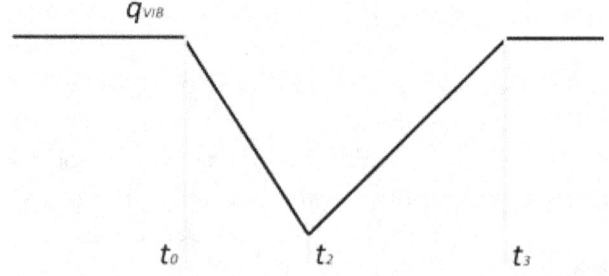

where q_{PPE} – hydro power plant efficiency indicator.
       t_0 – start of Power plant efficiency change.
       t_4 – end of Power plant efficiency change.
       t_5 – recovery of Power plant efficiency.

Figure 5.27. Graphical presentation of wind power plant efficiency indicator.

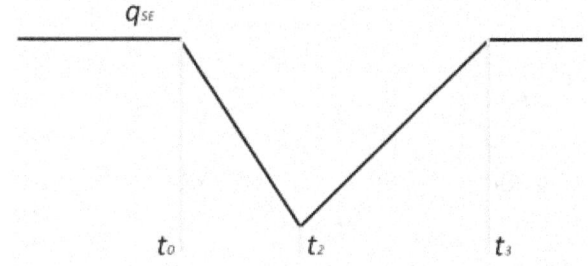

where

   qSE – social indicator
   t_0 – start of Social Indicator change
   t_2 – end of Social Indicator change
   t_3 – recovery of Social Indicator

Figure 5.28. Graphical presentation of hydro power plant social indicator.

The efficiency of the hydro power plant is defined with the two main parameters: hydrostatic height and water flow through the turbine (Figure 5.27). The change of either of these parameters is warning signal for the development of mailfunction of the hydro turbine power plant system. The decrease of the efficiency of HPP is relatively slow process and can be verified in due time.

d) Social Effect of Hydro Power Plant

The social aspect of the potential catastrophe development is the need for the social warning to the inhabitants in the vicinity of hydropower plant. It happens in several occasions that due to the limited capacity for the fast evacuation of neighboring population the death toll to have occurred. One of the very important indicators for the verification of the potential hazard in the surrounding of hydro power plant social is the readiness for fast evacuation.

The Total agglomeration of resilience index is an additive function of all individual resilience indexes measured in the same time scale (Figure 5.28).

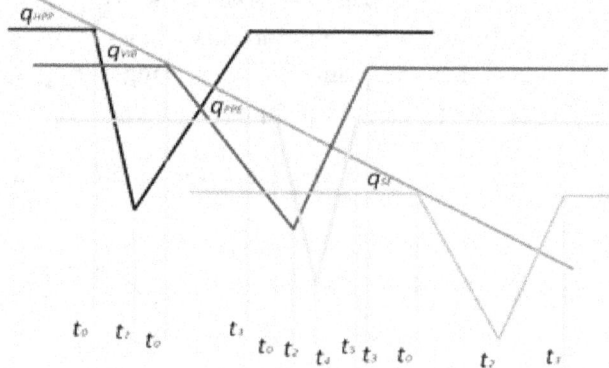

Figure 5.29. Graphical presentation of Resilience Indexes for Hydro Power Plant.

5.6.2 Assessment of the Resilience Index Agglomeration

In the evaluation of the potential hazard development on Hydro Power Plant the agglomerated Index is developed to be used as the parameter for the evaluation of the catastrophic event of Hydro Power Plant. In the evaluation of the potential catastrophe a following resilience indexes are used

1. resilience index for Power Plant Power Production
2. resilience index for Turbine Vibration
3. resilience index for Power Plant Efficiency
4. resilience index for Social Indicator

With the agglomeration of these four Resilience Indexes we will obtain the Total Resilience Index which is used for the assessment of the potential catastrophic event. The critical value of the Total Resilience is the upper limit before the catastrophic event will appear.

Mathematical it can be expressed that

$$R_{TOT} < R_{CRIT} \tag{5.24}$$

For the catastrophic event evaluation of Hydro Power Plant the main emphasize will be devoted to Resilience index for Power Plant Power Production. It is also necessary to verify the agglomerated value of the Total Resilience index to be compared with the Critical value of the Resilience Index corresponding to the Catastrophic event.

It has to be noticed that every overcoming of the Total agglomerated Resilience Index the Critical Resilience Index value it has e to be verified as the marker for the potential catastrophic event. So, it is imminent to every catastrophic event to be verified as the agglomerated resilience Index of all sudden change of respective indicators.

REFERENCES

[1]   Next big advance will be in catastrophe resilience, *The 2011 Stockholm Water Prize Laureate*, Prof. Stephen R. Carpenter.

[2]   N.H. Afgan, D.B.Cvetinovic, P.A. Andre, Sustainable resilience of Company Management, *Journal of Knowledge Management, Economy and Information Technology*, Issue 7, Dec. 2011

[3]   John M. Macdonald, at all, *Catastrophic Failure Evaluation Proceedings of the 7th Mediterranean Conference on Control and Automation (MED99) Haifa*, Israel - June 28-30, 1999

[4]   Daniel S. likes,*Resilience Capacity Index*, (http://brr.berkeley.edu/rci

[5]   *Fukushima Daiichi - A One Year Review, Tokyo Electric Power Company*, http://www.tepco.co.jp/en/nu/fukushima-np/review/index-e.html

[6]   Chernobyl Accident 1986, http://www.worldnuclear.org/info/chernobyl/health_impacts.html.

[7]   Risk management: A tool for improving nuclear power plant performance, iaea-tecdoc-1209.

[8]   StijnDenders,Fault Detection and Identification for Wind Turbine Systems:*University Master Theses*, University of Twente, Faculty of Applied Physics,2002.

[9]   BadrinathVeluri,Failure Modes Of Wind Turbine Components, *PhD Theses*, Aarhus University, http://www.au.dk/da/uni/ledstud.htm.

[10] J. Ribrant and L. M. Bertling, *Survey of Failures in Wind Power Systems with Focus on Swedish Wind Power Plants During 1997–2005 IEEE Transactions on Energy Conversion*, Vol. 22, No. 1, March 2007 167.

[11] Y. Amirat, V. Choqueuse and M.E.H.Benbouzid, *Wind Turbines Condition Monitoring and Fault Diagnosis Using Generator Current Amplitude Demodulation*, 2010 IEEE International Energy Conference.

[12]   *Wind Turbine Failure*, http://savetheeaglesinternational.org/

[13]   MohdHasan Ali, *Wind Energy Systems: Solutions for Power Quality and Stabilization*, OCR Press, ISBN 978-1-4398-55614-7.

[14]   *Geomagnetic Storms: An Evaluation of Risks and Risk Assessment*, Office of Risk Management and Analysis.

[15]   Kappenman, John G., et al., Solar Wind Monitor Satellite Crucial for Geomagnetic Storm Warning,*IEEC Power*,Engineering Review, 1990.

[16]   The Green Corona Index and Soft X-Ray Flux, The Green Corona Index and Soft X-Ray Flux, *Solar Physics*,Volume 1 / 1967 - Volume 277 / 2012,

[17]   Milli L., Qui Q.,Phadke A.G., Risk assessment of catastrophic failure in electric power system, *Int. J. Critical Infrastructure*, Vol.1, No.1,pp 38-63,

[18]   Thorp, J.S., Phadke, A.G., Horowitz, S.H. and Tamronglak, S. (1998) "Anatomy of power system disturbances: importance sampling', *Electrical Power & Energy Systems*", Vol. 20, No. 2, pp.147–152.

[19]   Board of Review (1997) *First Phase Report: System Blackout and System Restoration*, Edison, 13-14 July.

[20]   Board of Review (1997) *Second Phase Report: System Blackout and System Restoration*, ConEdison, 24 August.

[21]   Fang Yang,*Summary of research on hidden failures in protection systems*, Power Symposium, 2006. NAPS 2006. 38th North American,

[22]   Chi-Hsiang Wang et all,*Overview of resilience concepts, with application to water resource systems*, CSIRO Sustainable Ecosystems,2009Ge

[23]   Boyko and Sergey Popov, *Investigating the Sayano-Shushenskaya Hydro Power Plant Disaster*, EKRA-Sibir Ltd arbox.

[24]   Kenedy B., *China warns of catastrophe dam Three Gorges Dam*, Reurtes, Sept. 23,2007.

[25]   S.Kucukali, *Risk assessment of river-type hydropower plants by using fuzzy logic approach*, World Renewable Energy Congress 2011, Linkoping, Sweden, May 2011.

CHAPTER 6

EVALUATION OF ECOLOGICAL
CATASTROPHIC EVENTS

6.1. INTRODUCTION

According to the ICSU, for the period 1994–2003, floods represented 33 % of the natural hazards, storms 23 %, epidemics 15.2 %, droughts 15 %, earthquakes 7 %, tsunamis 7 %, landslides 4.5 % and volcanic eruptions 1.4 %, whereas avalanches accounted only for 0.7 % of the total number of events [1]. Hazards related to extreme weather conditions occurred most frequently and often affected the largest areas. Most of these events lead to disasters but did not led necessarily to environmental catastrophes.We could attempt to define an environmental catastrophe, such as a natural hazard combined with a large disaster, the latter including measurable human and economical costs (e.g. death, infrastructure destruction, cultural impact, financial loss). In its definition of natural disaster, the International Human Hurricane Katrina(Figure 6.1),was one of the most destructive natural disasters to occur in the United States and is likely to be the most expensive catastrophe loss that the global insurance industry has ever experienced. RMS estimates the event will ultimately result in insured in 40 to 60 Million dollars.

Dimension Programme (IHDP) stresses that it is more a function of vulnerable people than severity in the natural hazard Anenvironmental catastrophe also could be defined as a rapid departure from normality where humans and/or ecosystems cannot adapt. However, catastrophic events do not always occur rapidly. In addition, these events may be, in some cases, more pervasive at the societal scale and, retrospectively, seen as catastrophes. At times, it is difficult to separate catastrophes from normal environmental events, since the environment is never stable, but always undergoing modification: Not nature in balance, but nature in flux.

A large cause (environmental hazard) may produce only a small effect (disaster) and vice versa. Societal responses to external forces are non-linear in nature; hence, in the geoarchaeological record, assumption of causality between cultural transition and natural hazard often is questionable [2] and must be used with care. The three factors contributing to the amplitude of an environmental catastrophe include time, area and societal characteristics

Figure 6.1.Hurricane Katrina.

The time factor (sharp onset and overall duration) is an essential consideration in defining an environmental catastrophe. First, the usual high speed of change makes it impossible for humans to adapt unless preparedness plans are in place. Second, events of longer duration result in greater damage: for example an environmental change that extends beyond the food storage capacity of a society. Recent estimates indicate the global supply of grains, if not replenished, would last barely two months [3]. After a nuclear war or volcanic winter, it has emerged that the main cause of disaster would be destruction of global agriculture and food supply[4] After a year of severely reduced food supply, there would be mass starvation. Because a nuclear [or volcanic] winter might last two or three years, scientists concluded that this would threaten the continued existence of civilization (and possibly even our species).

An environmental catastrophe affecting a large area (typical of a drought), or a large proportion of a settlement, will be more difficult to overcome than one affecting a smaller area (typical of a flood, earthquake, volcanic eruption). People living in these areas must move further away to survive, but, most often, they have nowhere to go to escape the disaster. Of course, this predicament is exacerbated on small islands (e.g. Easter Island) and on densely populated continental areas. In terms of anthropological studies, some pronounced cultural changes have been connected to disasters encompassing large areas [5].

A flexible society and/or ecosystem will be able to adapt faster to environmental changes and thus suffer less. Societies can increase their inflexibility under conditions such as fixed hierarchies where one person cannot replace another, fixed religious rules that impose proscriptions, food prohibitions, fewer personal freedoms (e. g. to pursue innovative or parallel thinking), or tendencies to reject or despise other ways of life. For example,the Norse settlements in Greenland collapsed for various reasons. Because they despised the Inuit people, the Norsemen were hindered in learning how to survive in Arctic conditions by using skin boats, harpoons for hunting ring seal at sea and multilayered skin clothing [6].

6.2 RESILIENCE OF ECOLOGICAL SYSTEM

Resilience – a term that has roots in ancient thinking and was developed in mathematics and engineering – is slowly coming of age in today's arena ofenvironmental policy-making. Attempts to transfer this and related stability concepts beyond their original realms into domains of ecology and society are far from new. In particular it is of interest to understand essential concept of resilience.

Our scope is to attempt at establishing a conceptual framework that can help resolve some basic questions and problems with resilience and other stability concepts in terms of their validity when subjected to such transfer between realms. Undoubtedly, *analogy* transfers between science realms, and between science and policy, can be both powerful and helpful, and might offer common ground for inter-disciplinary endeavours. However, fundamental problems will arise ifanalogy is mistaken for *identity*. In these notes, we provide a brief account of the meaning of resilience, and directly related stability concepts, in the realms in which they were first developed and applied. We then briefly address the transfer ofsuch concepts that has occurred into the realm ofecology, and some ofthe conceptual and other problems that are then encountered.

It if great interest to introduce our understanding of the resilience concept. In this respect The concept of resilience provides a new and useful framework of analysis and understanding on how individuals, communities, organizations and ecosystems cope in a changing world facing many uncertainties and challenges. Sometimes change is gradual and things move forward in continuous and predictable ways; but sometimes change is sudden, disorganising and turbulent. The resilience approach focuses on the interaction between periods of gradual and sudden change, and provides better understanding on how society should respond to disruptive events and accommodate change. Resilience is an area of research under rapid development with major policy implications for sustainable development.

6.3. INDICATORS OF ECOLOGICAL SYSTEM

In order to define ecological system we have to introduce number of indicators in order to be able define the state of the system. As regards ecological system it is commonly used the EPA's Framework for Ecological Risk Assessment [6] (EPA 1992), indicators must provide information relevant to specific assessment questions, which are developed to focus monitoring data on environmental management issues.The process of identifying environmental values, developing assessment questions, and identifying potentially responsive indicators is presented elsewhere Nonetheless, the importance of appropriate assessment questions cannot be overstated; an indicator may provide accurate information that is ultimately useless for making management decisions.In addition, development of assessment questions can be controversial because of competing interests for environmental resources.However important, it is not within the purview of this document to focus on the development and utility of assessment questions.Rather, it is intended to guide the technical evaluation of indicators within the presumed context of a pre-established assessment question or known management application

In an international effort to promote consistency in the collection and interpretation of environmental information, the Organization for Economic Cooperation and Development (OECD) developed a conceptual framework, known as the Pressure-State-Response (PSR) framework, for categorizing environmental indicators.The PSR framework encompasses indicators of human activities (pressure), environmental condition (state), and resulting societal actions (response). The PSR framework is used in OECD member countries [7] (Adriaanse 1993) Within EPA, the Office of Water adopted the PSR framework to select indicators for measuring progress towards clean water and safe drinking water.EPA's Office of Policy, Planning and Evaluation (OPPE) used the PSR framework to support the State Environmental Goals and Indicators Project of the Data Quality Action Team,and as a foundation for expanding the Environmental Indicators Team of the Environmental Statistics and Information Division. The Interagency Task Force on Monitoring Water Quality [8]refers to the PSR framework, as does the International Joint Commission in the Great Lakes Water Quality Agreement [16]. Measuring management success is now required by the U.S. Government Performance and Results Act [9] of 1993, whereby agencies must develop program performance reports based on indicators and goals.In cooperation with EPA, the Florida Center for Public Management used the GPRA and the PSR framework to develop indicator evaluation criteria for EPA Regions and states.The Florida Center defined a hierarchy of six indicator types, ranging from measures of administrative actions such as the number of permits issued, to measures of ecological or human health, such as density of sensitivespecies. These criteria have been adapted by EPA Region IV, and by stateand local management groups.Generally, the focus for guiding environmental policy andviiidecision-making is shifting from measures of program and administrative performance tomeasures of environmental condition.

ORD recognizes the need for consistency in indicator evaluation, and has adopted many ofthe tenets of the PSR/E framework.ORD indicator research focuses primarily on ecologicalcondition (state), and the associations between condition and stressors (OPPE's "effects"category).As such, ORD develops and implements science-based, rather than administrative policy performance indicators.ORD researchers and clients have determined the need for detailed technical guidelines to ensure the reliability of ecological indicators for their intended applications. The Evaluation Guidelines expand on the information presented in existing frameworks by describing the statistical and implementation requirements for effective ecological indicator performance. This document does not address policy indicators or indicators of administrative action, which are emphasized in the PSR approach [10,11].

6.4 RESILIENCE INDEX OF ECOLOGICAL SYSTEM

By definition the resilience Index of the ecological system is the time integral of the indicator comprising sudden change to the specific level and its-recovery to primary state [12,13].

Mathematical definition of Resilience Index is

$$R_{tot} = \sum_{n} w_i \int_{t=0}^{t=t_i} q_i \left(\Delta t \right) \tag{6.1}$$

Where

w- probability of I – indicator
q – specific indicator

It is important to notice that R_{tot} is agglomeration of the all resilience indexes corresponding to the system under consideration. As regards ecological system it comprises resilience indexes for all indicators.

For the ecological system under consideration a following resilience indexes are taken into a consideration: :

a) Resilience Index for the Sudden Change of Atmospheric Temperature

$$R_{tot} = \sum_{n} w_i \int_{t=0}^{t=t_i} q_i \left(\Delta t \right) \tag{6.2}$$

Where

R_{AT}- resilience index for sudden temperature change
W_{at} – probability of resilience index for change of atmospheric temperature

q_{pr}– specific index for atmospheric temperature
t_2 – time for atmospheric temperature recovery

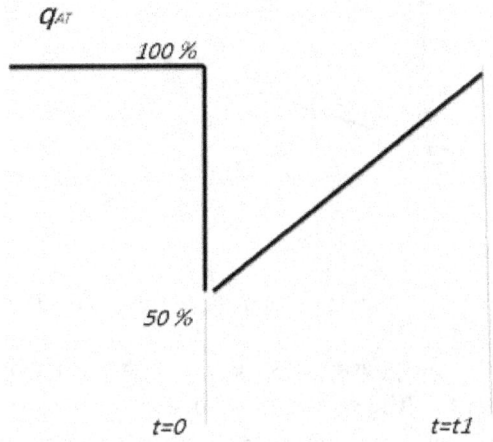

Figure 6.2. Graphical presentation of atmospheric temperature change.

This demonstration of sudden change of atmospheric temperatureFigure 6.2 shows the effect of climate change on the resilience index. It verifies a potential change of resilience index as the change of the capacity of the system to withstand eventual critical state of the system. If this is related to potential catastrophic event it may be considered as measurement of adverse effect of this change within the system

b) ResilienceIndex for the Sudden Pressure Change

$$R_{PR} = w_{pr} \cdot \int_{t=0}^{t=t_2} \left(1 - q_{pv}\right) dt \tag{6.3}$$

where
  R_{AT}- resilience index for sudden atmospheric pressure change
  W_{pr} – probability of resilience index for atmospheric pressure change
  q_{pr}– specific index for atmospheric pressure
  t_2 – time for atmospheric pressure recovery

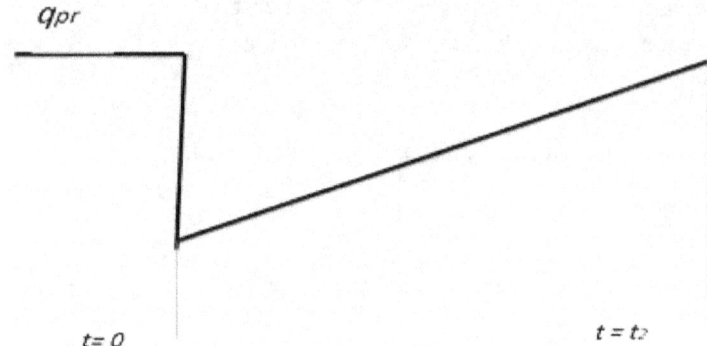

Figure 6.3. Graphical presentation of atmospheric pressure change.

The change of atmospheric pressure is very often related to the generation of strong movement of the atmospheric masses leading to hurricanes with storm tides of 3 to 10 meters Figure 6.3. If the is connected with the potential sudden change of other indicators of the systemit may lead to unpredictable catastrophe.

c) Resilience Index for the CO_2 Concentration Change

$$R_{co_2} = w_{co_2} \int_{t=t_3}^{t=t_4} \left(1 - q_{co_2}\right)$$

(6.4)

where

R_{CO}- resilience index for sudden CO_2 concentration change

w_{co} – probability of resilience index for change of CO_2 concentration change

q_{co}– specific index for CO_2 concentration

t_3– CO_2 concentration end

t_4 – time for CO_2 concentration recovery

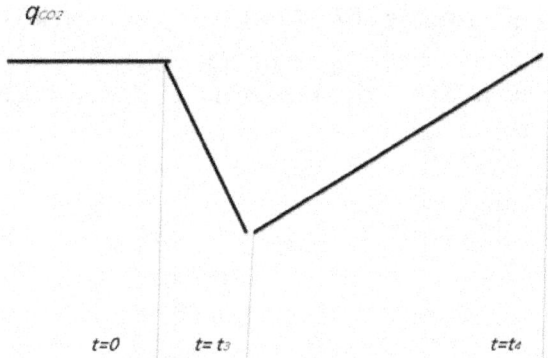

Figure 6.4. Graphical presentation of CO2 concentration change.

The CO_2 concentration indicator change is very dangers potential event. If is anticipatedto be changed within the noncontrollable time scale it may lead to large scale human disasterFigure 6.4. The recovery time of the CO_2 indicator is taking very long time it may produce high human adverse effect.

d) ResilienceIndex for GasVelocity Change

$$R_{GV} = w_{g\nu} \int_{t=t_5}^{t=t_6} \left(1 - q_{g\nu}\right) \qquad (6.5)$$

Where

    R_{AT}- resilience index for sudden gas velocity change
    w_{pr} – probability of resilience index for change of gas velocity
    q_{pr}– specific index for gas velocity
    t_5 – time for end of gas velocity
    t_6 – time for the gas velocity recovery

The sudden change ofair velocity is very often related the formation of the tsunami waves which very often connected with the high catastrophic events Figure 6.5. These catastrophic events are is very often leading to very large destruction of human dwelling.

6.5 Assessment of Ecological Catastrophe

The evaluation of the ecological system requires agglomeration of the individual resilience index

$$R_{TOT} = R_{at} + R_{ap} + R_{CO_2} + R_{gv} \qquad (6.6)$$

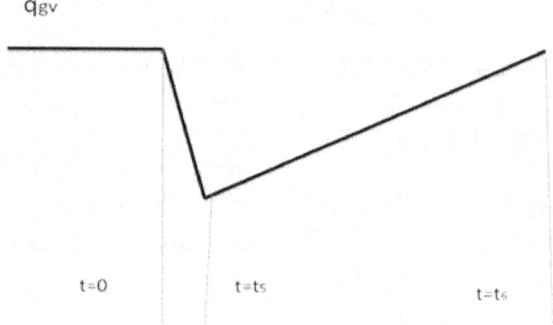

Figure 6.5.Graphical presentation of gas velocity change.

The assessment of ecological system catastrophic event is based on the comparison of the total resilience index and resilience index reflecting catastrophic event. If the total resilience index will overcome resilience of catastrophic index then the catastrophic event is expected.

Catastrophic event can be defined as

$$R_{TOT} > R_{CAT} \qquad (6.7)$$

In order to use this method for the assessment of the potential catastrophic event it necessary to verify potential cases when agglomeration of the resilience indexes lead to the expected catastrophic event.

As regards ecological catastrophic events it is of paramount expectation to verifythe need for the selection of the respective indicators to be included in the assessment of of the specific cases.

REFERENCES

[1] Leroy, S., Kazancı, N., Ileri, Ö., Kibar, M., Emre, O., McGee, E., Griffiths, H. I., 2002. Abrupt environmental changes within a late Holocene lacustrinesequence south of the Marmara Sea (Lake Manyas, N-W Turkey):possible links with seismic events. *Marine Geology* 190 (1-2), 531-552.

[2] ICCU, 2005. *Science and natural hazards.*http://www.icsu.org/6_memberzone/GA_documentation/9_Hazards.pdf

[3] Coombes, P., Barber, K., 2005. Environmental determinism in Holoceneresearch: causality or coincidence? *Area* (37.3), 303-311.

[4] Rampino, M., 2002. Supereruptions as a threat to civilizations on Earth-like planets. *Icarus* (156), 562-569.

[5] Sparks S. & Self S. et al., 2005. *Super-eruptions: global effects and future threats. Report of a Geological Society of London Working Group.*

[6] Torrence, R., Grattan, J., 2002. The archaeology of disasters: past and futuretrends. In: Torrence R., Grattan, J. (Eds.), *Natural Disasters and Culture Change.* Routledge, London, pp. 1-18.

[7] Diamond, J., 2005. *Collapse: How Societies Choose to Fail or Succeed.* Viking Press, New York, pp 575.

[8] ICSU, 2006. ICSU: *Dark Nature - Rapid natural change and human responses.* www.mun.ca/canqua/ICSU-DN/

[9] Leroy, S., Costa, P. (ed.), 2004. *Environmental catastrophes in Mauritania, the desert and the coast*, volume of abstract and field guide. ICSU Dark

[10] Leroy, S., Stewart, I. (Ed.), 2002. *Environmental catastrophes and recovery in the Holocene*, Volume of abstracts, conference held at Brunel University, West London, 28 Aug. – 2 Sept. 2002. 90 pp. http://atlas-

[11] Linnerooth-Bayer, J., Mechler, R., Pflug, G., 2005. Refocusing disaster aid. *Science* (309), 1044-1046.

[12] The National Tsunami Hazard Mitigation Program, 2005. www.pmel.noaa.gov/tsunami-hazard/[15] Scheffers, A., Kelletat, D., 2005. Tsunami relics on the coastal landscapewest of Lisbon, Portugal. *Science of Tsunami Hazards* 23 (1), 3-16.

[13] Stiros, S. C., 2001. The AD 365 Crete earthquake and possible seismic clustering: a review of historical and archaeological data: *Journal of Structural Geology* (23), 545-562.

CHAPTER 7

EVALUATION OF SOCIAL CATASTROPHIC EVENTS

7.1 INTRODUCTION

Catastrophic events are defined with the respective resilience of the system Figure 7.1. Direct measurement of resilience in social systems requires measuring the amount of change that the system can undergo before it is forced to reorganize to another alternate stable state, or the difference between the state of ecosystems and the thresholds.

Figure 7.1. French Revolution as social catastrophe.

Since the thresholds are hardly known, direct measurement of resilience in social systems is difficult. Alternatively, resilience can be estimated directly by monitorinng system properties which are related to the resilience of the system and are measurable. Resilience in social systems, from the perspective of system stability, increases with functional diversity and species richness. Species richness is the characteristics of the components of systems and can be viewed as the measurable system property related to the resilience of the system. It reflects diverse ecological functions of species, including regulations of the biogeochemical processes and regulations of ecological processes through interactions in tropic levels such as predation and parasitism. Therefore, species richness reflects the interactions between biotic and abiotic components in ecosystems.[1]

In current literature, resilience is defined as the capacity of a system to absorb disturbance and re-organize while experiencing change so as to maintain the same structures and functions. Many studies on resilience in social systems have emphasized the first part of this definition, i.e. the capacity of a system to absorb disturbance, or the buffer capacity for persistence. However, resilience is not only about being persistent to disturbance, but also about the opportunities that disturbance causes by reorganizing structures and processes. Therefore, resilience provides adaptive capacity that enables continuous development. Through self-organization, the system's adaptive processes that relate to the capacity to absorb changes emerge.

7.2 Resilience of Social System

Current studies of the resilience in social view is the capacity of the system to re-organize and incorporate the idea of adaptation, self-organization and learning. Research on resilience in Socio-ecological systems is still in the explorative stage. These studies perceive the response of the social system to ecosystem change from diverse perspectives, including understanding of social processes such as social learning, mental models and knowledge-system integration, visioning and scenario building, agents and actor groups and adaptive capacity [2,3]

Standards of living are difficult to measure, but indicators of social development are available. A basic measure, Gross Domestic Product (GDP) per capita, is the value of all goods and services produced within a region over a given time period, averaged per person. A more advanced metric, the Human Development Index (HDI), considers life expectancy, education and GDP. Many of the indicators discussed below are used to measure progress towards the Millennium Development Goals (MDG) - a set of targets agreed upon by United Nations member states as crucial for global human progress.

Indicators reflecting essential characteristic of the social system can be envisaged as the main parameters leading to the verification respective properties of the specific system, including: population, standard of living, food, water and sanitation, healthcare and disease, education and employment, and environment.

For many kinds of catastrophes, the distribution of event severity appears to follow apower law over a wide severity range. That is, sometimes the chance that within a many kinds of catastrophes, the distribution of event severity appears to follow a power law over a wide severity range. That is, sometimes the chance that within a small Our conclusions would apply directly to types of disasters that continue to be distributed as a power law even up to very large severity. Compare to this reference case, we should worry less about types of disasters whose frequency of very large events is below a power law, and more about types of disasters whose frequency is greater [4].

The essential characteristic of present world can be defined with introduction specific social indicators which are reflecting the main parameters of world social and economic system, including [5]:

7.2.1. Population

Global population is projected to reach 9.2 billion in 2050, with 6.3 billion people living in urban areas – 80% more than in 2010. Significant issues affecting population, as reported by governments around the world in2007 include: HIV/AIDS, infant and child mortality, maternal mortality, adolescenfertility, and life expectancy at birth. Life expectancy is below 50 years in many developing countries; it's 79 in the U.S.Fertility rate, or number of births per woman (of child-bearing age), is projected to fall from a global average of 2.52 in 2010 to 2.17 by 2050. Fertility rate is as high as 7 in some countries; in the U.S. it's 2.07.

7.2.2. Standard of Living

In 2005, 1.4 billion people lived below the world poverty line of $1.25 USD per day, down from 1.9 billion in 1981. The World Bank Chief Economist expects to achieve the MDG to cut 1990 poverty levels in half by 2015. In 2010 more than 15% of the U.S. population – 46.2 million – were living in poverty (income under $22,113, family of 4 with 2 kids).

For Hispanic and Black populations in the U.S., more than 26% of each group was living below the poverty line. Approximately 650,000 people were homeless in the U.S. in 2010.

7.2.3. Food

Average disposable income spent on food, beverages, and tobacco ranges from 17% in high-income countries to 53% in low-income countries. On average, Americans spend less than 10%, while Nigerians spend 73%.Globally, 30% of deaths of children under 5 are caused by under-nutrition. The Green Revolution led to large increases in agricultural yields, and helped feedthe rapidly growing global population in the second half of the 20 Century.

7.2.4. Water and Sanitation

2.6 billion people lack access to proper sanitation. Access is lowest in Southern Asiaand sub-Saharan Africa, where only 1 of 3 people have proper facilities. Urban areas also have better sanitation coverage – 76% compared to 45% in rural areas. In 2008, 87% of the world population had access to clean drinking water – 1.8billion more people than in 1990. However, in Oceania and sub-Saharan Africaonl 37% and 47% of the rural populations, respectively, have clean drinking water. Morethan a quarter of the population in several Sub-Saharan countries must travel 30+ minutes to collect water; most often women collect water in developing countries.

7.2.5. Healthcare and Disease

In 2007, 90% of national governments reported HIV/AIDS as aGlobally, 33.3 million were infected with HIV and 1.8 million died from AIDS in 2009. Most HIV cases – 22.5 million – are in sub-Saharan Africa. Incidence rate (annual number of new infections) and deaths are declining in many southern African countries due to behavior changes and better HIV treatment options. significant problem.

In 2009, 781,000 died from malaria, of which 91% were in Africa and 85% were children under 5. Preventive measures such as treated bed nets, indoor insecticide spraying, and anti-malarial drugs have reduced deaths. At least 2 dozen countries have officially eliminated malaria since 1960.Indoor cooking with fuelwood and animal dung results in 1.5 million deaths per year, more than 50% of which are children under 5.

Cardiovascular diseases are the leading causes of death in the world. A healthy diet, regular physical activity, and avoiding tobaccocould reduce premature deaths from cardiovascular diseases and strokes by 80%.

Globally, about 150 million people incur catastrophic healthcare costs each year (greater than 40% of household's capacity to pay).

7.2.6. Education and Employment

Global literacy is significantly improving. For example, youth literacy in-Southern Asia is 80%, up from 60% in 1990. However, in at least a dozen countries, including Afghanistan, Ethiopia, India, and Yemen, illiteracy rates are at least 25% higher for females than males. In Afghanistan female illiteracy is 87% – highest in the world. Cuba and Lesotho spend the highest percentage of GDP on education 13.6% and 12.4%, respectively in 2008. The U.S. spends around 5.5% of GDP each year.

Between 1991 and 2005, primary school enrollment in Sub-Saharan AfricaIn Least Developed Countries (LDCs), the average amount of schooling isincreased from 52% to 72%; the 2005 world average was 87%. 3.7 years. In the top 25 HDI-ranked countries, the averages are 9.7-12.6 years of school. Top employers in LDCs are agriculture (64%), services (26%) and industry (10%); 60% of jobs in LDCs pay $1.25 USD/day or less.

7.2.7. Environment

Most global warming is "very likely" (>90% certainty) caused by anthropogenic greenhouse gas emissions. In the 21 Century, natural and social systems will likely face increasing risks of extinction for 20-30% of plant and animal species; more coastal flooding and erosion, heat waves, droughts, tropical storm intensity; and health risks associated with malnutrition and water-related diseases. Declines in crop productivity in lower latitudes and freshwater availability are likely. Poor communities are especially vulnerable to climate change because of their low adaptive capacity and high dependence on climate conditions (e.g., rain for agriculture). The Stern Review found that investing 1% of global GDP annually in greenhouse gas (GHG) reductions could avert a permanentreduction of 5-20% GDP per capita due to climate change impacts.

7.3 Definition of Social Catastrophe Indexes

The concept of resilience has recently been introduced into fool security literature [6]. It aims to measure households' capability to absorb the negative effects of unpredictable shocks, as a legitimate component of vulnerability analysis. The definition of resilience to fool insecurity has a direct effect on the methodology used to measure it, and the model described in this document, considers resilience to be a latent variable defined according to four building blocks: income and food access; assets; access to public services; and social safety nets. Two additional dimensions – stability and adaptive capacity – cut across these building blocks and account for households' capacity to respond and adapt to shocks; these too are latent variables. To measure the whole system, two approaches can be pursued. The first measures each dimension separately using different multivariate techniques (factor analysis, principal components analysis and optimal scaling) before estimating the resilience index; the classification and regression tree (CART) methodology has also been used for the understanding of the process. The second approach measures all the dimensions simultaneously through structural equation models, and is based on normality assumptions on observed variables. As most of the variables in resilience measurement are ordinal or categorical, the first approach was adopted in this document. The role of the estimated resilience index in measuring vulnerability to fool insecurity was then assessed through a regression model with food consumption in logarithmic scale as a dependent variable and the resilience index and other household characteristics as independent variables.

Standards of living are difficult to measure, but indicators of social development are available. A basic measure, Gross Domestic Product (GDP) per capita, is the value of all goods and services produced within a region over a given time period, averaged per person. A more advanced metric, the Human Development Index (HDI), considers life expectancy, education and GDP. The highest HDI-ranked countries are Norway and Australia, with the United States ranked Many of the indicators discussed below are used to measure progress towards the Millennium Development Goals (MDG) - a set of targets agreed upon by United Nations member states as crucial for global human progress.[6,7,8]

Social Resilience Indexes

7.3.1. Population Indicator

Social population indicator is characteristic parameter used for the verification of the people distributed in the specific area. It is usually accepted to defined as the number of people living specific area. It is recognized to have social population indicator as measuring parameter for the specific area. It imply number of people living in the specific area. The definition of population indicator is

$$q_{po} = \frac{Q_{PO}}{Q_{TOT}}$$

(7.1)

where

Q_{po} – number of people in the region
Q_{tot} – total number of people

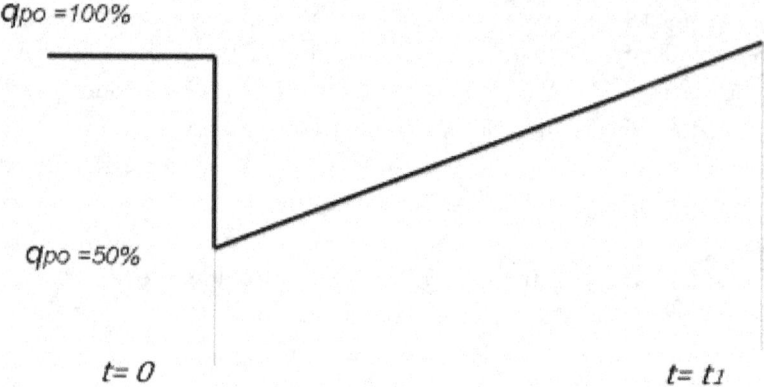

Figure 7.2. Graphical presentation of sudden change of population indicator.

Population indicator is parameter which reflects population in the region. Figure 7.2.

It is subject to sudden change if there is any adverse cause for its change. It may happen if it reflects sudden diesis which may contribute to the unpredictableloses of human life.

As it can be noticed, the sudden change of population indicator is defined by the time change at the t = 0 and indicator recovery at t =t_1

TheResilience Index is integral of the Sustainability Index between thetime of the sudden change in the respective indicator and thetime when it resumesa steady state value,The resilience index for an social system is.

$$R_j = w_i \int_{i=0}^{i=t} (1 - q_i)$$

(7.2)

where

j – resilience index
q_i –specific indicator
w_i- weight coefficient

7.3.2. Standard of Living Indicator

Standard of living indicator is characteristic parameter defining ranking a specific country by the poverty level in the specific time scale in the world scale

Figure 7.3. It is defined as the amount of income of the respective country.

$$q_{ST} = \frac{Q_{ST}}{Q_{TOT}} \tag{7.3}$$

where

Q_{ST} – specific income for standard of living
Q_{tot} – total income in the region

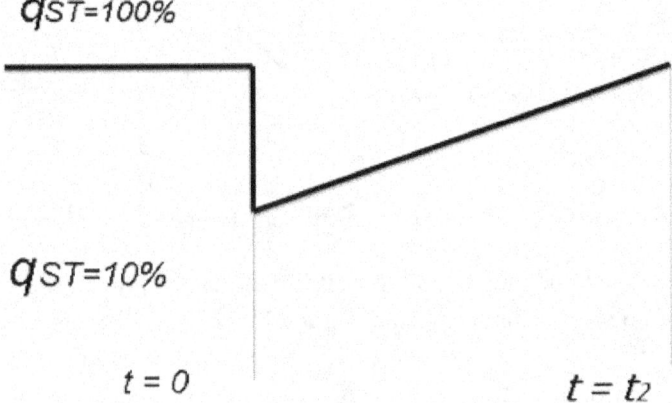

Figure 7.3. Graphical presentation of sudden change standard of life indicator.

The sudden change of standard of life indicator is demonstrated as the recovery of indicator with linear change in time to starting position Figure 3. It usually related to the loss of jobs and respective loses of household income.

7.3.3. Food Indicator

Food indicator is average income spent on food, beverages, and tobaccoFigure4.In itsspecific form this indicator comprise total expenses 'for single person.In evaluation of the sudden change of standard of life the specific value of indicator is defined as relative value of the standard of life forthe system.

$$q_{FO} = \frac{Q_{FO}}{Q_{TOT}} \tag{7.4}$$

where

Q_{FO} – specific income for food expenses
Q_{TOT} – total income in the region

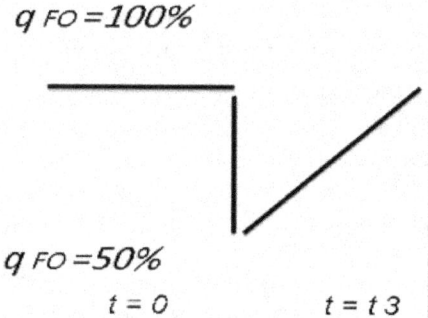

q FO =100%

q FO =50%

t = 0　　　　　　　*t = t 3*

Figure 7.4. Graphical presentation of sudden change of food indicator.

The sudden change of food indicator reflects drought in the region and corresponding loses human and animal food Figure 7.4. These loses are usually connected to some other causes which are result of unpredicted events effecting quality of human life.

7.3.4. Water and SanitationIndicator

The property of the water and sanitation is defined by the sanitation indicator. It comprise validation of the population expenditure for the water and sanitation per person.

$$q_{ws} = \frac{Q_{ws}}{Q_{TOT}}$$

(7.5)

where

Q_{WS} – specific income for water and sanitation
Q_{TOT} – total income in the region

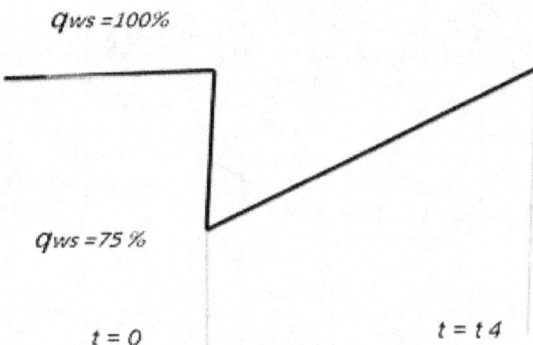

Figure 7.5. Graphical presentation of sudden change water and sanitation indicator.

Sudden deficiency of water for sanitation requires imply the need for fast recovery of this indicatorFigure 7.5. At the t =0 the change of sanitation indicator has to recover within the $\emptyset t_4$. This imply that the sudden change of sanitation indicator from 100% to 75% require respective time interval.

7.3.5.HealthcareIndicator

Healthcare expenditure indicator is defined as the unit expense for the single person Figure 6. It comprise expenses devoted to healthcare service in the specific area

$$q_{HEA} = \frac{Q_{HEA}}{Q_{TOT}}$$

(7.6)

where

Q_{HEA} – specific expenses for healthcare
Q_{TOT} – total income in the region

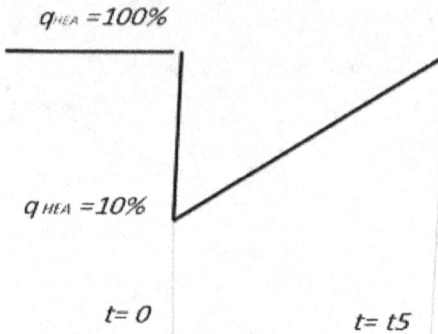

Figure 7.6. Graphical presentation of sudden change healthcare indicator.

The healthcare indicator is changed for 100 % to 10% and will be recovering with time interval∅t₅. Figure 6. It should be verified that the change of healthcare reflects rather high change of the indicator which means a high expenses for healthcare of the system.

7.3.6. Education and Employment Indicator

The education indicator is expenses devoted to Illiteracy improvement. It is an average expenses for schooling per person in the specific area

$$q_{ED} = \frac{Q_{ED}}{Q_{TOT}}$$

(7.7)

where

QED – specific income for education
QTOT – total income in the region

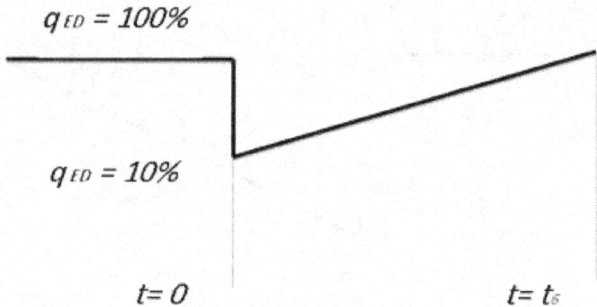

Figure 7.7. Graphical presentation of sudden change education indicator.

The expenses for household of the system under consideration includes education expenses. As it is shown on Figure7, the education expenses are10% total expenses of the system.

7.3.7. Environment Indicator

Global warming is "very likely" (>90% certainty) caused by anthropogenic greenhouse gas emissions. It shows expenses for vulnerability to climate change and its effect on the high dependence on climate condition Figure 7.8. It is defined as the expenses the per unit person of total population

$$q_{EN} = \frac{Q_{EN}}{Q_{TOT}}$$

(7.8)

where

Q_{ED} – specific expensesfor climate change

Q_{TOT} – total income in the region

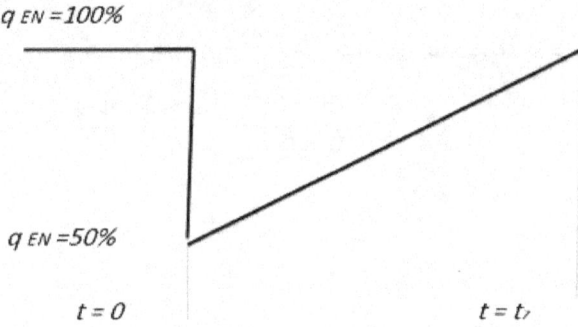

q EN =100%

q EN =50%

t = 0   *t = t,*

Figure 7.8. Graphical presentation of sudden change environment indicator.

The main part of the sudden change of environment expenses is defined with 50% of the total environment to be used for the for the climate change.

7.4 TOTAL RESILIENCE INDEX

The essential parameter for the assessment of the potential catastrophic events is the resilience index of the system. It comprise integral of the respective sudden change of indicators and their recovery to the primary state.

Resilience index is defined asintegral of the Sustainability Index between thetime of the sudden change in the respective indicator and thetime when it resumesa steady state value.The resilience index for an social system is composed of the following elements

$$R_i = \int_{t_0}^{t_1} \left[1 - q_i(t) \right]$$

(7.9)

where

    j − resilienceindex
    q_i −indicator
    w_i− weight coefficient

If we will take into a consideration number of indicators then the total R_{TOT} is obtained by agglomeration of the individual resilience indexes. In this case the total resilience index is defined as

$$R_{TOT} = \sum_{n=1}^{N} w_i \int_{t_0}^{t_1} \left[1 - q_i(t) \right]$$

(7.10)

Since the agglomeration index is a parameter for validation of the catastrophic event, it is adapted to use R_{TOT} for the assessment catastrophe even.

7.5 Social Catastrophe Assessments

As it is shown the social catastrophic event is validated by comparison the agglomeration of Resilience Indexes and the critical value of catastrophic event. [9,10.11].It should be recognized that there is possibility for different agglomerating resilience indexes composed by the resilience indexes corresponding to the different sudden change of the respective indicators.

In this respect a following criteria used to validate R_{TOT} in comparison with the R_{CRI} as the criteria for the definition of catastrophic event, in form

$$R_{TOT} > R_{CRI}$$

(7.11)

This criterion is the essential merits for the evaluation of the catastrophic event under consideration that the total resilience index is higher then the critical value of the resilience index defined for the system under consideration. In the definition of critical value of the system it has to be anticipated that the overriding of critical value means destruction of the structure and lose of its functionality.

If this applied to social system it will mean a total destruction leading to the catastrophe as war, culture of poverty, social unrest ect

REFERENCES

[1] *Handbook On Social Indicators*, ST/EBA /STAT Ser. F/19, United nation Publication, Sales No.6,87,XVII.6.

[2] Samoil H. Princ, *PhD Theses, Catastrophe and Social Change*, Faculty of Political Science, Cambridge University.

[3] Social Developed Indicators, *United Nation Development Progrem, Human DevelopmentReport*.

[4] Guy Sapirsteib, *Social resilience: Forget Element in Disaster Reduction, Organizational Rescue International*, Boston, Massachusetts, USA.

[5] J.L. Hooper Douglas, *Catastrophe Models: Some Illustration and Picture for Social Impact Assessment*, Brigham Young University, Prove, Utah, USA.

[6] Hansen R., 2007, Catastrophe Change and New Extinction, Gorge Mason University.

[7] SchautonM.,van der Haide M.,Heijman W., 2009, *Resilience of Socio-Economic Systems in European Rural Areas, Economic of Consumers and Households*,Wageningen University.

[8] Social Development Indicators, 2011, *Center for Sustainability Systems*, University of Michigan.

[9] Sapirstine G., *SocialResilience Forgotten Element in Disaster Reduction*, Organization Resilience Institute, Boston, USA.

[10] LingeA., ManeE.,Romano D., 2009, *Measuring Household of Resilience Food Insecurity*,FAO Agriculture Division Economy,(FAO-ESAF).

[11] Brenson-Lazan, G. (2003). *Group and Social Resilience Building*.URL: www.communityatwork.com/resilience/RESILIENCIAENG.pdf

CHAPTER 8

RESILIENCE OF GLOBAL WARMING

8.1 INTRODUCTION

Climate change isn't happening as single phenomena, there are numerous factors that interact in various ways, creating a new challenge. Furthermore climate change, superimposed on poverty, exacerbates existing problems. Whatever threatens the viability of ecosystems also ultimately threatens human societies, starting with people who most directly rely on natural resources for their livelihood.

New insights have been gained over last ten years about essential role of energy resilience for prosperous development of society. A grooving number of case studies have revealed the tight connection between resilience, diversity and sustainability of social and ecological systems. Moreover, energy limit have been identified as one of the 12 most serious environmental problems facing past and future societies.

The global system resilience refers to the capacity of a global system to withstand perturbations from e.g. climatic, economic, technological and social causes and to rebuild and renew itself afterwards

The resilience of global warming is the transient heat and mass transfer process leading to the increase of atmosphere temperature on our planet. It comprise a time dependent processes reflecting the heat and mass transfer processes between the sun and atmosphere.

Resiliency is the ability to avoid, minimize, withstand, and recover from the effects of adversity, whether natural or man-made, under all circumstances of use. The global warming resilience is the ability of global system to provide and maintain an acceptable level of service in the face of various and challenges to normal operation.

The resilience analysis of global warming processes comprises the evaluation of main parameters effecting the change of heat and mass transfer processes between sun and earth. Among parameters to be taken in this analysis are: earth surface temperature, atmospheric temperature, CO_2 concentration and radiation properties of the earth.

Global climate change is increasingly recognized as the key threat to the continued development – and even survival - of humanity [1]. The context obtained from earth history, as the pattern of global environmental change in the past provides an indispensable context to establishing likely trajectories of future climate change. The evidence for human-induced climate change is now persuasive, and the need for direct action compelling. The Ice Age climate change has been rapid, pervasive and frequent [2]. For instance, during the last 2.6 million years, the duration of the current Ice Age, there have been 104 major fluctuations between global cold and global warmth. Each of the major fluctuations was itself complex, encompassing 'minor' changes of up to 5 degrees centigrade in average annual temperature. As temperature rose and fell, so did global sea level, by up to 130 meters [3].

It is also undoubted that levels of CO_2 are now some 30% higher than at any time over the past 750 000 years,(with levels of methane having more than doubled) [4]. CO_2 levels are now increasing, seemingly inexorably, by nearly 1% a year, and the trend is accelerating. It is also beyond doubt that these increases are due to human activity, particularly the burning of fossil fuels, rather than being due to, say, volcanic activity. One track into this uncharted territory is to model, mathematically, the effects of increasing greenhouse gases on temperature. In these models, the earth and its various parameters need to be simplified, and there also remain considerable uncertainties. Most current models suggest global warming of between 2 and 6 degrees by the end of this century, to levels unprecedented in earth history over the past few million years [5].

In both of these, the influx of greenhouse gases has been demonstrated by changes in the ratios of carbon isotopes within fossils. The isotopes themselves do not say whether mainly CO_2 or methane was involved, but plausible scenarios suggest the involvement of both. Rapid warming of the order of between 5 and 10 degrees centigrade took place globally, the temperatures declining back to background values over many thousands of years, probably as the excess greenhouse gases were slowly drawn out of the atmosphere by reactions associated with rock weathering.

These geological examples strongly reinforce the modeled scenarios of global warming for later this century. Crucially, such temperature surges show the earth behaving in a non-linear fashion when reacting to environmental stress: that is, it tends to 'flip' from one quasi-stable state to another, and this kind of behavior is inherently difficult to model or to predict.

Sea level has constantly fluctuated in the geological past: its highest recorded level was in the Cretaceous Period, some 80 million years ago, when CO_2 levels were considerably higher than at present, and ice-caps were virtually absent from the earth. Then, sea level stood at least 200 meters higher than today, with most of the UK being submerged.

Less well known are the variable sea levels recorded in previous warm phases of the Ice Ages For instance, in the most recent of these, some 125 000 years ago, sea level reached some 6 m higher than at present. Such a difference is geologically modest, and reflects relatively minor differences in the extent of melting of land ice. We emphasize that it occurred in a world where levels of greenhouse gases, unaffected by humans, were lower than at present.

The problem can only be marginally (i.e. ineffectually) addressed by increases in alternative energy and energy efficiency, any likely savings being offset by population and economic growth [6]. And, given the huge energy and material demands in the construction of, say, wind farms, the ultimate value of these is debatable. More radical solutions to humanity's dilemma are necessary, and these might include:

- massive underground sequestration of CO_2. This is not yet a proven method on anything like the scale needed, but needs to be pursued with urgency.
- large-scale capture of CO_2 from the air and its conversion into a mineralized form, perhaps as carbonate minerals.
- a large-scale switch to civil nuclear power. This has the benefit of being proven technology. We are aware of the problems, and current public unpopularity of this route, but we consider the dangers posed by global warming to be orders of magnitude greater than those likely to be caused by the controlled use of nuclear power. This energy

source, additionally, could lie at the heart of future hydrogen-based transport systems.

8.2 FLUCTUATION

Global and land surface temperature fluctuation is shown on Figure 1. It can be noticed that fluctuation pattern is similar in the different time period. This implies that these fluctuations are result of the disturbances caused by the different processes [6,7].

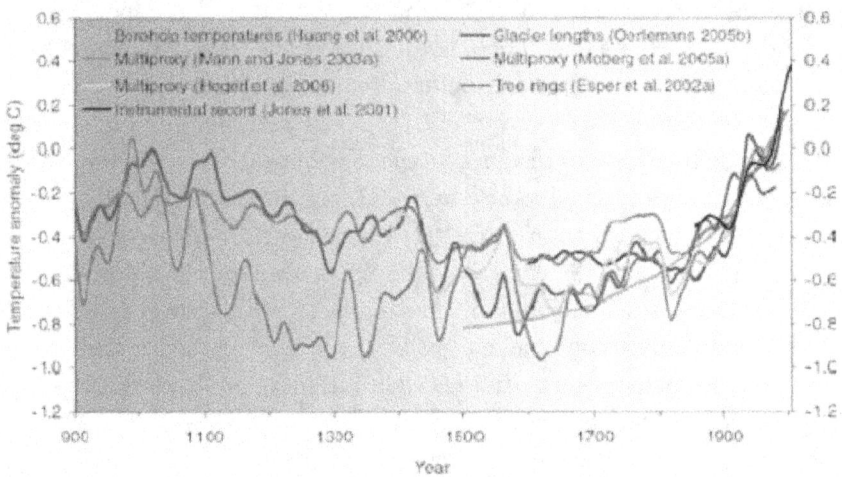

Figure 8.1. Global Temperature Fluctuation.

8.3 RESILIENCE OF THE GLOBLS SYSTEM

The resilience of a system relates to the magnitude of disturbance required to fundamentally disrupt the system causing a dramatic shift to another state of the system, controlled by a different set of processes [8,9]. When resilience is lost or significantly decreased, a system is at high risk of shifting into a qualitatively different state. The new state of the system may be undesirable. Restoring a system to it's previous state can be complex, expensive, and sometimes even impossible. Research suggests that to restore some systems to their previous state requires a return to conditions well before the point of collapse.

The global system resilience refers to the capacity of a global system to withstand perturbations from e.g. climatic, economic, technological and social causes and to rebuild and renew itself afterwards [10]. Loss of resilience can cause loss of valuable system services, and may even lead to rapid transitions or shifts into qualitatively different situations and configurations.

In general terms, the vulnerability of a system is assessed according to the concept of resilience, developed in the mathematics of non-linear differential equations. According to this frame, the opposite to the vulnerability of a system is its stability, its resilience, defined specifically as an attribute of a system. The system is like a net; it consists of a great number of not's, which are interlinked.

Resilience provides a new framework for analyzing economic, ecological, technological and social systems in a changing world facing many uncertainties and challenges. It represents an area of explorative research under rapid development with major policy implications for sustainable development.

Sometimes change is gradual and things move forward in roughly continuous and predictable ways. In other times, change is sudden, disorganized and turbulent reflected by climate impacts, earth system science challenges and vulnerable regions. Evidence points out to a situation where periods of such abrupt changes are likely to increase in frequency and magnitude

Resilience index of global warming can be modeled as processes defined with respective indicators including: global temperature, economic welfare, environment indicator and social indicator. Global temperature is the average atmospheric temperature. Economic welfare is defined with the average global income per capita. Environment indicator is average carbon dioxide concentration in earth atmosphere. Social indicator reflects poverty index as the average global income per capita.

.

8.4 ResilienceIndex for Global Warming

Resilience Index is integral of the Sustainability Index between the time of sudden change of the respective indicator and time when it resume steady state value. The resilience index for an global warming system is composed of the following elements: economic, environmental, technological and socialthe resilience indicators [11,12].

$$R_j = \sum_{i=1}^{i=k} w_i \int_{t=0}^{t=k} \left[100 - q_i \right] dt \tag{8.1}$$

where

$j(x)$ – resilience index
$q(x)_i$ –indicator
w_i- weight coefficient

The resilience index is composed of sub-indexes. In the same way the environmental, technological and social resilience element could be obtained, as follows. Under assumption that the sudden indicator change resumes starting state is linear function of time, than we can write

$$R_i = \frac{1}{2} w_i \left(\Delta q_i \Delta t \right) \tag{8.2}$$

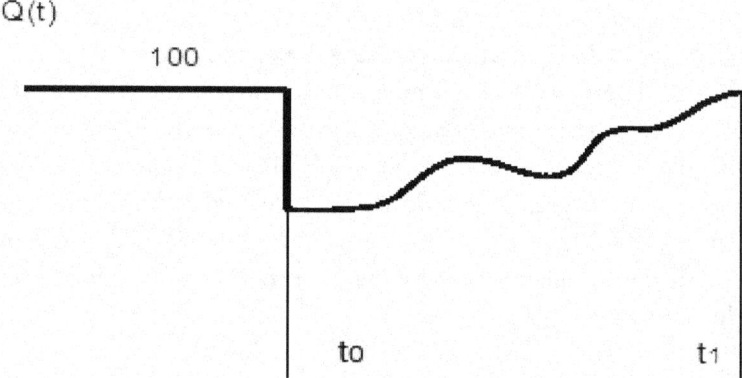

Figure 8.2. Graphical presentation of Resilience Index.

If it is assumed that the time interval for resuming starting state is equal for all indicators than the Resilience Index for the individual case is

$$R_j = \frac{\Delta t_o}{2} w_i \Delta q_i \tag{8.3}$$

The total Resilience Index is an additive function of all resilience Indicators as follows

$$R_{zt} = R_t + R_{en} + R_s + R_z \qquad (8.4)$$

In the evaluation of global warming processes following indicators are taken into a consideration.

Thermal process will be described with global surface temperature which is considered as essential parameter for the description of the global heat transfer process between sun and global surface. In the assessment of the resilience reflecting thermal process the global surface temperature is used as the characteristic parameter which define respective Global Warming Resilience Index component.

Global environment processes are including the emission of green house gases to the global atmosphere resulting from anthropological man activity on the earth. In simplification of these processes we will assume that only CO_2 gas is taken into a consideration. The Global Warming Resilience Index environment component is defined as the CO_2 emission flux.

Social processes on the earth are reflecting change in the social welfare on the planet It is assumed that the social commodity is the measuring parameter reflecting human life quality and it is defined by the average income per capita as the resilience social component of Global Warming Index.

Poverty generation is the immanent process on the globe. It reflects the increase of global population and deficiency of energy, agriculture and industrial products. In order to unified global poverty it is anticipated that the energy consumption is the main parameter to be used in the definition of the Global Warming Index component reflecting poverty generation on the globe. The Resilience of Global Warming Index component is the global average energy consumption per capita.

The Global Warming Resilience Index is defined as shown on Table 1. Numerical values for components are calculated for four options, namely: Option A, Option B. Option C, and Option D. Each of the option comprise values of indicators having Maximum, ¾ of Maximum, ½ of Maximum, ¼ of Maximum and zero value.

Option 1

Option 1 design is based on the assumption that the change of the indicators is defined with the maximum change of the surface temperature, 1/2 change of CO_2 emission, ¾ change of Income per capital and zero change of the energy consumption per capita. It is anticipated that all other changes are introduced in the same time with time and will last t time period.

Option 2

Option 2 comprise situation when the maximum change of the CO_2 emission is introduced at the same time as the ½ change of surface temperature, ¼ change of income per capita and zero change of the energy consumption per capita. It is of interest to emphasize that this option is reflecting major change of the CO_2 emission and is effect on the global warming. By the introduction of the maximum change of CO_2 emission the resilience index will reflect vulnerability of our planet. It is important to notice that if the sudden change of the CO_2 emission will override the maximum value of the resilience index it may be lead to the catastrophic event.

Option 3

If the sudden change of income per capita is introduced with its maximum value with other indicator changes corresponding to ½, 1/4 and zero, respectively, this option will correspond to potential social impact to the resilience index. As it was defined for other options, if the sudden change of income will lead to the unexpected change of the resilience index than the catastrophic even can be expected. Otherwise, this situation can lead to the social events which may be difficult to control.

Option 4

The energy consumption per capita is an indicator which reflects the economic advances in global welfare. The maximum change of energy consumption per capita is the measure of the potential change of the quality life on our planet. Introduction of other indicators change reflecting zero change will define the potential change of the global advances.

The procedure for the Global Warming Resilience Index determination is based on the assumption that options are defined by the agglomerated function with weighted arithmetic mean as the synthesized function. Each option is defined with the respective priority given to the individual option. Numerical values for the maximum of respective indicator are determined as specified in the Table 1.

8.5. DEMONSTRATION OF GLOBAL WARMINGRESILIENCE INDEX

GLOBAL WARMING RESILIENCE INDEX

Table 1.

Options	Surface temperature	CO_2 emission	Income per capita	Energy consumption per capita
	⊠ T/y	⊠ C/y	Euro/cap/y	kWh/cap/y
	°C/y	Kg/m³/y	€/cap/y	kWh/cap/y
Option A	5.0	0.15	1530	0.00
Option B	2.5	0.30	0.00	17000
Option C	1.75	0.00	6170	34000
Option D	0.00	0.075	3850	64000

Table 2. Multi-criteria Assessment of Global Warming

Options	CRITERIA
Option A	$ST>CO_2=IN=EN$
Option B	$CO_2>IN=EN=ST$
Option C	$IN>EN=ST=CO_2$
Option D	$EN>ST=CO_2=IN$

Table 3. Resilience Index for Different Option

Options	Resilience Indexes R_n			
Option A	2.50	0.135	0.125	0.00
Option B	1.125	0.57	0.00	0.25
Option C	0.825	0.00	0.50	0.125
Option D	0.00	0.135	0.25	0.50

8.6 MULTI-CRITERIAEVALUATION OF THE RESILIENCE INDEX OF GLOBAL WARMING

Multi-criteria resilience indexes are obtained as the agglomeration of the resilience indices multiplied of the respective probability of the resilience index for specific option.

$$R_M = \sum_M w_n R_n$$

The rating among the individual value of the resilience index for the global warming under constrain of the specific criteria. It is of interest to verify priority of the multi criteria resilience index under constrain as the measuring parameter for the indicators

Evaluation of the resilience index of the global warming includes analysis the several cases with priority devoted to the specific indicators.

CASE 1

Case 1 is designed with the aim to investigate effect of Surface Temperature Indicator under constrain that it has priority in comparison with other indicators having the same weighting coefficients. Under this constrain, it can be noticed that options rating is followed by the option numbering.

It is interest to verify that the constrain introduced with the Surface Temperature Indicator priority reflects the situation when the catastrophic events the most probable occurrence

Priority of Indicators – 1 -TEM> CO2 = IN = EN

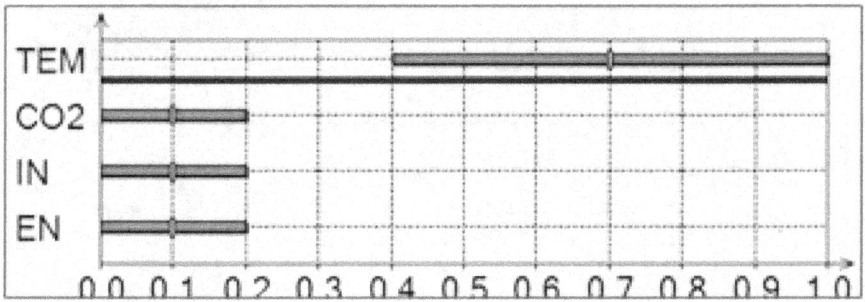

Option Rating of Resilience Index for the Case 1 - TEM> CO2 = IN = EN

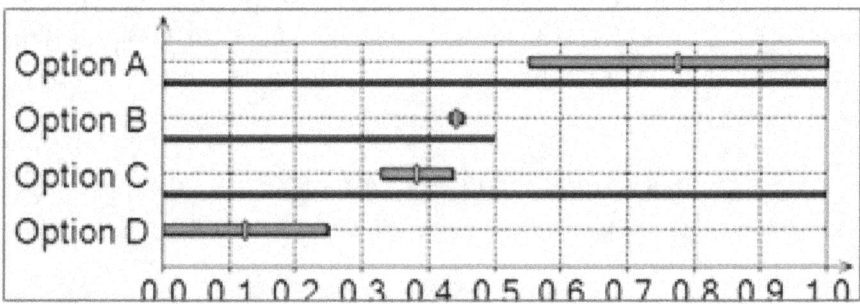

CASE 2

Case 2 is designed under constrain that the CO_2 emission indicator has priority in comparison with other indicators. Obtained rating among options has changed and priority is obtained for the Option D followed by Option C. Options A and B taking the lowest position on the rating list.

Priority of Indicators -CO2> TEM = IN = EN

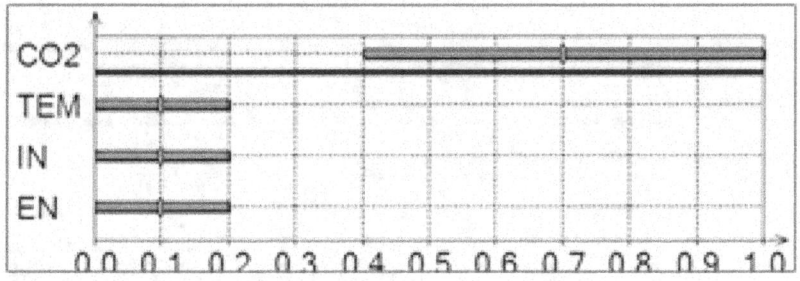

Option Rating of Resilience Index for the Case 2 – CO2> TEM = IN = EN

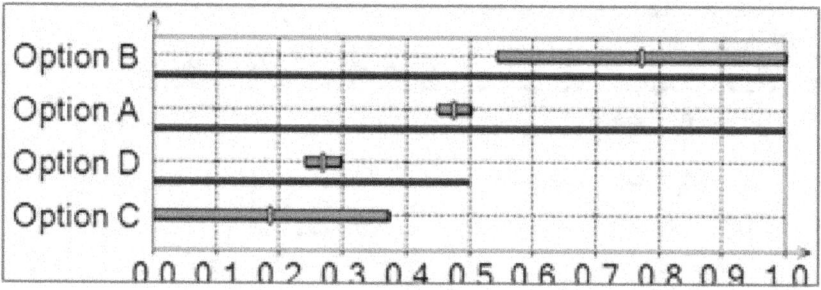

CASE 3

Case 3 includes preference to be given to income per capita indicator priority. It can be noticed that Option D is taking first place on the rating list. Options B, C, and D are with increasing number of option. This proves that Income per capita indicator priority does not substantial effect the stability of the system,

Priority of Indicators - IN > TEM = CO2 = EN

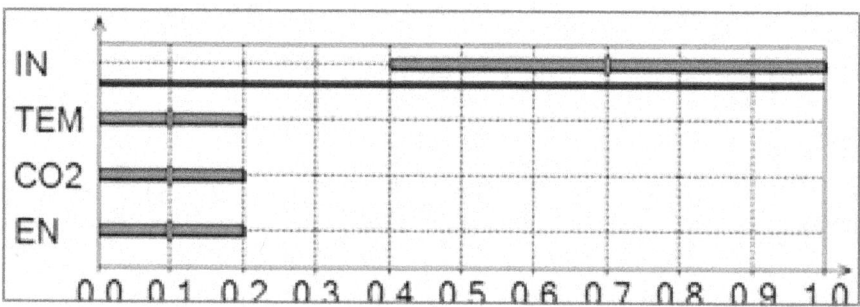

Option Rating of Resilience Index for the Case 3 - IN >TEM = CO2 = EN

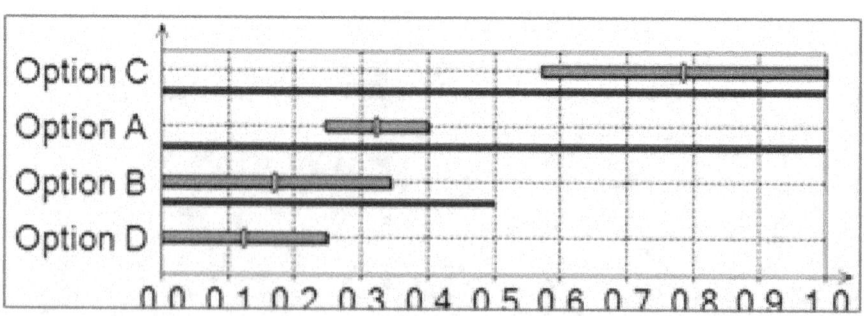

CASE 4

Case 4 reflects the situation when priority is given to Energy Consumption Indicator. It can be noticed that Case 4 is having the same rating list as the Case 1. Even indicators under considerationin this case are different the stability of the system is similar to the Case 2.This imply that stability of the system under*consideration is the same.*

Priority of Indicators Case 4 - EN > TEM = CO2 = IN

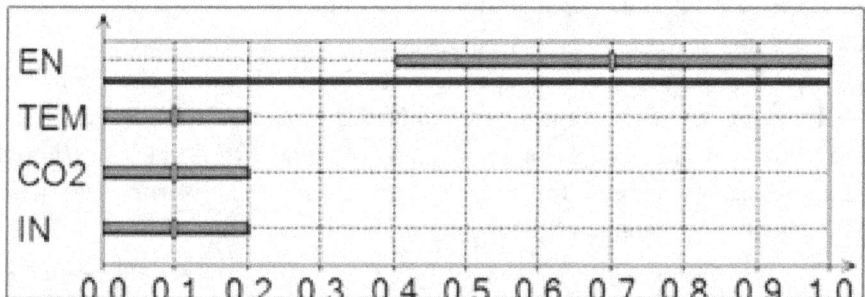

Option Rating of Resilience Index for the Case 4 - EN >TEM = CO2 = IN

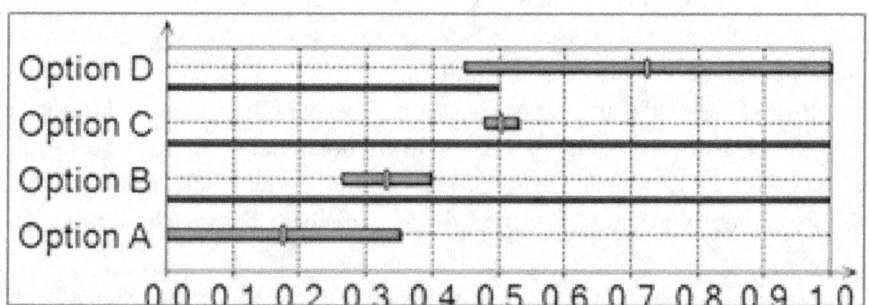

The multi-criteria assessment of the selected options comprise several steps, including : normalization of indicators, definition of constrain for weighting coefficients, and determination of the Resilience Index.

8.7 DISCUSSION OF THE RESULTS

Global warming is complex process including several interacting processes comprising hear transfer process from the sun to the earth, emission of green house gases, change of income per capita and energy consumption. These processes are identified by the respective indicators, including: surface temperature, CO_2 emission, income per capita and energy consumption. Each of the indicators are specified as parameters contributing to the resilience index of the global system.

In this evaluation we have assumed that each parameter of the system is contributing to the resilience of global system with weighting factor reflecting respective constrain imposed on the Cases in this analysis. In this exercise the multi-criteria method is applied in the determination of sustainability index and resilience index as the measure of system quality and stability.

In this evaluation six cases are taken into the consideration. First four cases are devoted to those situations when priority is given to the individual indicator with other indicators are having the same normalized value. Here, it should be emphasized that the rating list for each case is the measuring parameter which justify the stability of the system under specific constrain.

Global worming measured by the resiliency of the system is reflecting the effect of processes under consideration to the potential catastrophic events. Those events are the unexpected behavior of the system following interaction of the processes under consideration. It is of interest to recognize that the interaction of the processes under consideration lead to the agglomeration of the potential hazard effect of the individual process.

Study of global warming has been under very high attention of the scientific and human community in order to learn more about potential catastrophic events. So, it is of special interest to learn more about interaction of the different processes and potential hazard consequences of the resilience of global warming.

In this paper we have tried to develop the method for the evaluation resilience of global warming having in mind that the interaction of different processes may lead to the catastrophic events.

Obtained results of this exercise prove that the evaluation of the resilience can be used as qualitative measure of the potential hazard behavior of the global system leading to the instability of of the processes under consideration. It should be emphasized that the study of the global warming deserve special attention to the application of the multi-criteria assessment to this problem.

REFERENCES

[1]   *Climate Change Sciences: An Analysis of some Key Questions*, USA National Academy of Sciences, 2003.

[2]   Orester, N., Scientific Consensus on Climate Change, *Science*, Vol.306, p.1686,2004.

[3]   *Features: Global Warming: A Prospective from Earth History*, University of Lancaster, 2008/2009.

[4]   Facts Sheet,*Global Warming*, Environmental Defense, Jan.2003.

[5]   Royal Society and 15 others, *The Science of Climate Change*, London, United Kingdom.

[6]   Levensen Th. *Ice Time Climate Science and Life on the Earth*, New York, Harper and Row. 1989.

[7]   Landeberg H., Man-made Climates Changes, *Science*170, pp1265-1274.2002.

[8]   C.S. Holling, Resilience and Stability of Ecological System, *Annual Review of Ecology and Systamatics*, Vol.4, pp.1-23, 1973.

[9]   . Holbagel, P.Nemet, S. Dokker, *Resilience Engineering Perspective*, Ashgate, June 2008.

[10]   H.R. Gruenn,*Resilience and its Application to Energy System*, Springer Berlin/Heidelbrg, 2006.

[11]   N.H. Afgan, M.G. Carvalho, *Quality, Indicators and Sustainability of Energy Systems*,Begell House Publisher, New York, 2008.

CHAPTER 9

EVALUATION OF URBAN SYSTEM CATASTROPHES

9.1 INTRODUCTION

Urban systems are centered in urban areas; in terms of ecosystem services, urban areas are primarily sites of consumption. This contrasts with the other systems assessed in this chapter (such as cultivated systems, drylands, and coastal systems), which primarily generate and supply ecosystem services. Urban systems exist at several scales and can be identified with individual urban settlements or networks of such settlements.

9.2 URBAN AREA CATASTROPHE

Urban settlements are agglomerations of people and their activities; although urban areas may contain a wide variety of species, it is the humans that make them urban. About half the people in the world live in areas deemed as urban, up from less than 15% at the start of the twentieth century. Combined with population growth, this has meant an almost fifteenfold increase in the world's urban population, from 200 million in 1900 to 2.9 billion 100 years later. Over the same period, the rural population more than doubled, increasing from 1.4 billion to 3.2 billion. The share of Earth's land area that is urban is also growing, but it remains only about 2.8%

Urbanization and urban growth continue to be major demographic trends. The world's urban population increased from about 200 million (15% of world population) in 1900 to 2.9 billion (50% of world population) in 2000, and the number of cities with populations in excess of 1 million increased from 17 in 1900 to 388 in 2000. As people are increasingly living in cities, and as cities act as both human ecosystem habitats and drivers of ecosystem change, it will become increasingly important to foster urban systems that contribute to human well-being and reduce ecosystem service burdens at all scales.

Urbanization is not in itself inherently bad for ecosystems. Many ecosystems in and around urban areas are more biodiverse than rural monocultures are, and they can also provide food, water services, comfort, amenities, cultural values, and so on, particularly if they are well managed. Moreover, urban areas currently only account for about 2.8% of the total land area of Earth, despite containing about half the world's population. Urban demographic and economic growth has been increasing pressures on ecosystems globally, but affluent rural and sub-urban living often places even more pressure on ecosystems. Dense urban settlement is considered to be less environmentally burdensome than urban and suburban sprawl are. At the same time, urban centers facilitate human access to and management of ecosystem services through, for example, the scale and proximity economies of piped water systems. Climate change and its concomitant challenges are driving reassessments of the ways in which cities and urban regions are contributing to these issues. These reassessments focus on the influence of urban form, space, and operations on global social, economic, and environmental sustainability. While there are local cultural and physical issues distinct to individual situations, many of the challenges presented by urban growth and climate change are shared by cities and urban regions, regardless of location. These include resource scarcity, changing patterns of consumption and demographics, insufficient or inappropriate built environments, and outdated or ill-adapted systems of planning, management, and operational practice. Such problems can result in suburbanization of valuable peri-urban areas, spontaneous settlements, areas of urban decay, and social inequalities.

Urban development trends do pose serious problems with respect to ecosystem services and human well-being. Ecosystem processes that provide services to urban residents tend to be neglected as a result of the continued lack of understanding and appreciation of the complex processes involved, many of which take place at some distance from the urban consumers; the difficulties that private enterprises encounter in owning, trading, and negotiating over ecosystem services (and burdens), which rarely conform to property boundaries; the difficulties that public agencies encounter in managing and regulating ecosystem services, which also tend to cross administrative and sectoral boundaries; and the fact that the people most adversely affected by the loss of ecosystem services tend to be the least influential economically and politically (such as the urban poor, future generations, and residents living far from where the decisions are being made).

Models of urban systems, especially those enabled by recent developments in information and communication technologies (ICT), provide critical insights into how the various aspects of urban environments work, and how they can be best adapted to address social and environmental challenges. In addition, they support effective decision making regarding how to manage these interactions within cities and urban regions. They are thus becoming more important in a contemporary policy context that aims to steer urban change toward sustainability.

The development of ICT tools has resulted in a shift away from the holistic mega models that characterized the field from the The attributes of models may vary from place to place and are selected according to the understanding required or decisions to be made in a particular setting. Contemporary urban models employ an increasing range of visualizations tools, including for example, 3D and 4D representations of form, spatial, and operational relationships, and 2D objects such as charts, maps, and diagrams that correlate the data as indicators of performance within a bounded domain and present relationships across data sets. The process of selecting appropriate and specific indicators and data to model the performance of particular urban systems against sustainability criteria is of increasing significance.

1960s to the early 1990s, toward more specific models that investigate an identified cluster of relationships such as urban form, traffic, and greenhouse gas (GHG) emissions, or demographic distributions, service provision, and urban morphology. Models aim to represent complex relationships between operations in cities and urban regions. These models can be used to compare indicators and relationships from city to city, region to region, and nation to nation. Developments in urban metabolism and industrial ecology also provide new and simplified models of urban footprints, linking the overall GHG emissions associated with human activity within cities with their transboundary life cycle and supply chains.

Models of urban systems have been developed at different times and for different purposes. Many existing models are aggregations of preexisting methods and packages loosely integrated and adapted for particular situations, rather than being holistic tools applied generically as a standard set of tightly integrated methods. The expanding use of recently developed combinations of geographic information systems (GIS) and 3D and 4D visualization packages are examples of this process, although very few practical urban models have yet integrated these new methodologies.

The major urban modeling tools now include those developed by individual cities or groups of cities and urban regions, such as the VURCA, MUSCADE, and NEDUM projects in France, and THOR in Denmark. They also include commercially available generic modeling tools such as MATSim, Tranus, and UrbanSim. While tools are typically developed through collaborations between local or city governments (as the principle users) and research laboratories in universities (as the model makers), collaborations may also include commercial software specialists (e.g. IBM and Modelistica) and companies with an interest in urban construction or property management (e.g.,Eiffage'sPhosphore 2 in France).

9.3 DEFINITION OF URBAN AREAS AND POPULATIONS

In line with other MA systems (such as cultivated, dryland, and mountain terms of a metropolitan area; and still others in terms of a (usually larger) , urban systems are associated with particular spatial locations, urban agglomeration. These differences have persisted for many years. in this case urban areas. Urban areas are in turn associated with urban In the 2001 revision of the U.N. report, about half the countries in the settlements and populations. This Box focuses on how urban areas and world used estimates based on "city proper," with most of the remaining populations are distinguished from rural areas and populations. There are claiming to be applying the concept of urban agglomeration.no hard and fast rules on this; although conceptual clarity is important. Although country-specific definitions will remain central to defining and must also be recognized that the dividing line between urban and rural is assessing urban centers for many years to come, the basis for a more inevitably somewhat arbitrary. For example, many people move regularly uniform definition is emerging from work using remote sensing and geobetween locations classified as urban and rural. Graphical information systems. This chapter relies on two different delineaIt is generally agreed that urban agglomerations (cities and other urban tions of urban to examine urban conditions and trends: one based on the centers) tend to have larger populations than rural agglomerations (villages) country-specific definitions used by the United Nations, and the other do, are more likely to be the site of large facilities (such as hospitals) and based on a preliminary urban-rural split developed as part of a broader higher-level administrative functions (national or local government offices, mapping and indicator exercise being undertaken by the Center for Interfor example), and create comparatively densely settled areas, with a national Earth Science Information Network (Balk et al. 2004). higher share of built-up area. Furthermore, urban residents are less likely The country-specific definitions provide the basis for the statistics on to work in agriculture and more likely to work in industry or services. It is historic urban populations and short-term projections, as well as a number also agreed that there are more and less urban lifestyles and cultures. of the descriptive statistics on urban population, such as the share with There is no international agreement, however, on the defining characteris access to improved water sources. The geospatial estimates are used for tics of urban, nor are there any scientifically accepted criteria by which to the map in Figure 27.1 and for the Tables situating urban populations identify urban areas and populations. Moreover, many urban researchers in relation to coastal zones, dryland, mountains, and other MA system believe that the distinction between rural and urban is becoming less categories. Although the geospatial estimates remain provisional and are relevant and that the boundary definitions are inevitably unlikely to be adopted by national governments in the foreseeable future, somewhat arbitrary. they have a number of potential advantages, including better international Cut-off points for identifying urban areas or populations vary within comparability and local verifiability, as well as the ability to portray, for the different criteria. Minimum population density criteria commonly range example, how sets of urban centers themselves are concentrated spabetween 400 and 1,000 persons per square kilometer; minimum size critetially. typically range between 1,000 and 5,000 residents; and maximum ag- Many economic and social characteristics once considered quintesricultural employment is usually in the vicinity of 50–75%. In each case, sentially urban are increasingly found among residents of what must dehowever, cut-off points outside these ranges can easily be found. mographically be classier as rural areas. Alternatively, many people

According to a recent report on world urbanization prospects (United living in large cities do not have access to what is sometimes considered 109 of the 228 countries covered use an administrative defining "urban" infrastructure, such as piped water and sewerage. Such criterion to distinguish urban from rural localities, and 89 of these use it phenomena are important to recognize, but for the purposes of this chapas the sole criterion. Population size or density was used as a criterion inter people are identified as urban or rural depending on their primary 96 countries, and as the sole criterion in 46. The administrative and residence rather than their economic or sociocultural characteristics.

In line with other MA systems (such as cultivated, dryland, and mountain terms of a metropolitan area; and still others in terms of a (usually larger) systems), urban systems are associated with particular spatial locations, urban agglomeration. These differences have persisted for many years. in this case urban areas. Urban areas are in turn associated with urban In the 2001 revision of the U.N. report, about half the countries in the settlements and populations. This Box focuses on how urban areas and world used estimates based on "city proper," with most of the remaining populations are distinguished from rural areas and populations. There are claiming to be applying the concept of urban agglomeration. no hard and fast rules on this; although conceptual clarity is important, it Although country-specific definitions will remain central to defining and must also be recognized that the dividing line between urban and rural is assessing urban centers for many years to come, the basis for a more inevitably somewhat arbitrary. For example, many people move regularly uniform definition is emerging from work using remote sensing and geobetween locations classified as urban and rural. graphical information systems. This chapter relies on two different delineaIt is generally agreed that urban agglomerations (cities and other urban tions of urban to examine urban conditions and trends: one based on the centers) tend to have larger populations than rural agglomerations (villages) country-specific definitions used by the United Nations, and the other do, are more likely to be the site of large facilities (such as hospitals) and based on a preliminary urban-rural split developed as part of a broader higher-level administrative functions (national or local government offices, mapping and indicator exercise being undertaken by the Center for Interfor example), and create comparatively densely settled areas, with a national Earth Science Information Network higher share of built-up area. Furthermore, urban residents are less likely.The country-specific definitions provide the basis for the statistics on to work in agriculture and more likely to work in industry or services. It is historic urban populations and short-term projections, as well as a number also agreed that there are more and less urban lifestyles and cultures. of the descriptive statistics on urban population.

According to a recent report on world urbanization prospects (United living in large cities do not have access to what is sometimes considered 109 of the 228 countries covered use an administrative defining "urban" infrastructure, such as piped water and sewerage. Such criterion to distinguish urban from rural localities, and 89 of these use it phenomena are important to recognize, but for the purposes of this chapter the sole criterion. Population size or density was used as a criterion inpeople are identified as urban or rural depending on their primary 96 countries, and as the sole criterion in 46. The administrative and residence rather than their economic or sociocultural characteristics. Thus, population-based criteria are themselves different in different countries: for example, a Kansas farmer living in a rural area a university for example, the lower limit above which a settlement was considered degree, hooked up to the Internet and a fax machine, with a barn full of urban ranged between 200 and 50,000 persons. expensive machinery, who keeps strict accounts and sells his grain.

There are also differences in the manner in which localities would be identified as a rural person fied and settlement populations calculated. Some countries report city with the accoutrements of an urban lifestyle rather than an urban person populations on the basis of the boundaries of the city proper; others in living in a rural locationfied and settlement populations calculated.

9.4 Urban System Indicators

Before addressing the specific problems in urban systems, it is useful to understand the specific parameters to be used for the identification of the system. We can verify a number of specific indicators describing the state of the system. In the design of urban system models, utilization of specific indicators are pilots for the urban system definition.

Population Density

For humans, population density is the number of people per unit of area; usually per square kilometer or mile (which may include or exclude cultivated or potentially productive area). Commonly this may be calculated for a county, city, country, other territory, or the entire world.

Land Use per Household

The household is the basic unit of analysis in many social, microeconomic, and government models. The term refers to all individuals who live in the same dwelling. Land use indicator per household is defined as the utilization of the land to be devoted to respective quality of life. It comprises total area of the household. It is defined in km²/household.

Water Use

Water as essential for human life is defined as water consumption for the specific household. In this evaluation, we consider only sanitation and drinking water in the total water consumption. *Energy consumption.* Household energy consumption is defined using data for a single building with three members in the family. Energy consumption is the potential consumption for all appliances used in the specific urban household. *Household size.* Household size is determined by the number of family members in the household.

Income per Household

In this analysis, income per household is determined in accordance with the average income in the European Union as defined by the respective evaluation of Eurosat data. Income in a single household is between 20,000 and 30,000 Euros.

9.5 RESILIENCE OF THE URBAN SYSTEM

Urban resilience is defined as the "capability to prepare for, respond to, and recover from significant multihazard threats with minimum damage to public safety and health, the economy, and security" of a given urban area.

Contemporary academic discussion of urban resilience focuses on three distinct threats: climate change, natural disasters, and terrorism. This chapter will initially focus on the challenges and disasters specific to climate change, and future additions on counter-terrorism; other disasters (earthquakes, tsunamis, solar flares, etc.) and sustainable energy strategies are welcome and encouraged.

The urban impacts of climate change vary widely across geographical and developmental scales. This chapter will define and discuss the challenges of heat waves, droughts, and flooding. Resilience-boosting strategies will be introduced and outlined. Resilience is especially important in urban areas, because over the past century there has been a considerable increase in urbanization and urban sprawl. Half of the world's population now lives in cities, a figure that is set to rise to 80% by 2050. Mass density of people makes them especially vulnerable both to the impacts of acute disasters and the slow, creeping effects of the changing climate; all making resilience planning critically important.

By definition, resilience index is the time integral for the respective indicator. It is anticipated that after a sudden change of indicator the resilience index returns to the starting position. In this respect, resilience index can be envisaged as the potential capacity of the system.

$$R_i = w_i \int_{i=0}^{i=t} (1 - q_i)$$

(9.1)

There are two methods for the definition of resilience index. If it is assumed that the sudden change of indicator returns to the starting point with linear function in time, resilience index

$$R_i = \left(\frac{\Delta q_i \Delta t_i}{2} \right)$$

(9.2)

Where

Δq_i is the sudden change of specific indicator

Δt_i is the time interval for specific indicator recovery

Restoring a system to its previous state can be complex, expensive, and sometimes even impossible. Research suggests that to restore some systems to their previous state requires a return to conditions well before the point of collapse.

Definition of the resilience index for every indicator can defined as follows.

Resilience index for population density indicator

$$q_{PD} = \frac{Q_{PD}}{Q_{TOT}}$$

(9.3)

where

Q_{PD} is the population density in the region
Q_{TOT} is the total number of people

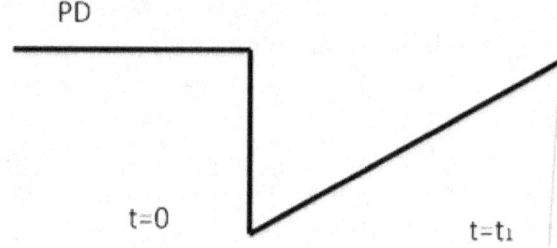

PD

t=0   t=t₁

Figure 9.1. Graphical representation of sudden change population density indicator.

As we can see, the sudden change of population density indicator is defined by the time change at the $t = 0$ and indicator recovery at $t = t_1$

Land use per household

$$q_{LU} = \frac{Q_{LU}}{Q_{TOT}}$$

(9.4)

where

Q_{LU} is the land use in the region
Q_{TOT} is the total number of people

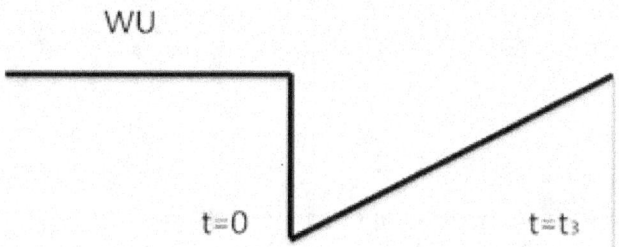

Figure 9.2. Graphical representation of sudden change of land use indicator.

As we can see, the sudden change of land use indicator is defined by the time change at time $t = 0$ and indicator recovery at $t = t_2$

Water use

$$q_{EC} = \frac{Q_{EC}}{Q_{TOT}}$$

(9.5)

where
Q_{WU} is the water use in the region
Q_{TOT} is the total number of people

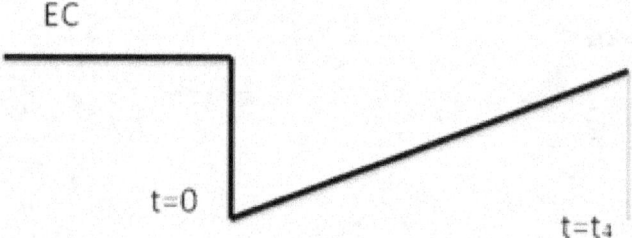

Figure 9.3. Graphical representation of sudden change water indicator.

As we can see, the sudden change of population indicator is defined by the time change at time $t = 0$ and indicator recovery at $t = t_1$.

Energy consumption

$$q_{HS} = \frac{Q_{HS}}{Q_{TOT}}$$

(9.6)

where
    Q_{EC} is the energy consumption in the region
    Q_{TOT} is the total number of people

Figure 9.4. Graphical representation of sudden change energy consumption indicator.

As we can see, the sudden change of population indicator is defined by the time change at time $t = 0$ and indicator recovery at $t = t_4$.

Household size

$$q_{HS} = \frac{Q_{HS}}{Q_{TOT}}$$

(9.7)

Where
    Q_{HS} is the household in the region
    Q_{TOT} is the total number of people

Figure 9.5. Graphical representation of sudden change household size indicator.

The resilience of the sudden change of household indicator is the measuring parameter of the household expenses It reflects the expenses for the household and definition of household indicator.

Income per household

$$q_{IN} = \frac{Q_{IN}}{Q_{TOT}}$$

(9.8)

Where

Q_{IN} is the household income in the region
Q_{TOT} is the total number of people

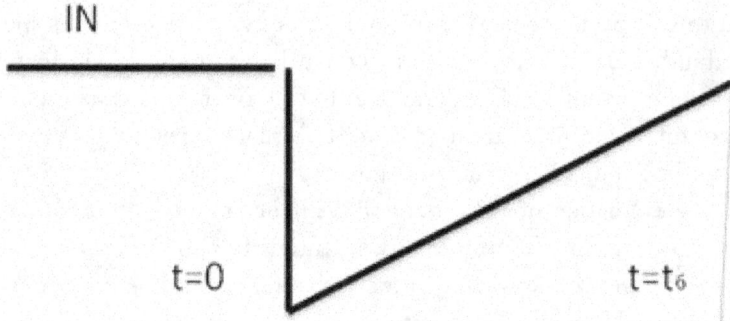

Figure 6. Graphical representation of sudden change household income indicator.

Household income is the total income of the system under consideration (It represents income of all members living in the same house. The change of household implies the expenses for the household.

9.6 Assessment of Urban System Catastrophe

The concept of resilience is connected to the ability to transform and re-transform urban spaces. [1-11] Resignation or submissiveness, which sometimes give the impression of being strong or tolerant when facing poverty, are in fact considered the absence of resilience. In fact, it is important not to equate resilience with humble and stoic gestures facing increasing adversities. The so-called resilience in facing natural or man-made adversities could include the most significant and recent examples of Lower Manhattan with its project to reconstruct, renovate, and reequip the area destroyed by the September 11, 2001 attacks; the coastal Asian cities destroyed by the 2004 tsunami; the floods in New Orleans; or the areas in India and Pakistan devastated by earthquake in 2005; among many others. From a long list of disasters, selected merely by the visibility they get in the international media, we can notice both rich and poor cities, but all with an incredible ability to articulate immediate reconstruction aid action.

Taking resilience as the indicator for the recovery of the wasted urban area, it is of primary importance to define resilience index as the quantitative and qualitative merit of the catastrophe to be evaluated. Also, resilience index is the capacity of the urban system to full recovery.

In this respect, the urban system disaster evaluation requires specifically defined indicators that are relevant to the urban system. The resilience index is, in general, an appropriate parameter to use for the assessment of potential catastrophic events in an urban system. It is usually recognized as the agglomeration of the individual resilience indexes.

In the evaluation of agglomerated resilience indexes for an urban system we have to anticipate differences of time interval for all indicator changes and verify the differences between eventual individual cases designed for evaluation of the potential catastrophic events.

The following criteria are used to validate R_{TOT} with R_{CRI} as the criteria for the definition of the catastrophic event:

$$R_{TOT} > R_{CRI} \qquad (9.9)$$

This criterion is the essential merit for the evaluation of the catastrophic event under consideration where the total resilience index is higher than the critical value of the resilience index defined for the system. In the definition of critical value of the system, the overriding of critical value means destruction of the structure and loss of its functionality.

REFERENCES

[1]   J. Kawede, *Characteristics of Urban Natural Disasters and its Seismic toward Catastrophe*, 2007.

[2]   Young F., Shao D., Shao D., Tan X., Estimation of Catastrophe Measurement Agents Natural Disasters, *Journal of Natural Disasters Science* Vol. 9, No.1, 1996.

[3]   Assessment of urban water scarcity based on catastrophe theory, No.3,. *Water Science technology*, Vol. 66 (3), pp.486–595, 2012.

[4]   *Vulnerability Assessment Indicators for Climatic Change*, ETC/ACE, Technical page, 2010, Dec. 2010.

[5]   D. Brown, K Saito, R. Spence and Y Torwong. *Indicators for Measuring, Monitoring and Evaluation Disaster Recovery*, Cambridge University, 2008.

[6]   *Indicators of Sustainable Development*, United Nation Publication, 2007.

[7]   C. Martinas, Assessment of Urban Resilience, *MS Thesis*, University of Auckland, 2010.

[8]   Pali Lucy Lin, Urban Resilience, *PhD Thesis*, National Taipei University, Taiwan, 2006.

[9]   Carpater S.R., Wesley F., Turner G., *Surrogate for Resilience of Social-Ecological System, Ecosystem*, 8, pp. 1–3, 2002.

[10]   Peterson G.D. 2002 Estimating Resilience across Landscape, *Conservation Ecology*, No.6, 1-14.

[11]   Ultinari G., Rozande D.A., 2009, *Urban Resilience and Slow motion Disaster, City and Time*, 2,(3), URL: http://www.ch.cecci.br.org.

[12]   Masten, A. S., and J. Obradovi . 2008. Disaster preparation and recovery: lessons from research on resilience in human development. *Ecology and Society* 13(1): 9. [online] URL: www.ecologyandsociety.org/vol13/ iss1/ art9/

CHAPTER 10

CATASTROPHIC RISK OF POWER PLANTS

10.1 RISK ASSESSMENT OF POWER PLANTS

Risk management is a process for identifying, assessing, and prioritizing risks of different kinds. [1,2,3] Once the risks are identified, the risk manager will create a plan to minimize or eliminate the impact of negative events. A variety of strategies is available, depending on the type of risk and the type of business. There are a number of risk management standards, including those developed by the Project Management Institute, the International Organization for Standardization (ISO), the National Institute of Science and Technology, and actuarial societies.

There are many different types of risk that risk management plans can mitigate. Common risks include things like accidents in the workplace or fires, tornadoes, earthquakes, and other natural disasters. It can also include legal risks such as fraud, theft, and sexual harassment lawsuits. Risks can also relate to business practices, uncertainty in financial markets, failures in projects, credit risks, or the security and storage of data and records. [4,5,6]

The idea behind using risk management practices is to protect businesses from being vulnerable. Many business risk management plans may focus on keeping the company viable and reducing financial risks. However, risk management is also designed to protect the employees, customers, and general public from negative events such as fires or acts of terrorism that may affect them. Risk management practices are also about preserving the physical facilities, data, records, and physical assets a company owns or uses.

While a variety of different strategies can mitigate or eliminate risk, the process for identifying and managing the risk is fairly standard and consists of five basic steps. First, threats or risks are identified. Second, the vulnerability of key assets such as information to the identified threats is assessed. Next, the risk manager must determine the expected consequences of specific threats to assets. The last two steps in the process are to figure out ways to reduce risks and then prioritize the risk management procedures based on their importance.

There are as many different types of strategies for managing risk as there are types of risks. These break down into four main categories. (1) Risk can be managed by accepting the consequences of a risk and budgeting for it. (2) Another strategy is to transfer the risk to another party by insuring against a particular event, such as fire or a slip-and-fall accident. (3) Closing down a particular high-risk area of a business can avoid risk. (4) Finally, the manager can reduce the risk's negative effects, for instance, by installing sprinklers for fires or instituting a backup plan for data.

Technical risk management tends to concentrate on the prevention of plant failures, which can cause unscheduled downtime, safety incidents, and loss of income. Actions to minimize such threats typically comprise development of risk-based maintenance and inspection strategies, together with design and operation reviews, and analysis of the likelihood and consequences of failure. Such analysis is often backed up by detailed condition assessments and inspections, reviews of operation and maintenance histories, and design (code-based or by analysis, e.g., finite element). Full scale physical testing in controlled environments can also be appropriate when analytical design does not provide sufficient reassurance that the plant will operate reliably and safely. The suitability of these strategies can vary depending on a number of factors including operating regimes and demands of licensing authorities and regulatory bodies.

Business risks that may adversely affect profitability can be more difficult to identify and therefore more difficult to quantify and manage. Any aspect of an asset's operation that limits output from design conditions is a business risk, but justification to devote resources to address such issues can be very difficult. The situation often demands a step out in faith to encourage those involved to explore where improvements could be made, without introducing additional risk. A constructive working relationship between the asset owner and other organizations with appropriate specialist skills can contribute greatly to improving the business performance and mitigating risks to mutual benefit.

Mitsui Babcock Company has developed a risk-based approach to identify the aspects of the plant that may require modification to ensure safe and reliable service during periods of cyclic operation. Optimization of operational procedures especially during transients is also integrated into the assessment. Mitsui Babcock Company applies a health check approach, which comprises a combination of reviewing the design, the historical operating conditions, and the current condition. Table 10.1 shows a typical likelihood and consequence analysis and Figure 3 provides an overview on a typical power plant of how priorities can be presented, with certain issues being generic in nature and others more plant specific. This risk-based approach has proved invaluable as a rationalization and prioritization tool, ensuring resource is devoted to the areas that really are at risk. Owner operators can use the results of this approach to plan their long-term strategies for the asset, while also minimizing difficulty gaining insurance cover.

To serve the growing demand for electricity, utilities and power plant developers sometimes look to new coal-fired power plants as a resource option. As of late 2007, the cost of constructing a new coal-fired power plant was between $2000 and $2500 per kW of generating capacity, which means that a 500-MW plant would cost between $1 billion and $1.25 billion. Running a coal-fired power plant would also incur fuel, operating, maintenance, and environmental compliance costs for around 50 years. This chapter examines the risks of not fully recovering the costs of new conventional coal-fired power plants. Cost recovery, including sufficient revenues to pay interest or dividends and to pay a market return on capital, is a central consideration for utilities, developers, regulators, and investors. Factors that might imperil cost recovery include:

Table 10.1. Typical Likelihood and Consequence Analysis

	Likelihood (L)	Consequences (C)	
		Time Cost Safety/Performance/Life	
High	L > 70%	Immediate shutdown after 4 hrs; I week lost availability	>$500K
Medium	30% < L < 70%	Shutdown with up to 3 months lost availability	>$100K
Low	10% < L < 30%	Minimal lost availability or continue production with additional monitoring	<$100K

- Escalating construction costs
- Increased fuel costs
- Excess generating capacity
- Unexpected costs of complying with greenhouse gas emission reduction regulations.

When regulators approve power plant construction, place a power plant in a utility's rate base for ratemaking purposes, or approve a long-term power purchase contract, they commit consumers to pay for new power plants, without much certainty about what the costs may be over the life of the power plant or purchased power contract. Such approval sends a signal to investors that cost recovery is likely. In deregulated wholesale or retail electricity markets, cost recovery is more likely if the power plant owner has long-term contracts with electricity buyers that commit the buyers to paying for capacity and energy over a long time period.

To understand the risks of introducing new conventional coal-fired power plants into the generation portfolio, it is useful to look back at similar circumstances in the past and to look forward at anticipated new risks.

Historically, utility regulatory commissions have made large disallowances for coal and nuclear power plants. Recently, in the deregulated wholesale market, excess capacity of new gas-fired power plants has led to the sale of some of these plants at a price below the cost of constructing the plant.

Looking forward, an important new risk is the cost of complying with potential greenhouse gas emission regulations. The cost impact is currently uncertain, but if compliance costs are high, regulators may rethink the wisdom of passing along all those costs to ratepayers. In the deregulated sector, given the additional costs of complying with greenhouse gas emission regulations, coal-fired plants may be less competitive with other generation technologies and energy efficiency measures, which emit lower amounts of carbon dioxide or none at all.

10.2 Risk Assessment of Coal Fired Power Plants

Recognition of the risks associated with investments in new conventional coal-fired power plants is beginning to occur. For example, Fitch Ratings predicts that a company's ability to recover any future compliance costs associated with greenhouse gas emission regulations will have important implications for its credit rating. The *Wall Street Journal* reported that some coal-fired plant investments have been cancelled because of climate change and cost risk. [7]

Coal is a major energy source for electric power generation. In 2006, coal-fired generation capacity in the United States was about 313,000 MW, and that capacity produced about half the electric energy (in kilowatt-hours, or kWh) generated in the United States. Coal-fired power plants typically provide baseload or intermediate power, as reflected in their high average net capacity factor of 74% in 2005.

Coal-fired power plants are relatively expensive to build, but generally have low fuel costs. As indicated, a new 500-MW coal generating unit may cost over a billion dollars to construct. In 2006, the electric power sector paid, on average, $1.69 per million Btu (MMBtu) for coal as compared to $6.94 per MMBt for natural gas.

A 500-MW conventional coal-fired power plant would emit about 174 million metric tons of carbon dioxide over a 50-year operating life. The average carbon dioxide emission rate of new coal-fired power plants is slightly less than one metric ton per MWh generated, which is by far the highest of any widely used power generation technology.

10.3 RISK ASSESSMENTOF A NUCLEAR PLANT

Radiation occurs naturally in our environment; a typical person is, and always has been struck by 15,000 particles of radiation every second from natural sources, and an average medical X-ray involves being struck by 100 billion. While this may seem to be very dangerous, it is not, because the probability of a particle of radiation entering a human body to cause a cancer or a genetic disease is only one chance in 30 million billion (30 quintillion).

Nuclear power technology produces materials that are active in emitting radiation and are therefore called *radioactive*. These materials can come into contact with people principally through small releases during routine plant operation, accidents in nuclear power plants, accidents in transporting radioactive materials, and escape of radioactive wastes from confinement systems. We will discuss these separately, but all of them taken together, with accidents treated probabilistically, will eventually expose the average American to about 0.2% of his or her exposure from natural radiation. Since natural radiation is estimated to cause about 1% of all cancers, radiation due to nuclear technology should eventually increase our cancer risk by 0.002% (one part in 50,000), reducing our life expectancy by less than one hour. By comparison, our loss of life expectancy from competitive electricity generation technologies, burning coal, oil, or gas, is estimated to range from 3 to 40 days. [11]

There has been much misunderstanding on genetic diseases due to radiation. The risks are somewhat less than the cancer risks; for example, among the Japanese A-bomb survivors from Hiroshima and Nagasaki, there have been about 400 extra cancer deaths among the 100,000 people in the follow-up group, but there have been no extra genetic diseases among their progeny. Since there is no possible way for the cells in our bodies to distinguish between natural radiation and radiation from the nuclear industry, the latter cannot cause new types of genetic diseases or deformities (e.g., bionic man), or threaten the human race. Other causes of genetic disease include delayed parenthood (children of older parents have higher incidence) and men wearing pants (this warms the gonads, increasing the frequency of spontaneous mutations). The genetic risks of nuclear power are equivalent to delaying parenthood by 2.5 days, or of men wearing pants an extra 8 hours per year. Much can be done to avert genetic diseases utilizing currently available technology; if 1% of the taxes paid by the nuclear industry were used to further implement this technology, 80 cases of genetic disease would be averted for each case caused by the nuclear industry.

The nuclear power plant design strategy for preventing accidents and mitigating their potential effects is "defense in depth"—if something fails, there is a backup system to limit the harm done; if that system should also fail there is another backup system for it, and so on. Of course it is possible that each system in this series of backups might fail one after the other, but the probability for that is exceedingly small. The media often publicizes a failure of a particular system in a plant, implying that it was a close call on disaster; they completely miss the point of defense in depth, which easily takes care of such failures. Even in the Three Mile Island accident where at least two equipment failures were severely compounded by human errors, two lines of defense were still not breached—essentially the entire radioactivity remained sealed in the thick steel reactor vessel, and that vessel was sealed inside the heavily reinforced concrete and steel lined "containment" building which was never even challenged. It was clearly not a close call on disaster to the surrounding population. The Soviet Chernobyl reactor, built on a much less safe design concept, did not have such a containment structure; if it did, that disaster would have been averted.

Risks from reactor accidents are estimated by the rapidly developing science of *"probabilistic risk analysis* (PRA). A PRA must be done separately for each power plant (at a cost of $5 million) but we give typical results here. A fuel meltdown might be expected once in 20,000 years of reactor operation. In 2 out of 3 meltdowns there would be no deaths, in 1 out of 5 there would be over 1000 deaths, and in 1 out of 100,000 there would be 50,000 deaths. The average for all meltdowns would be 400 deaths. Since air pollution from coal burning is estimated to be causing 10,000 deaths per year, there would have to be 25 meltdowns each year for nuclear power to be as dangerous as coal burning.

Of course, deaths from coal burning air pollution are not noticeable, but the same is true for the cancer deaths from reactor accidents. In the worst accident considered, expected once in 100,000 meltdowns (once in 2 billion years of reactor operation), the cancer deaths would be among 10 million people, increasing their cancer risk typically from 20% (the current U.S. average) to 20.5%. This is much less than the geographical variation: 22% in New England to 17% in the Rocky Mountain states.

Very high radiation doses can destroy body functions and lead to death within 60 days, but such "noticeable" deaths would be expected in only 2% of reactor meltdown accidents; there would be over 100 in 0.2% of meltdowns, and 3500 in 1 out of 100,000 meltdowns. To date, the largest number of noticeable deaths from coal burning was in an air pollution incident (London, 1952) where there were 3500 extra deaths in one week. Of course, the nuclear accidents are hypothetical and there are many much worse hypothetical accidents in other electricity generation technologies; for example, there are hydroelectric dams in California whose sudden failure could cause 200,000 deaths.

The radioactive waste products from the nuclear industry must be isolated from contact with people for very long time periods. The bulk of the radioactivity is contained in the spent fuel, which is quite small in volume and therefore easily handled with great care. This "high level waste" will be converted to a rock-like form and emplaced in the natural habitat of rocks, deep underground. The average lifetime of a rock in that environment is 1 billion years. If the waste behaves like other rock, it is easily shown that the waste generated by one nuclear power plant will eventually, over millions of years (if there is no cure found for cancer), cause one death from 50 years of operation. By comparison, the wastes from coal burning plants that end up in the ground will eventually cause several thousand deaths from generating the same amount of electricity.

The much larger volume of much less radioactive (low level) waste from nuclear plants will be buried at shallow depths (typically 20 feet) in soil. If we assume that this material immediately becomes dispersed through the soil between the surface and ground water depth (despite elaborate measures to maintain waste package integrity) and behaves like the same materials that are present naturally in soil (there is extensive evidence confirming such behavior), the death toll from this low-level waste would be 5% of that from the high level waste discussed in the previous paragraph.

The effects of routine releases of radioactivity from nuclear plants depend somewhat on how the spent fuel is handled. A typical estimate is that they may reduce our life expectancy by 15 minutes.

Potential problems from accidents in transport of radioactive materials are largely neutralized by elaborate packaging. A great deal of such transport has taken place over the past 50 years and there have been numerous accidents, including fatal ones. However, from all of these accidents combined, there is less than a 1% chance that even a single death will ever result from radiation exposure. Probabilistic risk analyses indicate that we can expect less than one death per century in the United States from this source.

Mining uranium to fuel nuclear power plants leaves *mill tailings*, the residues from chemical processing of the ore, which lead to radon exposures to the public. However, these effects are grossly over-compensated by the fact that mining uranium out of the ground reduces future radon exposures. By comparison, coal burning leaves ashes that increase future radon exposures. The all-inclusive estimates of radon effects are that one nuclear power plant operating for one year will eventually avert a few hundred deaths, while an equivalent coal burning plant will eventually cause 30 deaths.

10.4 RISK ASSESSMENT OF WIND POWER PLANT

We are experienced in wind farm preconstruction environmental risk assessment, especially for birds and bats. [12] The experience includes work on sites with high visibility and significant stakeholder interes.

10.4.1. How Is an Ecological Preconstruction Risk Assessment Conducted?

The major focus of the risk assessment is on birds and bats. We initially identify heavy bird-use areas by surveying the property at different times of the day and at different seasons. It is then map those areas using both GPS-groundtruthing, aerial photography of the property, and GIS software. We quantify usage by implementing a variety of methodologies, such as point counts and transect counts during daylight hours, and radar, infrared cameras, and bat detectors during the night. By combining older methodologies with newer methodologies and technology we compile a data set that not only can be directly compared with data from older projects, but that can improve the accuracy of the assessment and provide a benchmark for post-construction studies.

Good wind quality often means few trees. As a general rule, fewer trees mean fewer migrating raptors. Surveys specifically address this issue. Upland game birds—turkey, dove, grouse, pheasant and quail—typically fly low to the ground and are unlikely to ever be threatened by a turbine blade. In contrast, ducks and geese routinely fly at rotor heights, often making daily flights between roosting and feeding areas. Their routes, however, mainly depend on historical usage and are generally confined to narrow flight corridors. At other wind farms located in close proximity to waterfowl areas, the birds seem to have high avoidance ability, and are rarely struck. Daily and seasonal bird traffic is one of the most important characteristics we identify and define for establishing optimal and safe turbine siting.

10.4.2. What about Threatened or Endangered Species?

Determining the status of threatened or endangered species is a prime objective of the area surveys. If threatened or endangered species are discovered, every effort is made to define their range and to determine if breeding occurs. Although the focus is on birds, some properties may support other species that have to be evaluated.

This is arguably the most important factor affecting wind farms in areas with significant ecotourism. It is a difficult question to answer as little study has been done in the past. We have far more experience than anyone else in studying this question. In addition to daytime visual surveys, thedeploy of infrared camera and/or radar systems to monitor the night-time avian (and bat) migration flights. Many songbirds migrate at night, and infrared cameras are the only sensor that has 100% detection capability for individual small birds flying in the rotor zone. We also are always prepared to respond on short notice to the occurrence of abnormal weather events by putting multiple observers in the field. Such events can create conditions that are most likely to increase the strike risk of migratory songbirds. By observing the flight patterns during these events we can better predict the strike risk.

10.4.3. Who Has the Final Say on whether a Project Is Safe Enough?

As of 2008 in Texas there are no regulations or permits necessary for placing wind turbines on private property. It provides an estimated risk based on analysis of the data collected during the surveys. A prudent developer also consults regularly with government agencies, such as U.S. Fish and Wildlife, U.S. Army Corps of Engineers (primarily on wetlands issues), and state agencies such as Parks and Wildlife. The developer considers all the inputs, and makes a decision based on them. We assist the developer in communicating with the government agencies and interested stakeholders.

10.4.4. Wind Farm Post-Construction Ecological Risk Assessment

Once a wind energy facility is in operation, post-construction studies are conducted to validate the estimated risk from the preconstruction assessment. Traditionally, the most significant aspect of post-construction monitoring has been based on carcass searches. This can be very manpower intensive. We have been working to better incorporate the latest technology into post-construction assessments to not only reduce overall costs, but to achieve a more accurate assessment.

10.5 RISK ASSESSMENT OF HYDRO POWER PLANT

Hydro power plants, like any other business, encounter risks in all areas of operations, but especially in the areas of producing and marketing electricity. As the electricity supply industry reforms unfold, the resultant deregulation brings in several market regulatory and trade-related risks. The general risks affecting power utilities and place particular emphasis on hydropower plant operations by analyzing the effect of maintenance and operations quality in power plant risk management.

Electric power companies and their insurers/insurance advisors are required to understand and manage risk. Risk management is commonly seen as considering security, insurance, and safety issues only. It is however a broad management methodology that includes all areas and aspects of the organization. There are many elements that contribute to risk management: behaviors, management systems and practices, processes, and cultures. A comprehensive risk management framework and structure is necessary to ensure that all participants in an organization's business think, live, and breathe risk management. The most important contributor are employees' understanding of how all the elements of the system fit together, that is, how work practices, their knowledge, skills, and attitudes make the whole risk management system work. [13]

10.5.1. Risks Evaluation of the Hydro Power Plant

The risks of hydro power plant financing comprise several elements that have to be considered as they depend on geographical, political, and economic assessment of the country. [14] Financing a hydropower project is very heavily dependent on the prudent management of various types of risks. This involves identification of various risks associated with a project and assessment. However, the most important step lies in arranging measures to mitigate such risks including an effective insurance program. In the following subsections we discuss certain important risks from the perspective mentioned here.

10.5.2. Foreign Exchange Risk

A developer can borrow locally or from foreign institutions and the conditions with regard to security will be same. However, the borrower's exposure to certain risk will be different if the source of debt is overseas. There are mainly two types of risks that a borrower needs to be aware of while borrowing from a foreign lender. This risk materializes with the devaluation if revenue is denominated in local currency while having to service the loan denominated in foreign currency. Similarly, this risk also manifests in rising cost of imports. This risks can be mitigated by either (1) having the loan denominated in local currency, or (2) having the rate of revenue denominated in foreign currency. In the case of increase in the cost of imports, an insurance coverage against cost escalation would mitigate this risk.

10.5.3. Repatriation Risk

Another risk associated with foreign loan is *repatriation risk*. This becomes of greater concern to a lender if it is not able to repatriate the proceeds of debt servicing. Generally, governments of development countries, in their quest to attract foreign investment, have enacted legislation guaranteeing repatriation. If such a guarantee is not available, either the lender will not make a loan or will make it subject to an exorbitant rate of interest.

10.5.4. Sovereign Risk (Country Risk)

A foreign entrepreneur investing in exposed to risk such as those associated with the government's creditworthiness, the possibility of confiscation, expropriation and nationalization (CENRisk), changes in the local political environment, and enforceability of contracts. These types of risk are known as *sovereign* and *country risk*. The Multilateral Investment Guarantee Association (MIGA), a member of the World Bank Group, ensures against such risk for a fee. However, the availability of such insurance is limited only to foreign investors.

10.5.5. Interest Rate Risk

Lenders offer two kind of interest: (1) floating rate and (2) fixed rate. Floating rate entails changes in the interest rate during the term of the loan, thereby introducing an element of uncertainty or risk for the borrower. Banks prefer floating rate as they need to be able to adapt to changes in financial market as well as cover their own exposure to the vagaries of changing interest rates (including bank rates). For a developer, fixed rate is the best way to mitigate this risk. However, banks tend to add a margin to the then prevalent rate to cushion their own risk.

10.5.6. Inflation Rate

The real value of a unit of nominal currency tends to depreciate over time with inflation. Even hard currency is subject to this risk. Escalation in the rate of tariff is the only answer, short of trying to hold down the inflation with one's bare hands.

10.5.7. Market Risk

It is common knowledge among engineers that energy requires a guaranteed market due to the constraints with regard, primarily, to storage and transmission. A simple way to mitigate this risk is to sign a long term Power Purchase Agreement (PPA) with the utility. Developers are known to ask the government to issue a counter guarantee to cover the payment risk. This basically entails a government standing surety to the fact that the utility pays its dues to the developer in time, and in the case of a utility's failure to meet its obligations, the government is required to promptly make payment to mitigate the delinquency of the utility. Nowadays multilateral funding agencies such as the World Bank take a dim view of a government issuing a counter guarantee. Having a letter of credit put in place by the utility with the IPP as the beneficiary is another way of mitigating this risk over the short term.

10.5.8. Construction Risks

Time and cost overrun risks are one group of construction risks. Time overrun risk results in loss of revenue and may also raise the cost due to inflation. It also raises the total amount of interest during construction of the debt financing and may even attract penalties for late delivery of energy. Other construction risks are force majeure risk, socioeconomic/environmental risk, geological risk, performance risk, design risk, and so on. One can arrange insurance coverage against such risk like CAR, TAR, EAR, professional liability, and so on, including "advance loss of profit insurance" that can be complemented by signing a "fixed price" turnkey contract (or EPC contract) and incorporating a clause for imposition of liquidated damages on the contractor for delayed substantial completion or commissioning of the plant.

10.5.9. Hydrological Risk

In hydro power plants all energy produced by a plant, depending on the availability of water, irrespective of whether the season is dry or wet, shall be turned into cash. However, if there is no water to generate energy due to the change in the level of precipitation, climatic reason, or change in the hydrology of the catchments area, then these projects are on their own. This risk emanates from the fact that seasonal rainfall patterns affect the amount of water available to a hydropower plant and generation may fall below contract levels in any season.

Obviously, a dry year will be an unmitigated disaster for a hydropower plant. It is very effective way to mitigate hydrology risk is to gather hydrological data for a reasonable number of years in the past and design the project accordingly, after having selected a project with better hydrological potential as well as information. For the future assessment of the hydrological potential it is necessary to develop respective method for the evaluation and assessment of the hydrological risk.

REFERENCES

[1]   D. Scott, M. Grins, Ch. Fayforth, D. Lachman, N. Lucas, D. Clark, B. vanGils, C. Buck, L, Backer D. Harison, M.Elliot, E.Scharaner, J. Steger, *Ernst and Young*, Business Risk Report, 2010. (www.maplecroft.com)

[2]   Maplecroft,*Terrorism Risk Index*, 2010. (www.maplecroft.com) Course Program.

[3]   Mortimer, *ECR-Euro Money Country Risk*, 2010. (www.euromoney.com)

[4]   Zavadskas, E.K., Turskis, Z., Tamosaitiene, J., Risk assessment of construction projects, J. *Civil Engineering and Management*, 16, 2010, 33–46.

[5]   Mustafa, M.A., and Al-Bahar, J.F., Project risk assessment using the analytic hierarchy process, IEEE Transactions on Engineering Management, 38, 1991, 46-52. [6] Murray Neal,. (1996). *Risk assessment& management: A definitive method for proactive risk manipulation.* United States of America: Targeted Security Consultants Ltd.

[6]   Barry D. Investment risk of coal fired power plant, Western Resource Advocates, 2008.

[7]   Risk Management: A tool for improving nuclear power plant perform-
        ance, IAEA-TECHDOC-1209, IAEA, 2001.

[8]   Cepin M., *Development of Criteria for Risk-Informed Decision-Making*,
        NECE 2004, Portorož, 2004.

[9]   P. Samantha, I. S. Kim, T. Mankamo, W. E. Vesely,NUREG/CR-6141,
        Handbook of Methods for Risk-Based Analyses of Technical Specifications, US
        NRC, 1995.

[10]   Cepin M., Development of Risk Criteria in Nuclear Power Plants –
        Problems and Solutions, *International Journal of Materials & Structural
        Reliability* Vol. 4, No. 1, March 2006, 53–63.

[11]   *Risk assessment for 100 MW wind farm in Jilin Province*, Case study,
        UNEP Project, 2007.

[12]   Kucukal S. I, *Risk assessment of river-type hydropower plants by using fuzzy
        logic approach,*Word Renewable Energy Congress,May 2011, Linkoping,
        Sweden.

[13]   G.Huges, W. Diego, E.Eoliver, A. Dlugolecki, *Financial risk management
        institute for renewable energy project*, United Nation Environment Pro-
        gram, 2004, ISBN 92-807-2445-2.

[14]   P. Samanta, I. S. Kim, T. Mankamo, W. E. Vesely NUREG/CR-6141,
        Handbook of Methods for Risk-Based Analyses of Technical Specifications, US
        NRC, Sept. 2009.

INDEX

cyclones, 76

D

damages, 5, 9, 22, 26, 39, 108, 192
danger, 14, 21, 129
data processing, 73, 74, 110, 111
data set, 172, 189
data transfer, 27, 120
database, 26, 38, 55
deaths, 2, 9, 10, 11, 17, 46, 52, 100, 149, 150, 187, 188
debt service, 68
debt servicing, 191
debts, 1, 35
decay, 24, 116, 117, 119, 172
decision makers, 36, 37
decoupling, 37
defects, 108
deficiency, 17, 155, 164
deficit, 77
degradation, 28, 49, 52, 57, 66, 93, 105, 121
delinquency, 192
Denmark, 30, 107, 173
Department of Defense, 14
Department of Energy, 28, 30, 97, 121
Department of Transportation, 47
dependent variable, 151
depression, 2
depth, 67, 187, 188
deregulation, 190
destruction, 6, 11, 13, 15, 17, 18, 22, 137, 138, 143, 158, 181
detection, 25, 26, 30, 47, 106, 189
determinism, 144
detonation, 100
devaluation, 191
developed countries, 27, 120
developing countries, 149, 150
deviation, 25

diet, 150

differential equations, 38, 56, 78, 162

dinosaurs, 16

direct action, 159

direct measure, 148

disaster, 2, 6, 11, 12, 14, 17, 39, 46, 47, 48, 49, 50, 51, 52, 76, 137, 138, 143, 145, 181, 187, 193

diseases, 150, 186

disorder, 12

dispersion, 90

disposable income, 149

distribution, 27, 29, 68, 69, 82, 120, 129, 148

diversity, 38, 40, 44, 45, 55, 148, 159

doping, 77

dream, 21

drinking water, 140, 149, 176

drought, 37, 138, 154

drugs, 150

E

early warning, 40

earthquakes, 2, 33, 47, 137, 176, 183

Easter, 138

Eastern Europe, 3

ecological indicators, 140

ecological processes, 148

ecological systems, 2, 12, 35, 36, 41, 53, 54, 148, 159

ecology, 1, 46, 50, 139, 173

economic change, 59, 122

economic crisis, 92, 103

economic development, 82

economic growth, 36, 40, 160, 171

economic indicator, 17, 57, 58, 63, 66, 85, 122

economic systems, 36, 37, 39, 41, 48, 51

economic welfare, 162

economical cost, 137

economics, 27, 46, 50, 120

F

H

hydrogen, 18, 54, 100, 161
hysteresis, 129

I

ideals, 13
identification, 36, 40, 175, 190
identity, 39, 139
illiteracy, 150
image(s), 47, 116, 117
Impact Assessment, 158
imports, 43, 44, 45, 191
improvements, 53, 184
impulsive, 116, 117
incidence, 187
income, 17, 39, 149, 151, 152, 153, 154, 155, 156, 162, 163, 164, 167, 168, 176, 180, 184
independence, 27, 29, 120
independent variable, 151
India, 15, 150, 180
individual character, 61
individuals, 14, 33, 39, 40, 48, 51, 139, 176
industry(s), 21, 22, 24, 25, 26, 44, 67, 77, 101, 120, 137, 150, 174, 175, 187, 188, 190
inflation, 192
information technology, 16
infrastructure, 22, 23, 27, 37, 38, 40, 43, 44, 45, 46, 47, 48, 50, 52, 55, 76, 120, 137, 174, 175
initial state, 111, 123
injuries, 2, 10, 20, 46, 47, 52
insecticide, 150
insecurity, 35, 151
insertion, 91
inspections, 184
instinct, 33
institutional change, 35, 56, 89
institutions, 27, 40, 46, 47, 50, 51, 191
insulation, 76

M

O

S

U

X

Y

Z